FRIENDS
IN DEED

FRIENDS IN DEED

RECOVERING THE LOST ART
OF BEING A GOOD NEIGHBOR

DON HAWKINS

MOODY PRESS

CHICAGO

*This book is dedicated to my parents,
Jim and Juanita Hawkins, who taught and modeled
the biblical principles on which* Friends in Deed
*is based, and to whom I owe a huge debt of gratitude
for their impact on my life. I consider it
providential that the release date for this book
coincides with the month they celebrate
fifty years of marriage.*

CONTENTS

FOREWORD

Some books are manufactured out of thin air; although they entertain you for a while, they don't change you.

Many books are manufactured from other books. An author does a lot of studying and writing, but the only thing new about the book is the title. You've seen the contents before, and you feel cheated. Recycling old ideas just doesn't excite us.

This book came out of life, *real* life, and it won't take you long to find that out. It also came out of the author's serious encounter with the Bible and what it says about loving others and helping them when they need it most. *Friends in Deed* didn't emerge from the comfortable library of an ivory tower. It was lived and written on the battlefield.

A veteran preacher, counselor, writer, and radio host, Don Hawkins meets all kinds of people in all sorts of situations; and in these pages, you'll meet them too. Best of all, you'll meet *yourself* in these pages. And you'll discover how Jesus Christ can change your life and make an encourager out of you.

Thanks, Don, for *living* this book and then writing it so we can discover the excitement and enrichment of living like Good Samaritans. I hope all of us will put these clear biblical principles into practice and start making a difference in this dangerous and difficult world.

Warren W. Wiersbe
Author, conference speaker

ACKNOWLEDGMENTS

Y ou expect authors to admit that a book is the product of more than one person. It always is. I'm grateful to many who, directly or indirectly, have played a role in *Friends in Deed.*

My wife, Kathy, has not only been a stellar example as my best friend, she has helped me shape concepts and words. I've also received valuable help from other ministry colleagues, including Woodrow Kroll, Herb Epp, Mark Brunott, and Warren Wiersbe.

Jim Bell and the Moody Press team, including Greg Thornton and Bill Thrasher, played a significant role in shaping the concept. Ruth Ann Franks did her usual masterful job typing the manuscript, and Cheryl Dunlop put in many hours editing and re-editing. Susan Hertzler helped me tremendously with her proofreading skills.

The contribution of others who are part of our ministry team at Back to the Bible has helped me finish this project while keeping other responsibilities moving. These include but are not limited to Brian Erickson, Tom Schindler, Herman Rohlfs, Neal Thompson, Kirk Chestnut, Craig Sovereign, LeRoy Rock, Dan Waldo, Lyle Swedeen, Herb Potter, Rachel Derowitsch, and Elizabeth Erlandson. Our Life Perspectives team, including Wayne Collins, Cindy Walters, Kirk, Craig, and Kathleen, also provided significant help. Cathy Strate played an important role in coordinating schedules, communication, and workload.

INTRODUCTION

Have you ever needed a Good Samaritan?

Have you ever been the victim of a violent criminal act and desperately needed someone to come along to help you? That's what happened to Tina Hayes. Bleeding to death, body riddled with bullets, Tina crawled from a basement apartment onto the dark streets of the Crown Heights neighborhood in Brooklyn. Several people apparently saw her and turned away, unwilling to get involved or to help.

Perhaps your experience was more along the lines of thirty-five-year-old Susan B., her sixty-four-year-old mother, Margaret, and Susan's three children, ages six, four, and eighteen months, who because of a blown tire were left stranded one evening along a busy stretch of freeway in suburban Dallas, Texas.

Or perhaps you went through something like Gerald did. A quiet, unassuming businessman sitting in a waiting area of the world's busiest airport, Gerald, who had been a diabetic since his youth, found himself going into insulin shock. Desperately in need of help, he was unable to communicate his dilemma. Since no one around him seemed interested, he could easily have died.

Then there was Richard, who phoned our nationwide radio call-in program "Life Perspectives." "Nobody seems to care about me," he said. "I've tried everything! Even when I reach out to other people, no one seems interested." Further conversation revealed that Richard had been deeply hurt during his early years by a wide range of abuses. Now he admitted to being driven to try to control others, while at the same time feeling paranoid over whether or not they cared about him. As a result, he felt lonely and disconnected without, as he put it, "a single healthy relationship in the world."

Some years ago while spending a weekend in New York City, my wife and I visited the Crown Heights area and had dinner in an Italian restaurant not far from where the Tina Hayes shooting would occur. I have driven countless times the busy stretch of freeway where Susan and her mother were stranded. And I've spent more hours than I would like to recall sitting in the very bank of seats at O'Hare International Airport where Gerald found himself in a diabetic coma. I've visited the beautiful Midwest city in which Richard lives and met numerous friendly people, many of them members of an evangelical church where I had the privilege of ministering.

But I'm not the common thread that links their varied experiences.

Tina, Susan and her mother, Gerald, and Richard are symptomatic of why I feel the need for a book like *Friends in Deed*. For although we live in a global village today, people with whom I talk seem for the most part to feel less connected, more isolated, than ever before.

It's ironic, isn't it? The Berlin Wall has come down, the Cold War has ended, and global hostility has been reduced in many areas. Yet growing conflict and increasingly weakened relationships continue to mark the world of the end of the twentieth century. Brother battles brother in Bosnia, Somalia, and Palestine; marriages in the Western world deteriorate; children suffer incredible abuse; and families engage in bitter feuds worldwide. Neighbors look the other way when individuals are victimized by criminals—and these are just a few of the external symptoms of what has become an arid wasteland of human relationships.

NEEDED: AUTHENTIC LOVE

Burt Bacharach and Hal David wrote a song in the seventies entitled "What the World Needs Now . . . Is Love, Sweet Love." Although the lyrics of the song indicate a less than precise view of what love really is, the general idea behind them is an accurate one. Jesus Christ, the ultimate authority on life, once pointed out to an inquiring lawyer that our major life purposes could be summarized in the verb "love."

Several years ago, after considering Jesus' response to questions about what is the greatest or most important commandment, I became convinced that our major life purposes could be summarized in two mandates: to love God wholeheartedly and to love our neighbor unconditionally, or as ourselves.

THIS BOOK IS DESIGNED TO ENCOURAGE OUR WILLINGNESS TO HELP THE STRANGER CHANGE THE FLAT—AND ALSO TO EXERCISE LOVE IN THAT SOMETIMES DIFFICULT RELATIONSHIP WITH A PARENT OR SPOUSE, FELLOW WORKER OR FRIEND.

If we are to fulfill these mandates, we must first grasp what Jesus meant by the verb "to love." Unfortunately, as reflected in so many of the songs, poems, novels, and screenplays of our day, our contemporary perception of love as either a sentimental feeling or a sexual attraction seems to have clouded our thinking about this supremely essential character quality.

Friends in Deed has been written to provide the refreshing water of a word from God about how to reach out to others, to relate, to care. After all, God invented relationships in the first place. Furthermore, it was man—not God—who withdrew in isolation and fear after tasting the forbidden fruit in the Garden of Eden. Men and women have been hiding from God and from each other ever since.

Throughout the book we will use as our basis of consideration the story Jesus told of a man who reached out to help his neighbor when others looked the other way—a man we have labeled "the Good Samaritan." However, in using this biblical foundation it's important that we not fall into an applicational trap. It's easy to segment "being a Good Samaritan" into occasional acts of kindness —sort of like the old "doing my good deed for the day" that the Boy Scouts recommend.

Now there's nothing wrong with doing a good deed. Yet some of us may find it easier helping a stranger fix a flat tire or assisting a neighbor in picking up garbage scattered by a dog than learning to apply daily the important relational principles we will discuss in this book that relate to problem children, in-laws, or even a wife or husband. This book is designed to *encourage* our willingness to help the stranger change the flat—and also to exercise love in that sometimes difficult relationship with a parent or spouse, fellow worker or friend. After all, these relational principles are often the hardest to apply with those to whom we're closest.

Our focus in this book will be on love—wholehearted love for God and unconditional love for people. Whereas most of us seem to agree with the need for wholehearted love of God, sometimes even Christians disagree about unconditional love for people. Creatures of extreme, we tend to practice either a weak-kneed, codependent kind of love or a "tough love" almost completely stripped of feeling.

The kind of love we're talking about is not "Walk all over me, Baby; I'll still love you. Do you need me to pick up some more wine when I go to the store?" Nor is it "I have no feeling left for you, you reprobate. All you ever do is drink and complain. Give it up!"

I like the balance suggested by my editor, Cheryl Dunlop: "I won't always like your actions, and sometimes I may lovingly—even angrily—tell you so. But I love you enough that, even if you wind up in prison—and you deserve to be there—I'll still come see you." Incidentally, practicing this kind of love seems to be the best way to avoid having to visit a loved one in prison: The other person is more likely to care what effects his or her actions will have on the loved one.

It is my prayer that *Friends in Deed* will promote authentic, balanced love in all our human relationships, both with strangers and neighbors, friends and family.

DEARTH OF RELATIONSHIPS

Why such a dearth of relationships? Why so much hesitation to "by love serve"? Why such weakness in those relationships that exist? For one thing, life in the nineties is just too busy. We all have far too many "important" things to do to be able to take the kind of time necessary to cultivate close relationships or to reach out to help someone in need.

In addition, we live in fear. Crime and violence, from random freeway shootings to kick-down-the-door home robberies to drug-motivated attacks on pizza delivery people, cause us to hide behind our triple-locked doors and avoid contact even with those who live nearby. Ours is a day of mega-metropolitan areas with millions of people living practically on top of each other, yet in almost complete isolation. We bolt our doors, arm our electronic home security systems, and often sleep with our hands just inches from a firearm. No wonder we find it hard to reach out!

The quest for possessions has also hindered the development of relationships in numerous ways. Couples work long hours to be able to take the kind of dream vacations described in the brochures that picture lush resorts and lavish cruise ships, then they wonder why the vacations they take are filled with acrimony, bitterness, loneliness, and isolation. Perhaps we are living the observation from Solomon's song, so busy cultivating the vineyards of others that we have neglected the personal vineyard of our own relationships.

Another factor keeping many of us from reaching out to others is intense hurt suffered in the past. Abuse of various kinds, including childhood sexual trauma, is rampant in our world today. As one well-known psychiatrist put it, "When you've been hurt over and over, it's difficult to distinguish paranoia from insight." Still hurting from the past, fearful of being hurt again, we simply withdraw. Dysfunction in families, generation after generation, has produced an epidemic of unhealthy relationships and a climate of control or be controlled, manipulate or be manipulated.

Yet another factor lives right with us, under our own skins. Few of us like to admit it, but we're really far more interested in ourselves than we are in others. When you consider how selfishness parallels insecurity, it's easy to see why few relationships get past the "cocktail party conversation" level, or why much of what might be called "Good Samaritanism" has been reduced to dialing 911.

Finally, there's a breakdown of basic societal bonds—proliferating divorce, the absence of the nuclear family due to modern patterns of moving, and a growing single-adult population. These factors have left more people with neither role models for intimacy nor homes in which to incubate it.

A FOUNDATIONAL PARABLE

The story of the Good Samaritan, recognized as the best-known parable in Luke's gospel and perhaps the entire New Testament, provides a solid foundation for exploring various aspects of strengthening relationships in order to become an authentic good neighbor. *Friends in Deed* is designed to explore this parable in order to unfold principles designed to help us understand and apply the concept of loving service.

Richard, Gerald, Susan and her mother Margaret, and Tina all shared a desperate need for encouraging, loving relationships and/or service-motivated help. In short, they all needed a Good Samaritan.

Although my radio guest and I encouraged Richard to seek out a Christian counselor who could help him work on the pain of his early life and then look for a supportive network of Christian friends at a local church, we're not sure what ultimately transpired in his life.

For Gerald, it seemed like an eternity before someone finally noticed he had passed out. His wallet and briefcase had been stolen, and he literally had been left lying by the side of the modern counterpart to the busy road between Jerusalem and Jericho, near the point of death. Finally, an elderly black man who worked on the cleaning and maintenance staff noticed Gerald and summoned help. Rushed by ambulance to a nearby hospital, he was cared for and he ultimately recovered. His question during his days of convalescence was, "Why did it take so long for someone to notice?"

For Susan and Margaret, spending more than an hour beside a busy freeway during and after a thunderstorm and listening to the seemingly endless complaints of three exhausted children left them feeling frustrated, angry, and not a little bit fearful. Their ordeal finally came to an end when two men who were en route to a meeting decided to take the time to stop, help them change the tire, and get them on their way.

And for Tina Hayes, hope came from a fifty-four-year-old rabbi named Israel Shemtov.[1] The rabbi and father of ten, who also runs a clothing store, started to call 911, then decided there was no time to wait for an ambulance. Aided by an unnamed bystander, he lifted the woman into his car and sped to nearby Kingsbrook, a Jewish hospital. Doctors later affirmed that the rabbi's quick action saved Tina Hayes's life. The spot where the shooting occurred was only blocks from where, two years earlier, a Jewish driver had struck and killed a seven-year-old black boy, touching off racial riots in the Crown Heights area. When asked why he risked his own life by taking the action he did, Rabbi Shemtov replied, "Color, race, or religion have no bearing on helping a human being."

Caring enough to see those around us who are hurting . . . stopping to get involved to help . . . putting ourselves at risk . . . becoming involved, even on a long-term basis. These are among the marks of Good Samaritans—both in Jesus' day and ours.

It is my prayer that this book will help motivate more of us to become authentic Good Samaritans.

NOTE

1. *Lincoln Journal Star* (13 August 1993), 4.

CHAPTER ONE

THE TEST: THE QUESTION ABOUT ETERNAL LIFE

And behold, a certain lawyer stood up and tested Him, saying,
"Teacher, what shall I do to inherit eternal life?" He said to him,
"What is written in the law? What is your reading of it?"
(Luke 10:25–26)

Good was not an adjective many people used when talking about Floyd. Quick with sarcasm, at times outrageously outspoken, he very soon became one of the least popular individuals on the campus of the Christian college he attended. Shunned by many who considered themselves spiritual, Floyd seemed to bend over backward to avoid winning any popularity contests.

With flashing dark eyes, a swarthy complexion, and a physique resembling Lou Ferrigno of *The Incredible Hulk,* Floyd went out for basketball and soon was given the role of team intimidator. As a freshman he scored very few points but was always assigned to guard the other team's offensive star, and usually he succeeded in taking him out of the game mentally or physically. Long before trash talking and "dissing" were popularized in professional and collegiate sports, Floyd had mastered those dubious skills, both on and off the basketball court. As a result, the primary question raised on campus wasn't how well Floyd would perform on the basketball court. It was would he be thrown off the team or thrown out of school altogether?

BEHIND AN INTIMIDATING STYLE

Few people took the time to get to know Floyd. After all, he generally wasn't a pleasant person to be around. Spending time with Floyd always entailed the risk of being insulted. At times his confrontations with fellow students and faculty alike led him to the brink of expulsion.

But there was a reason for Floyd's gruff exterior. Few of us realized how deeply he had been hurt in childhood or how serious and frequent the pain that had left him scarred physically, emotionally, and even spiritually.

That Floyd had made it to Bible college was a miracle in itself. Childhood abuses included slaps to the head that ruptured eardrums and created permanent hearing loss. There were times when his hand was held on a hot stove as punishment. These were just some of the painful abuses to which Floyd was subjected in the dysfunctional home where he spent his early years and in the orphanage to which he was taken after his family disintegrated.

Yet somehow, beneath that gruff exterior, Floyd had developed a heart—a heart for God and a heart for people. Like a flickering candle on a foggy night, it was hard to spot. Few people dared get that close. They were afraid of intimidation or just simply found his words and actions too distasteful.

That's why, for much of his college life, Floyd was treated by most people like the Jews of Jesus' day treated the Samaritans.

RACIAL INTOLERANCE

I grew up in a part of the country where some people were viewed as second-class citizens because of the color of their skin. They were forced to use different drinking fountains and restrooms, sit at the rear of the bus, and put up with epithets and insults from individuals who simply happened to have been born with a different racial background. In our post-civil rights era, groups ranging from Neo-Nazis to the Ku Klux Klan are working feverishly to reintroduce racial bigotry and intolerance as the social order of the day.

However, such individuals have nothing on the Jewish attitude toward the Samaritans.

More than once the gospels reflect the fierce hatred between Jews and Samaritans.[1] Irate Jewish leaders bent on discrediting Jesus used the term "Samaritan" to insinuate their belief in the illegitimacy of His birth (John 8:48). Two of Jesus' closest followers once suggested calling down fire from heaven on a Samaritan village because of its lack of hospitality (Luke 9:54). The village was inhospitable because Jesus had made it clear that He was headed to Jerusalem. By Jesus' day, the hostilities between Jews and Samaritans had grown far beyond theological or racial differences.

The general area of the Northern Kingdom of the Old Testament was first called Samaria during the rule of the Persians, the third to fifth centuries before Christ.

There were two major theological differences between Jews and Samaritans. The Jews considered Jerusalem the appropriate place to worship, whereas Samaritans viewed Mount Gerizim as the right place (John 4:20). Furthermore, while Jews and Samaritans both anticipated a coming Messiah—the Samaritans referred to Him as *Ta'eb*—only the first five books of the Bible, those authored by Moses, were accepted by Samaritans. Jews were forbidden to eat what was slaughtered by a Samaritan, or to drink from their cups or vessels. Biased Jews included Samaritans among the list of categories—along with Gentiles and women—for which they were thankful they were not a part.

The parable known as the story of the Good Samaritan was recorded in the gospel written by a physician named Luke. It is likely, though not certain, that Luke was a Gentile.[2] In his gospel record, Luke includes three references to Samaritans, the middle of which presents a Samaritan traveler as the hero of a parable Jesus presents during a discussion with one of the religious leaders of his day. Although neither Jesus nor Luke used the term "good" to describe the Samaritan, the term has become associated with both the parable and its hero—the man who acted kindly toward the unfortunate robbery victim.

Even in our society today, the term "Good Samaritan" is used to refer to one who takes the time to go out of his way to serve others, to offer assistance in times of personal trouble and mass tragedy. Network television and news magazines carry frequent stories of individuals who risk their lives to aid victims of shootings, hurricanes, floods, and earthquakes. Carefully produced television docudramas, such as *Rescue 911,* regularly chronicle the accounts of Good Samaritans who assist victims of traffic mishaps, rush into burning buildings to rescue those who are overcome by smoke, or leap into icy waters to pull half-dead victims of plane crashes to safety.

UNLIKELY GOOD SAMARITAN

Although few of his contemporary collegians knew or suspected it, Floyd was a Good Samaritan.

I learned this when, in what some people would call random chance and others would recognize as the sovereignty of God, Floyd and I became roommates.

I'll never forget the first time I saw Floyd in this unusual light. It was a cold, rainy evening. We had all been to a service at the downtown rescue mission, where we had ministered to those who were "down and out." After fulfilling our evening's service for God, we had a bit of extra time before we had to be back in our dorm to meet curfew. So we decided to stop off at a nearby drive-in where greasy burgers, onion rings, and thick shakes were the order of the evening.

Just a few blocks before we reached the warmth and safety of the drive-in, we spotted a car pulled off to the shoulder of the road, with an obviously flat tire. Floyd spoke first, "Let's stop and help."

Immediately the other three of us in the car presented our arguments:

"We'll ruin our good clothes."

"It's too cold and wet."

"We won't have time to stop at the drive-in."

Floyd remained insistent, and in the end he prevailed. We stopped, helped change the tire, and sent the elderly couple safely on their way.

During the years Floyd and I were roommates, I saw this pattern repeat itself numerous times. Even though he was respected by few of his contemporaries—and many were outwardly hostile toward him—Floyd never showed off his "Good Samaritan trait."

When he became engaged to Pam, a sensitive girl with a birth defect that caused her to have to wear artificial legs and use crutches or a walker to get around, their loving relationship developed out of Floyd's willingness to help Pam with such mundane things as getting her car repaired. Not surprisingly, some of those who had looked down on Floyd began to see him differently when his romance with Pam blossomed.

However, the day came when bad news spread like wildfire across the campus. Floyd and Pam had broken up. Instantly his stock plummeted with almost everyone to a ranking somewhere between Hitler and Idi Amin. How could this uncouth, uncaring individual break up with sweet, compassionate, helpless Pam?

Yet as Floyd and I discussed the matter over coffee late one evening, his rationale made sense to me.

"Don, I have to be sure I really love her. I need to know that I don't just feel sorry for her because of her disability. If we're going to spend a lifetime together married, I have to know that my love for her is real."

It wasn't too long after that conversation that Floyd and Pam announced the renewal of the engagement which led to their marriage. Today, even though my wife and I only see them about once every five or six years, we count them among our best friends.

Authentic, Unconditional Love

What is it about Floyd that I particularly liked? Not his gruff exterior, I don't think. Nor his bombastic approach to basketball or his frequent disregard for the rules. What I saw in Floyd early in our relationship was something I sensed God wanted to develop in me and in others: an authentic unconditional love for people that leads to genuine service. It's a rare trait, yet one I'm convinced God wants to develop in our lives today.

Now don't get me wrong. Floyd certainly wasn't perfect. In fact, even though he's grown incredibly since his days in college, Floyd still has rough edges and areas of weakness. But then again, so do the rest of us. A guy I see in the mirror every morning has just as many areas that need attention and growth as Floyd has.

SOMEWHERE BETWEEN THOSE WHO DEMAND "NO-SELF" THINKING AND THOSE WHO CALL FOR "SELF-FOCUSED" THINKING, WE NEED TO FIND A PLACE TO STOP THE PENDULUM AT A POINT OF BALANCE.

Good Samaritans are still around. From time to time we see them in action—doing their thing, serving God and people. But there are just not enough of them. And that's the major factor that has motivated me to write *Friends in Deed.* During more than twenty-five years of ministry of various kinds, I've been privileged to meet some authentic servants—true-to-life Good Samaritans. You'll read about some of them in the pages of this book. But it is my prayer that many more who read these pages will accept the challenge to become real Good Samaritans, to commit to serving Christ and people.

But being a servant isn't a popular thing. Few of us have considered "servant" as one of our major career options. Even those of us who wind up in vocational ministry don't always remember that "minister" means servant. And even when we do, we don't always fulfill that service in practice.

The Pendulum Factor

One reason I believe we need a book like this is that, in recent years, the pendulum has swung away from selfless service toward looking out for self. Some of this has been healthy. I believe the body of Christ has benefited from recognizing the need to take care of ourselves, to deal with family of origin issues and the deep emotional pain that so often caused us to equate being a servant with being a doormat. Such service is often motivated not by love or even godly obedience, but by guilt and fear. I think it has helped to address issues such as codependency and enabling, especially when viewing them from a biblical perspective.

However, the pendulum factor has affected the body of Christ. For years Christians were exhorted to forget about self, serve God and others, and be willing to sacrifice. Often this call was both biblical and healthy, although sometimes the call went beyond the biblical, outside the realm of the healthy. In recent years we have seen the pendulum swing toward self-protection, self-fulfillment, and self-actualization.

We can see this at work in Christian circles today. Browse through your average Christian bookstore. On one shelf are books that talk about how dangerous, how wrong, how ungodly it is to consider or think of self. On a nearby shelf, other books by people equally convinced of their biblical foundation encourage healthy self-esteem, even considering it as essential to fulfill God's will in serving others. Some of these might even go so far as to suggest that you can't really be in fellowship with God unless you have a strong sense of positive self-esteem.

Somewhere between those who demand "no-self" thinking and those who call for "self-focused" thinking, we need to find a place to stop the pendulum at a point of balance.

It is not my purpose to criticize others who may differ with me on this issue. However, it is interesting to observe that Luke presents Jesus' account of the Good Samaritan as an outgrowth of the command to love your neighbor as yourself. For the sake of discussion, let me make two observations.

First, Scripture doesn't instruct us *not* to think of ourselves, but does make it clear *how* I am to think of myself. Writing to explain the gospel of the grace of God, Paul says in Romans that, based on the grace God has extended to us, none of us is to think of himself more highly than he should (Romans 12:3). Instead, we are to think "soberly," or realistically, based on the fact that God has given to each of us a measure of faith. Since we are a part of God's family through the loving initiative of the Lord Himself, our view of ourselves is not to be as "junk," but as His unique creation, fallen sinners who have nonetheless been called into the family of God. In short, we are God's kids.

From this flows a second observation. Most of those who say we should never love ourselves don't take the time to address the issue of what love really is. Many have been guilty of constructing then attacking a straw man, an argument which is built up by design in order to be destroyed. The "love straw man" they have developed is an emotional, even unbiblical definition of love.

We'll examine this further in the following chapter, but love is an act of will, a choice. It makes a commitment to what is best for the one loved. Since Christians realize that what is best is Christlikeness, authentic love seeks to move the object of love toward an increasing measure of Christlikeness.

FOCUS: LOVING SERVICE

However, the focus of *Friends in Deed* is not self-esteem, but loving service, the kind Paul called for in Galatians 5:13. As he reiterated the Lord's word to the lawyer in the account of the Good Samaritan, the apostle reminded his readers, "The entire law is summed up in a single command: 'Love your neighbor as yourself'" (Galatians 5:14 NIV).

Luke's narrative develops around three key questions. The first, voiced by a first-century expert in theology and Mosaic Law, is just as important today as it was in Jesus' day: "Teacher, what shall I do to inherit eternal life?" (Luke 10:25).

As a baseball fan who lived in Texas for many years, I took great delight in watching Nolan Ryan pitch. I never had the privilege of seeing one of his seven no-hitters in person, but I watched several innings of his last one on television. Although he was known primarily as a fastball pitcher, "Big Tex" was at his best when he had mastery of his curve.

The curves thrown from the mound by major league pitchers of the caliber of Nolan Ryan had a lot in common with the curve thrown by this Jewish lawyer in the question he tossed to Jesus. Luke is careful to point out that his purpose was to test the Lord. Even a casual reading of the dialogue of the gospels shows that, whether they were pitching fastballs high and tight or sharp curves like this one, the Pharisees and their enemies, the Sadducees, were always out to trip Jesus up or get Him out.

One of the teachers was apparently sincere when voicing a similar question near the end of Jesus' life: "Of all the commandments, which is the most important?" (Mark 12:28 NIV). Perhaps there were mixed motives here—a sincere question, yet in the context of a desire on the part of the young lawyer to please his superiors, who had made no secret about their desire to get Jesus any way they could.

When Jesus countered the religious teacher with a question— "What is written in the Law? How do you read it?" (Luke 10:26 NIV)—the summary answer He received was undoubtedly the one for which He was looking. In the next two chapters we'll consider the two foundational truths of his answer, which I like to refer to as wholehearted love for God and unconditional love for people.

A Profound Question

Jesus' reply to the young man's response raises an important theological question, since He responds, "You have answered correctly. Do this and you will live" (v. 28 NIV).

The question raised is both simple and profound. Simple in that Jesus' words are not in the least obscure. The importance of the question raised can be seen when we consider the overwhelming evidence of the New Testament that salvation is a free gift, one that cannot be *earned* by keeping the law or doing any good works. Yet Luke's context is clear. The question raised by the lawyer is about eternal life. And Jesus replied, "Do this and you will live."

So how do we put all this together? Was Jesus telling him, or us, that salvation can be earned?

Two Central Commandments

The answer, quite simply, is that the Savior lovingly took the lawyer just as far as he was willing to go. As a point of fact, Jesus' statement was absolutely accurate. If this man or anyone else perfectly kept these two cardinal principles upon which Jesus would later affirm—"All the Law and the Prophets hang on these two commandments" (Matthew 22:40 NIV)—he would have *earned* eternal life.

However, James, Jesus' half-brother, helps us solve this apparent confusion with a statement in his epistle: "For whoever keeps the whole law and yet stumbles at just one point is guilty of breaking all of it" (James 2:10 NIV). And Romans 3 tells us that without exception *all* have sinned.

PEOPLE IN THE ISRAEL OF JESUS' DAY HAD ARBITRARILY DETERMINED TO ELIMINATE FROM CONSIDERATION AS NEIGHBORS THOSE WHO WERE FROM A DIFFERENT RACIAL BACKGROUND.

When we examine the young lawyer's second question, and notice Luke's explanation of his motivation—he wanted to justify himself—it's apparent what is going on. This young lawyer could easily have fit into the typical mold of many of the baby boomer generation today. Authorities who have studied the phenomenon we refer to as baby boomers point out how one of the fundamental characteristics is a preoccupation with self, often to the exclusion of other people.[3]

However, it's all too easy to point the finger of accusation toward boomers. In reality selfishness is the virus that affects every generation alive today—plus those that preceded us and those that may follow. Henry Ward Beecher observed, "Selfishness is that detestable vice which no one will forgive in others, and no one is without in himself."[4]

In first-century Israel, a similar self-focused mentality was reflected in extensive discussion over the concept of who were neighbors. Gentiles were not considered neighbors, neither were Samaritans. While the term for neighbor, *plesion,* refers to "one who is near," people in the Israel of Jesus' day had arbitrarily determined to eliminate from consideration as neighbors those who were from a different racial background. Perhaps in the mind of the young man talking with Jesus, and of others who were listening, was the thought, *Sure, I can love my neighbors as myself. So the command demands that I love them unconditionally? No problem, as long as I can draw the boundaries of where my neighborhood ends.* Ironically, while the young lawyer and many of his contemporaries were interested in shrinking the boundaries of "neighbor" to fit their prejudices, Jesus was about to stretch those boundaries beyond anything they could have imagined.

In first-century Palestine, people lived primarily in either cities such as Jerusalem or in villages. Even though the society was agricultural, people didn't live in the kind of isolated farmhouses found in much of rural America.[5] Most of those who farmed the land lived in villages and walked back and forth to their fields to till the ground rather than driving individual, isolated vehicles in heavy traffic the way we do today. In addition, their living quarters did not have the kind of high privacy fences designed to keep out neighbors and others which have become characteristic of so much of suburban America. As a result, there was generally more contact with neighbors in Jesus' day than in ours.

Now it doesn't take a theological genius to figure out who one's neighbor is. I remember the quiet emphasis of Dr. Charles Ryrie many years ago as I sat in a class at Dallas Seminary. In response to a question he replied, "A neighbor is anyone who is nearby and who has a need." Does that mean that we in America can be safely unconcerned about Haitian refugees, since they are not our "neighbors"? Not at all. In our global community, we are aware of, and should be concerned with, needs all around the world. Yet proximity remains a valid check: As distance increases, my responsibility and involvement decrease. I cannot try to take responsibility for people in Africa while I ignore the fact that my next-door neighbors just lost their house.

PROLIFERATION OF DISASTERS

In the numerous disasters, natural and otherwise, in the recent history of the United States, opportunities for Good Samaritans to help their neighbors have proliferated. In August 1992, Hurricane

Andrew ripped across a twenty-five-mile front in Florida, taking fifteen lives, devastating three hundred square miles, with property losses estimated at twenty billion dollars.[6] Earlier that summer, riots left portions of Los Angeles, south of the downtown area, resembling a war zone. Millions watched on live television as a young man was pulled from his truck at a busy intersection and beaten almost to death. The following summer, devastating floods took forty-five lives in the Midwest, forcing seventy thousand people to be evacuated.[7] Then on Monday, January 24, 1994, millions of southern California residents were awakened to the shock of an earthquake measuring 6.6 on the Richter scale—not quite strong enough to be considered a "major quake," but leaving several of the nation's busiest freeways ruined and useless, and between fifty and fifty-five people dead, many crushed in their beds in the Northridge Apartments near the quake's epicenter. Property damage was estimated by the governor of California at up to thirty billion dollars, eclipsing the previous record disaster price tag placed on Hurricane Andrew. The Los Angeles quake prompted the revival of an old joke about Los Angeles's four seasons: earthquake, fire, flood, and drought—to which some sarcastic wags added a fifth, riot. During the same time period, frighteningly destructive cold weather in the Midwest and East took the lives of more than 142 individuals.[8]

Yet each of these disasters prompted action by individuals who could be accurately labeled "Good Samaritans." Thirty-year-old Joseph Tyler, a business major at Cal State Northridge, spent the moments after the earthquake rescuing the woman who lived next door, risking his own life rather than rushing to the relative safety of nearby ground still reeling with aftershocks.[9] Twenty-seven-year-old Wendy Sheeler escaped her third floor apartment and joined with other quietly heroic neighbors to spend the next hours helping others crawl from the wreckage. Robert Horton, who lived next door to the Northridge Apartments, found a ladder, which he and three other men used to help dozens of people climb to safety.

As Wendy Sheeler put it, "To know that strangers put themselves at risk to come into your building and help you—well it just restores my faith in human kind. We have all these driveby shootings, and gangs, and lousy people, and then somebody you have never met saves your life."[10] Even during the worst of the Los Angeles violence, several individuals, some of whom had been watching on television, rushed into the busy intersection to grab the young man who had been beaten and kicked and pull him to safety. At the risk of their own lives, they saved his life then rushed him to the hospital.

Yes, Good Samaritans are still active in the final decade of the twentieth century.

During the icy Midwest winter of early 1994, people risked their lives to help stranded motorists find safety and shelter. In the 1992 Miami hurricane, neighbors pitched in to help each other clear the rubble, after others had risked their lives to help neighbors find shelter during the brief moments while the eye of the hurricane passed over.[11]

And following the flooding that devastated the Midwest during the spring and summer of 1993, President Clinton presented Certificates of Commendation to nineteen individuals who "in this time of crisis . . . risked their lives to save children and parents, to pull people from troubled waters or trapped vehicles, to feed the hungry, to provide water to people who literally could not have had safe living conditions otherwise. And most importantly, a lot of them are committed to staying involved in this for the long haul."[12]

As the president went on to note in his speech, there were hundreds of thousands of others who might just as well have been recognized, who took on the raging rivers to stick up for friends, neighbors, and even strangers.

WHAT ABOUT THOSE WHO ARE UNLOVELY? WHAT ABOUT THOSE I DON'T KNOW? DO I REALLY CARE ABOUT THEM?

No, Good Samaritans are not totally missing from the twentieth century.

However, one of the applications we might draw from the Good Samaritan passage is that all too frequently, Good Samaritans surface from the ranks of those who have not followed the biblical path to a personal relationship with Christ. In His day, it was not the priest—who should have been the guardian of divine law—who helped. Nor was it the Levite, who was actively involved in what was recognized as service to God. Rather, it was an individual who followed an unorthodox religion, who worshiped in a place and in a manner not recognized as following the fundamentals of the biblical faith of that day.

It seems to me that Jesus used this parable to call on those of us who would secure eternal life through faith in Him, and would then seek to obey Him, to practice what we might label the art of Good Samaritanism—to become involved compassionately, even when risk is present, in the lives of others. Is this not the thrust of the Savior's final words to His young challenger? "Go and do likewise."

MANDATE FOR BELIEVERS TODAY

Sadly, many Christians are frequently all too willing to pass on the opportunity to be of help and service to others. Sometimes the reason may be fear, as in the case of a woman driving alone through what appears to be a dangerous neighborhood who encounters a stranded motorist. Perhaps she should not stop to render aid. But she could find a place to call for assistance or use her mobile phone if she has one.

For others, the reason for uninvolvement may be busyness. After all, most of us today have far more to do than we have time in which to do it. There just isn't time for interruptions. Yet throughout His lifetime, the Savior demonstrated a willingness to be interruptible, even while refusing to lose sight of His ultimate goal. His final trip to Jerusalem, toward which He was headed as Luke recorded his narration (Luke 9:51), provided the occasion for an interruption by two blind beggars, one of whom was identified as a man named Bartimaeus (Mark 10:46). The Savior compassionately stopped to heed their cries and meet their needs, then went on to fulfill His mission of giving His life for the world. Surely if He wasn't too busy to perform the actions of a Good Samaritan, how can we possibly claim to be?

A third reason, perhaps at the heart of both fear and busyness, is simply a lack of compassion, a deficiency in authentic love. It's difficult for me to look in the mirror and ask myself honestly, candidly, *Do I really care that much about other people?* Obviously, there are some people—those who are close to me, those I am related to, those I work with or minister or serve with—for whom I'm willing to take the time. What about those who are unlovely? What about those I don't know? Do I really care about them?

I hope this book will help each of us face that question honestly, while motivating us to consider the pointed message of our Savior, generating an authentic loving response. Thus motivated, we will step forward as Good Samaritans, caring enough to move into the lives of friends and strangers alike, willing to care, willing to serve, willing even to develop caring relationships. After all, as Dick Wulf so clearly put it, "In God's eyes, people are the most important commodity in the whole world, and they are to be handled with care."[13] Wulf sees God as in the people-building business, and the apostle Paul makes clear that, by both words and actions, we are to be building up those around us (Ephesians 4:29). Unfortunately, ours is a world which, in general, still buys the philosophy of looking out for number one, taking care of ourselves at all costs. Even the Christian community today seems to have bought into that philosophy to a degree. Wulf rightly notes that "we cannot develop a true godly self-respect unless we respect others. Right relationships with other people are necessary for an honorable self-respect." The phrase from the prayer of St. Francis of Assisi years before—"for it is in giving that we receive"—expresses this vividly.

Perhaps rather than focusing so much on our feelings toward ourselves, our esteem or love for ourselves, we will find this commodity developed as we begin to love our neighbor as ourselves.

After all, the text does not command us to love ourselves. The command is to love our *neighbor*. This is not to say that it is wrong to love ourselves. A later chapter will give consideration to what seems almost paradoxical. However, here the bottom line is a focus not on self but on others—a focus that calls on us to be humble servants, servants of God and of others for His sake.

The desperate need for such servants is illustrated by a story relayed by Pastor Arthur Rouner.

> One wintry night on a straight lonely stretch of Wyoming highway, an area where the distance between towns ranged between thirty and forty miles, a man's car had run into trouble and he had pulled to the side of the highway. The temperature was close to zero.
>
> The man waved frantically at the infrequently passing cars, desperately begging for a ride or for help.
>
> No one stopped.
>
> The next morning, the Wyoming highway patrol discovered his body beside the car. The man had shot himself with a gun he kept in his car.
>
> Pinned to his coat was his own handwritten message of judgment on the world.

"My car broke down. I waited here eleven hours trying to stop someone to help me. I was freezing to death, but no one would stop."[14]

Where are the Good Samaritans?

NOTES

1. Gerhard Kittel, *Theological Dictionary of the New Testament* (Grand Rapids: Eerdmans, 1971), 7:88–91.

2. For a discussion of Luke's Gentile background, see *The Expositor's Bible Commentary*, ed. Frank E. Gaebelein (Grand Rapids: Zondervan, 1984), 8:799.

3. For an excellent discussion of both boomers and busters, see George Barna, *Baby Busters: The Disillusioned Generation* (Chicago: Moody, 1994). The typical boomer attitude toward self and others is specifically discussed on pages 35–39 and 109.

4. Cited in Herbert V. Prochnow and Herbert V. Prochnow, Jr., *5100 Quotations for Speakers and Authors* (Grand Rapids: Baker, 1992), 506.

5. Vine, *Expository Dictionary of New Testament Words,* 789.

6. "Inside Hurricane Andrew," *Reader's Digest* 142, no. 849 (January 1993), 62–65.

7. "Remarks on Signing Flood Relief Legislation at a Tribute to Flood Heroes in St. Louis, Missouri (speech by President Clinton on August 12, 1993)," *Weekly Compilation of Presidential Documents* 29, no. 33 (23 August 1993), 1619–23.

8. "After the Quake," *Newsweek* CXXIII, no. 5 (31 January 1994), 25–33.

9. *People Magazine* (31 January 1994), 34–35.

10. Ibid., 35.

11. "Hurricane Andrew," 62–65.

12. "Flood Relief Legislation," 1619.

13. Dick Wulf, *Find Yourself, Give Yourself* (Colorado Springs: NavPress, 1983), 35.

14. Arthur Rouner, Jr., *How to Love* (Grand Rapids: Baker, 1974), 112.

CHAPTER TWO

THE PREREQUISITE: WHOLEHEARTED LOVE FOR GOD

So he answered and said, "'You shall love the Lord your God with all your heart. . . .'"
(Luke 10:27)

S uppose you were to take a clipboard and survey sheets, drive to the nearest large shopping mall, and spend several hours interrupting men and women in pursuit of many people's favorite pastime: shopping. You ask them the question: "What really matters in life? What is your most important priority?"

What kind of answers do you suppose you might get?

The answers would probably be as varied as the people you would encounter. Some would say making a living. Others, spending what they make. Still others, taking care of family and friends. Perhaps a few might even include God in their lists of priorities.

To be honest, I don't like to be interrupted by a survey-taker when I'm in a shopping mall. Perhaps you don't either. But there are some questions in life that need to interrupt us—that need to jolt our attention away from the urgent, pressing matters of daily living—to cause us to step back a pace and consider the bigger picture.

This chapter and the one following it are designed to help us do that.

THE SETTING

Step back in time, if you will, to the word pictures painted by Luke the physician. Jesus of Nazareth, recognized sporadically by His disciples as the Messiah, rejected by religious leaders of Israel, is on His way to Jerusalem for His final confrontation and sacrificial death. Jesus began instructing His disciples, using three individuals who sought to become a part of Jesus' entourage to underscore the importance of absolute commitment to Him on the part of His followers (Luke 9:57–62). As He continued up the dusty roads toward Jerusalem, Jesus sent out seventy of His followers to invite the inhabitants of nearby towns to respond to this message: "Just as God promised, Messiah has come." As part of His message, Jesus warned against the consequences of rejecting Him and His Father (Luke 10:16).

As Jesus expressed joy over the positive response of many individuals from all walks of life to His message, He was confronted by an incident characteristic of the rejection He faced from the religious leaders of His day. Like the leaders of Isaiah's time centuries before, they honored the Lord with their lips but had removed their hearts far from Him (Isaiah 29:13).

A learned expert in Jewish law stepped out of the crowd of those listening to Jesus with a question designed to test Him. Although the interaction between Jesus and this man bears similarities to an incident Matthew and Mark describe which took place later in Jerusalem, in this telling it is the young man who responds with the priority of loving God and one's neighbor that Christ later articulates in Matthew 22 and Mark 12.

Using a term of respect, Rabbi, the man voiced a question designed to test Jesus or trip Him up, a motive consistent with the agenda of the organized religious leaders. The question itself was not ambiguous or theoretical. It is in fact a question asked by thinking people of our day as well.

However, as suggested earlier, the question contained a subtle yet deadly assumption that eternal life could be secured by doing some action or work. Like many today, the questioner thought that some action or good work could make it possible for men to attain immortality.

This man and others like him had devoted themselves to intensive study of the Old Testament law, constantly evaluating and questioning the priority of the more than six hundred Old Testament commandments. The question asked Jesus was not an unusual one, but rather, one frequently discussed and debated.

Not an Affirmation

When Jesus responded with a question of His own, it might have been easy to assume that the Savior was affirming that the man's presupposition was correct, that somehow it might be possible to secure a right standing before God by keeping the law. Actually, Jesus' intention was to expose him to the true nature of the law he so highly respected. Christ's response was not intended to justify, but to expose all of us to our personal deficiency—our complete inability to keep God's law or to gain God's favor through personal action (Romans 3:20). It takes *absolute perfection* to live by the law, a standard no human being could meet.

This is important, for it is essential that we recognize that no Good Samaritan ever earned a right standing before God through an act of kindness, love, or mercy. Nor can any religiously active individual earn a right standing before God through acts of devotion.

Down through the centuries there have been heroes, some of whom were willing to be burned at the stake because of religious convictions, others who were motivated to do incredible acts of kindness and benevolence. Some, like St. Bernard of Clairvaux, who wrote the beautiful hymn "Jesus, the very thought of Thee with sweetness fills my breast," have led lives of sacrifice and devotion to God. Others, like Mother Teresa of Calcutta, have been recognized as the epitome of good works toward others, leading lives of selfless sacrifice. Yet James made it clear that whoever keeps the entire law but fails in one point—one single omission of a good deed, one single commission of a bad deed, word, or even thought—that individual is as guilty as if he broke the entire law (James 2:10).

So Jesus cut through the confusion of the question to drive this man back to where he had to respond to the real answer to his question. There were two parts to the counter-question Jesus asked. First, what specifically does the law itself say about this question? Second, how do you personally interpret it or read it?

The religious authority quoted from the most familiar words of the Old Testament Torah, verses we currently identify from Deuteronomy 6:5: "You shall love the Lord your God with all your heart, with all your soul, and with all your might." Without hesitation, he adds familiar words from an earlier statement of Moses, from Leviticus 19:18, "and your neighbor as yourself."

Two Magnificent Peaks

I'll never forget the time when these words came home to me with full force. I had been a student of the Scriptures for many years, attended Bible college and seminary, pastored, and spoken at conferences.

But one day during a trip to Colorado, seated outdoors in the fresh morning air with Bible in hand, reading from the parallel passage in Mark 12:29–31, I looked up and noticed the beauty of God's creation before me. Against a majestic range of mountains, two peaks stood out, taller than the others. As I looked from the printed words of Scripture to the magnificence of the surrounding creation, it suddenly hit me. What the Savior was articulating here were the two ultimate responsibilities, the two major priorities—the two highest peaks—we should all seek in life. His words were clearly bottom-line statements, summing up every area of personal responsibility—not only for those under the law, but for those of us under grace as well.

Excited, I began thinking this concept through. Could it be that this was an important insight I had somehow overlooked in my previous years of walking with the Lord? Perhaps, like an individual who lives in the shadow of Pikes Peak, I had somehow come to take for granted what was clearly one of the high points of God's self-manifestation.

I began reading through the New Testament, making note of all the imperatives that had application for believers today. I worked my way through the gospels to the Book of Acts, looking for principles that might somehow fit outside the broad scope of these two priority commandments.

Finding none in those books, I moved on to Paul's writing, then to Peter, James, John, and Jude. Again, I discovered not a single command that could not be included under either the category of loving God wholeheartedly or loving people unconditionally. It became clear that the relevance for us today was no different than when Jesus told the legal expert in Matthew 22:40, "On these two commandments hang all the Law and the Prophets." He was *not* stating something that was true then but isn't valid today.

Lowest Common Denominator

Decades before, in elementary school, I had sat staring out the window, occasionally daydreaming about recess, hearing Miss Aycock or Miss Hafner remind my class, "Always reduce your fractions to the lowest common denominator." Although I learned many other important principles during my school years, this one was to have significant spiritual implications, as I discovered from meditating on the parallel principles found in Matthew 22:35–40, Mark 12:28–34, and Luke 10:25–28. For here were the lowest common denominators of fulfilling God's will for our lives.

Some time later my daughter Karen and I went out to eat on a father-daughter date. The subject of a possible life partner came up in the course of discussion.

> LOVE GOD WHOLEHEARTEDLY. LOVE PEOPLE UNCONDITIONALLY. THESE ARE THE ULTIMATE BASICS, THE TWIN PEAKS THAT TOWER OVER THE LANDSCAPE OF RESPONSIBILITY TO GOD.

Telling her about what I had learned from Jesus' two statements, I suggested, "Why don't you look for two things in a man, Karen. First, find one who loves God wholeheartedly. Then make sure he loves you unconditionally. I think when you find that man, you'll have discovered Mr. Right."

Years later, during Karen's days in junior college, her mother was enrolled at Dallas Seminary. One day Karen told my wife, Kathy, "Mom, I'd like to go down to seminary to class with you today. I have the day off from classes, and who knows, maybe God will lead me to the man I'm supposed to marry."

That very day, Karen was noticed by a young man with an engaging smile and red hair. Later she learned his name was Thom. Although she claims not to have remembered noticing him that day, it wasn't long before he called to invite her out—and she accepted. Their friendship blossomed into romance, and within months they were telling his parents and us their conviction that God was leading them to marry.

When I asked her why she had chosen Thom, Karen smiled and nodded enthusiastically, "It's exactly the way you said, Dad. I found a man who loves God wholeheartedly and loves me unconditionally."

In a day and time when people are calling for a return to basics in construction materials, foods, clothing, education, and just about every area of life, here's a return to basics that shouts at us from Scripture. Love God wholeheartedly. Love people unconditionally. These are the ultimate basics, the twin peaks that tower over the landscape of responsibility to God.

But I'm not claiming to have arrived in these two strategic areas. The longer I live, the more I realize how far I have to go in loving God unreservedly and how deficient I can be in loving others around me.

However, let me encourage you to pause and ask yourself the following questions, as I now try to do on a regular basis:

- Where do I stand with regard to loving God wholeheartedly?
- How am I doing when it comes to loving others unconditionally?

If you're like me, you probably sense a need to become more focused in both areas.

LOVING GOD: THE PREREQUISITE

Incidentally, I do not think it is accidental that the gospels of Matthew, Mark, and Luke identify these two mandates in this particular order. After all, how can we possibly love people apart from loving God? For as the apostle John said clearly, "We love because he first loved us" (1 John 4:19 NIV). Following this dramatic observation, John immediately asserts, "If anyone says, 'I love God,' yet hates his brother, he is a liar. For anyone who does not love his brother, whom he has seen, cannot love God, whom he has not seen. And he has given us this command: Whoever loves God must also love his brother" (vv. 20–21 NIV).

There are the same two major imperatives, repeated by the pen of the aged apostle, so beloved by the Savior, who leaned on Jesus' breast, who heard firsthand His words of rebuke when he and his brother James had wanted to call down fire on the Samaritan village.

Love God.

Love your neighbor.

I pray that if these twin peaks—or twin towers—of the first century language of the Word of God haven't yet permeated your mind, gripped your heart, and affected your life, they soon will.

As we consider loving God wholeheartedly (as we shall do for the balance of this chapter) and loving our neighbor unconditionally (as we shall in the next), several questions immediately come to mind. First, what is love? It's essential that we understand this often discussed but less often understood ingredient that has been said to "make the world go round." What is *wholehearted* love? What does it mean to love God with all your heart, soul, mind, and strength? For that matter, how can we understand Him? After all, we can't really love Him unless we know Him. Of course, when we understand the definition of love and have come to know and love God, we are in position to grasp what it means to love people.

LOVE IN THE OLD TESTAMENT

Before a person can really understand and apply this concept of love today, it is necessary to understand it in the same way Jesus communicated it in His day. After all, when Jesus affirmed the religious scholar's statement quoting Deuteronomy and Leviticus, there was no question but that the concept He had in mind was that of love based in the Old Testament.

So back to the Old Testament I went, seeking to get a handle on the Hebrew root *ahav* and the lesser-used *rahem,* the two most common words translated "to love" in the Old Testament. In a rather detailed discussion of these words, I came across the statement, "From this analysis, we learn that love in the Old Testament is basically a spontaneous feeling which impels to self-giving."[1]

As I surveyed a variety of Old Testament passages, four descriptive concepts surfaced with regard to love. First, such love is *passionate.* What I love I feel passionate about. That's why it's been said that the opposite of love is not really hatred, it's indifference.

The passionate character of love in the Old Testament is first seen in the love of God for Israel. Using the words to describe a husband-wife relationship, Jeremiah delivers God's message that His love for Israel is eternal and provides a foundation for His faithfulness and loyalty (Jeremiah 31:3). Likewise, the prophet Hosea illustrates by his own intense pursuit of an unfaithful wife just how passionately God loved the nation Israel (Hosea 3:1). With graphic language not only true of Israel in his day but having implications for the religious community represented by the man confronting Jesus, God is pictured as lovingly but relentlessly pursuing His wandering people (Hosea 2:16–17) and securing an eternal loving relationship

(v. 19) leading to an intimate knowledge of the Lord Himself (v. 20). Later, Hosea shifts to the motif of a father loving a child, writing:

> When Israel was a child, I loved him, and out of Egypt I called My son. As they called them, so they went from them; they sacrificed to the Baals, and burned incense to carved images. I taught Ephraim to walk, taking them by their arms; but they did not know that I healed them. I drew them with gentle cords, with bands of love, and I was to them as those who take the yoke from their neck. I stooped and fed them. (Hosea 11:1–4)

Here is yet another vivid picture of God's passionate concern that leads to action—and is not dependent on response from the object of love, since God said, "My people are determined to turn from me" (v. 7 NIV). Hosea describes the actions of a loving parent reaching out to a child, teaching him, meeting his every need, all out of a heart of caring.

Passionate Concern

Both of my daughters have children. Donna has three sons, Chris, Albert, and Brandon. Karen has two daughters, Karissa and Hannah. Whenever I talk with them, I sense the passionate concern each of my girls has for her children. Seldom do I need to ask how Chris is doing in school or how Albert's carefully constructed car did in the most recent pinewood derby, of Karissa's latest addition to her vocabulary or Hannah's most recent increase in weight. No, it's natural that passionate mothers, involved in the lives of their children, talk about what they care about. Such passionate care is present in love—of any kind—which is described in the Old Testament: God for people (Jeremiah 31:3), people for God (Deuteronomy 6:5), husbands and wives for each other (Song of Solomon 8:6–7), friend for friend (1 Samuel 18:1, 3), or person for neighbor (Leviticus 19:18).

This observation carries tremendous practical significance in a day of bland indifference, of seeming unconcern. I saw this illustrated vividly during a recent radio call-in broadcast. My friend Dr. Dan Allender was discussing principles from his book *Bold Love*. A woman phoned the broadcast to discuss her plight, which involved years of marriage to an abusive, harsh, controlling husband. She made it clear that she was at the point now where she no longer cared. She was ready to give it all up, and she felt she should forget about trying to confront him. Even though she thought she might still love him, she was just too tired of all the abuse and pain. She was ready to withdraw.

My guest didn't consider that an option at all. "Oh, but you must confront him," Dan challenged. "Genuine love always confronts, even surprises those who are evil and who treat us in an evil fashion, with a taste of both the goodness and wrath of God, of His mercy and His anger. If you really love him, as you say you do, you cannot allow the abuse to continue. Nor can you simply indifferently withdraw. Genuine love is always involved, even when its only option is to confront."

ALL GENUINE LOVE, ALL THAT IS TRULY PASSIONATE, WHETHER COMING FROM BELIEVERS OR UNBELIEVERS, ULTIMATELY FINDS ITS ORIGIN IN THE LOVING NATURE OF THE GOD WHO MADE US.

Passionate love, the missing ingredient in the essential quality, clearly originates in God. After all, we love because He first loved us (1 John 4:19). Decades after Jesus' conversation with the religious leader, John, who was present, would write, "And so we know and rely on the love God has for us. God is love. Whoever lives in love lives in God, and God in him" (v. 16 NIV). Just to make sure his readers, both in his day and in ours, didn't miss the point, he repeated the phrase twice: God is love. Love originates in God (v. 16), flows into the lives of human beings (v. 7), is given back in response to God (vv. 19 and 20), then is passed on to those around us (vv. 11 and 20).

One of the best illustrations of this process is the solar-powered house. Rays from the sun strike the house with all their magnificent splendor, providing warmth, heat, light, and power in far greater measure than can ever be captured or even understood. Yet the house reflects the sun's light, making it visible to those around— not because of any intrinsic light, but because of the light from the sun itself. Furthermore, as the power of the sun's light is assimilated by the solar panels, it is converted to energy so the house and the lights and appliances within it can function according to design. So it is with God's love.

Both Scripture and observation make it clear that all genuine love, all that is truly passionate, whether coming from believers or unbelievers, ultimately finds its origin in the loving nature of the God who made us, who sacrificed His Son for us, who gives us the sunshine and rain, and who gently yet relentlessly pursues us for a personal relationship with Himself.

This passionate element in love transcends the romantic. It can be seen with crystal clarity in the friendship Jonathan extended to David, who could have been viewed as a rival, but was loved "as his own soul" (1 Samuel 18:1). Later, David eulogized his fallen friend with the observation that "your love to me was wonderful" (2 Samuel 1:26). These two men genuinely cared for each other, pursuing their friendship with the intensity with which God pursues us and with which He desires that we pursue Him.

Powerful Love

A second characteristic I discovered as I studied love in the Old Testament is that it is *powerful.* This concept differs from passionate in its focus. *Passionate* describes the energy by which I respond in love. *Powerful* describes the energy of love itself. Perhaps the most clear, forceful expression of the strength of love can be found in Solomon's words at the close of his hymn to marital love:

> Place me like a seal over your heart, like a seal on your arm; for love is as strong as death, its jealousy unyielding as the grave. It burns like blazing fire, like a mighty flame. Many waters cannot quench love; rivers cannot wash it away. If one were to give all the wealth of his house for love, it would be utterly scorned. (Song of Songs 8:6–7 NIV)

In these words the overwhelming power of the love between the lovers is clearly articulated. There's an attraction, an energy that goes beyond even understanding.

Shakespeare captures something of this attraction in his romantic tragedy *Romeo and Juliet,* as he describes how these two young lovers from families at bitter enmity with each other choose to take their lives rather than be separated.

Think of just how powerful the love of Jonathan for David was. It was strong enough to overlook the possibility that Jonathan's friend would, in fact, wind up occupying the throne that should by inheritance have belonged to Jonathan. It refused to bow to the hostile threats of an angry, paranoid father who insisted that Jonathan turn his friend in and who actually attempted to kill his son when Jonathan refused to follow Saul's demands.

Like the incredible energy of the sun, which provides energy in a moment's time sufficient to light the largest of human cities for years, love has power far beyond what we may imagine.

Many of us have read with deep appreciation the writings of Robert McCheyne, the Scottish pastor and author whose brief ministry left him recognized as "the holiest man in Scotland." People would flock to his church hours before the announced service time in order to hear him explain the Scriptures.

However, Robert hadn't always been interested in spiritual things. His older brother David provided an example of loving devotion, spending time helping with family chores and reading Scripture while Robert spent much of his time partying.

Once after an evening of revelry, Robert returned home to find David kneeling in prayer. "I heard you call my name, Dave," Robert sneered. "Am I really that bad?"

David gently replied, "We're all sinners who need to trust Christ." Robert shrugged and turned away.[2]

The future appeared bright for the career of Robert's choice. After Robert enrolled in the University of Edinburgh, David continued to pray for his brother, even while struggling with the illness that would ultimately take his life.

It was only after David's death that Robert, affected by the power of the love of Christ evidenced by his older brother, finally came to trust and love the Savior, who then became the driving force of his own life.

Love That Permeates

A third thing I learned about love from examining the Old Testament Scriptures, is that, like the rays of the sun, it is *permeating*. Not only is God's love to be responded to, but love is to govern every human relationship. This spontaneous powerful feeling which leads to self-giving was to affect every relationship of life.

Moses the patriarch had been invited up into the presence of God on Mount Sinai to receive the Law, God's regulation for life. After mandating holy living based on His own holy character (Leviticus 19:2), God presented Moses with an impressive array of precepts affecting every area of life: respect for parents; keeping the

Sabbath; avoiding idolatry; following instructions for sacrifices; leaving remnants of the harvest for the poor; dealing honestly; avoiding profanity; dealing fairly and with integrity toward employees, the handicapped, the poor, and the rich. In short, to treat your neighbor rightly (v. 15) meant avoiding gossiping, guarding and valuing your neighbor's life, and not harboring hatred or bitterness or taking revenge rather than honestly confronting your neighbor. All this was included.

It's interesting to wonder what must have gone through the mind of Moses as he heard these words from God. He had judged between so many of his fellow Israelites, mediating disputes in their daily lives. Perhaps he felt pleased, even refreshed. Maybe he shook his head, wondering how they might respond to the statement, "Do not hate your brother in your heart. Rebuke your neighbor frankly so you will not share in his guilt. Do not seek revenge or bear a grudge against one of your people, but love your neighbor as yourself. I am the Lord" (Leviticus 19:17–18 NIV).

Sadly, by Jesus' day, there had been a concerted attempt on the part of the scribes to draw an exclusive border around the application of this principle. The term neighbor, a very general Hebrew word, had come to be used only of those who were both nearby and of the same racial or national origin. Gentiles were certainly not considered neighbors, nor were the despised Samaritans.

LOVING ONE'S NEIGHBOR AND EXPRESSING THAT LOVE IN A TANGIBLE, PRACTICAL WAY WERE NEVER INTENDED TO BE LIMITED TO THOSE WE LIKE, THOSE OF OUR PARTICULAR ETHNIC BACKGROUND, OR THOSE WHO ARE CLOSE TO US.

The faultiness of such exclusivistic thinking may be seen in comparing two other statements contained in Moses' writing. In Deuteronomy 22:1–4, love for neighbor is expanded to include taking the time to pursue and return a brother's or neighbor's lost livestock or clothing. You were to treat your brother's property as your own, caring for it until he came looking for it. That this principle extended beyond one who is immediately nearby or of the same race can be seen in the statement, "If the brother does not live near you or if you do not know who he is . . ." (v. 2 NIV). Clearly the concept includes any fellow human being, without regard to residence or race.

Earlier Moses expanded this statement even further, explaining, "If you come across your enemy's ox or donkey wandering off, be sure to take it back to him. If you see the donkey of someone who hates you fallen down under its load, do not leave it there; be sure you help him with it" (Exodus 23:4–5 NIV).

Solomon reminded Israel, "If your enemy is hungry, give him food to eat; if he is thirsty, give him water to drink. In doing this, you will heap burning coals on his head, and the Lord will reward you" (Proverbs 25:21–22 NIV).

Even-Your-Enemy Love

Clearly loving one's neighbor and expressing that love in a tangible, practical way were never intended to be limited to those we like, those of our particular ethnic background, or those who are close to us. Even our enemies are included.

I discovered just how vividly the implications of this principle can hit home some years ago during a pastoral counseling session with a couple who had come to see me as their last stop en route to the divorce court. Making it clear that whatever love they had once shared had evaporated, they sat on opposite sides of the room, throwing hostile glances and bitter words toward each other.

Remembering how seriously this young man had taken Scripture, I reminded him of his commitment to its authority, then proceeded on a tack I thought might bring about a breakthrough. I asked the husband, "But don't you love your wife? After all, you vowed to love her as your life partner."

"Not anymore," he retorted angrily. "For the past few months, she's meant no more to me than the neighbor next door."

Quickly I reminded him, "But the Scripture says you're to love your neighbor as yourself."

Without hesitation he retorted, "But I wouldn't even consider her a neighbor anymore. She's more like an enemy than anything."

Although I had never thought of it before in that context, I immediately responded—it seems the Lord gave me the words— "Scripture still doesn't let you off the hook." Calling his name, I continued, "Jesus even told us to love our enemies."

Not surprisingly, he didn't immediately break down and repent. However, a gradual thaw started, and years later this couple is still serving God together. Like glimmers of sunlight in a seemingly darkened room, God's love permeated and rekindled what seemed to be the lifelessness of their love.

A fourth thing I learned about love from the Old Testament is its *priority.* In Luke's gospel as well as in the discussion of these two commandments in Matthew and Mark, Jesus underscored what every person present already knew. There was no more foundational statement from the Old Testament. Every individual knew and could recite the *shema Israel:* "Hear, O Israel: The Lord our God, the Lord is one. Love the Lord your God with all your heart and with all your soul and with all your strength" (Deuteronomy 6:4–5 NIV). Followed closely by a mandate for parents to teach and model these principles (vv. 6–9), these words were to be the fundamental "stone of remembrance" to prevent them from forgetting the Lord who lovingly drew them from the bondage of Egypt (v. 12).

Even though the principle had degenerated into a meaningless ritual, a caricature of what it was intended to be, the principle of the priority of love, both for God and for people, was still present in the awareness of both the one who spoke with Jesus and those who stood nearby and listened.

So it is with us today. When it comes down to loving God wholeheartedly and people unconditionally, our major problem isn't understanding. It's response. Though sometimes we misunderstand because we haven't considered the biblical principles involved, the major issue isn't understanding, it's application. It has been said by more than one Bible teacher that we need not fear what we don't know about Scripture nearly as much as we should fear what we do know that we don't apply.

In Greek, the language in which Luke recorded the words of Jesus, who spoke Aramaic, there were three most common words used to express love of various kinds: *eros,* a passionate love which desires someone or something for its own enjoyment;[3] *philos,* a noble kind of love for a brother or friend; and *agape,* a word seldom used by extra-biblical writers, and often meaning no more than to be satisfied with, to greet or to honor, to prefer or esteem.[4] Yet *agape* would become the predominant word used in the New Testament for God's kind of self-sacrificing, passionate, priority love.

There isn't space in this book to consider every aspect of New Testament love. So let me summarize several important observations.

First, authentic love involves a choice of the will. It is not simply an emotion. As Jesus saw the multitudes, He was moved with compassion (Matthew 9:36), then He acted and called upon His disciples to act (v. 37). Later Paul would repeat that "Love *[agape]* does no harm to its neighbor. Therefore love is the fulfillment of the law" (Romans 13:10 NIV). Paul himself, in stating his passion for evangelizing the lost, demonstrates how love originates in the will, not simply the emotions. He writes to the Corinthians, "For Christ's love compels us, because we are convinced that one died for all, and therefore all died" (2 Corinthians 5:14 NIV). His knowledge of Christ's sacrificial death and of the human dilemma prompted him to choose to give his life to reach out in service to God and those who did not know Him.

Furthermore, love motivates toward action. This was expressed nowhere more vividly than the familiar John 3:16, "God so loved . . . that He gave . . . ." Thus, love becomes the passionate motivation that drives us to make the relationship a priority (Galatians 5:13) by serving one another in love. Aware of its motivating power, Christ demonstrated to His disciples the serving nature of love by washing their feet on the night before His death. Then He explained to them how love was to be their badge of discipleship. By this one thing— "if you love one another," He told them—they were to be known as His disciples (John 13:35). Not even personal conduct, church affiliation, or righteous deeds were to provide that ultimate badge for the follower of Christ. Such love was to be as much a part of the character and conduct of first-century believers as their clothing (Colossians 3:14), the ultimate expression of their obedience (1 Timothy 1:5), an evidence of healthiness in faith (Titus 2:2), and the antidote for wrongs and conflicts (1 Peter 4:8). Sixteen times in the New Testament we are instructed by Christ or the apostles to love one another.

In addition, love always seeks the highest good for the one loved. The ultimate example is God: He was willing to seek our highest good by giving His Son in our place. Just as Jonathan demonstrated authentic love by seeking the highest good for David in the Old Testament, so Christ sought what was best for His followers, lovingly washing their feet to give them an example of selfless, serving love (John 13).

From Paul's Ephesian statements comparing the love of husband for wife with that of Christ for the church we learn two additional important insights. Authentic love is unselfish and sacrificial, willing to lay down its life as Christ did (Ephesians 5:25; compare

1 John 4:16). Just as a husband should love his wife to the point where he is willing to lay his life on the line to protect her as Christ gave His life to secure life for the church, so we are to be willing to lay down our lives for our brothers and sisters.

Yet on a more practical level, just as Christ provides for all our needs, a husband is to love his wife as himself, providing nourishment and valuing or cherishing the one he loves (Ephesians 5:28–29; compare 1 John 4:17). So we are to reach out compassionately whenever we are in a position to meet the specific needs, material and emotional as well as spiritual, of those around us. Otherwise, John asks, how can we claim to have God's love abiding in us?

One final thought about love: Genuine love models after Christ in His sacrificial love, and moves the object of love toward Christ. In short, when we love other people, whatever we are doing in response to their needs should move them toward trusting Christ, knowing Him better and serving Him.

WHERE LOVE LEADS

If I love God wholeheartedly, what will be the result? And if I love people unconditionally, where will it lead? In the next chapter, we will develop these two important concepts and see how these two essential priorities can lead to a life of loving service.

So how can a person tell if God's love is present in his life? He will feel passionate about his relationship with God and about his relationships with people. He will be unable to take the cynical or blasé approach to relationships so many do today. The power of God's love will grip his life, much as it did Paul's, constraining him to become involved in his relationship with God and with people. God's love will permeate every aspect of his life. He won't simply segment his relationship with God to an hour or two on the weekend or a few minutes reading the Scripture. Rather, like Moses, he will endure life as seeing "him who is invisible" (Hebrews 11:27 NIV). In short, although he does not see Him, God will be present with His love, permeating everything he does. This, in turn, will cause him to care more about others and become involved in their lives.

Ultimately, such love will become a priority—more accurately, *the* priority—for, as Paul said, "And now these three remain: faith, hope and love. But the greatest of these is love" (1 Corinthians 13:13 NIV).

Peter agreed with Paul, emphasizing, "Above all, love each other deeply" (1 Peter 4:8 NIV). We might accurately translate his words, "Make it your passion to love each other."

Growing up in a critical, uncaring home, Mona had never experienced authentic love. Harshly abused by actively religious parents who painted a picture of a God sitting on a judgment throne in heaven—waiting to get her whenever she did wrong—one of her most vivid memories was of a picture of Christ her parents had placed near the door in her bedroom. "He's watching you, Mona," they repeated to her day after day.

It was no surprise that Mona had turned away from God and found it almost impossible to care about people. As she put it, "Most of the time I just felt numb."

Over a period of time during her college years, Mona began to come in contact with a Christian roommate who didn't preach at her but who loved her in a sacrificial manner from day to day. After months of declining invitations, Mona finally agreed to attend a campus Bible study with her friend. Drawn into a loving, warm circle of collegiate Christians, Mona soon became interested. A few months later, at the close of one of the Bible studies, she talked with the leader and indicated her desire to trust Christ.

While attending this Bible study, she met a young man who was passionate about his relationship with God. Although the two of them were clearly attracted to each other, because of the abuse in her life, Mona still found it difficult to believe anyone would really care about her. At the recommendation of another friend, she began seeing a Christian counselor who helped her work through the pain and baggage she carried and to understand what love and forgiveness were all about. Finally, Mona was able to commit herself in love, responding to the young man, and they became husband and wife.

Indeed, when it originates in God, love is the most powerful force in the universe. And it's the driving power behind every truly good Samaritan.

NOTES

1. *Theological Dictionary of the New Testament,* ed. Gerhard Kittel and Gerhard Friedrich, trans. Geoffrey Bromiley (Grand Rapids: Eerdmans, 1964), 1:22.

2. Paul Lee Tan, *Encyclopedia of 770 Illustrations* (Rockfield, Maryland: Assurance, 1979), 760.

3. Ibid., 35.

4. Ibid., 36.

CHAPTER THREE

THE HEART OF THE MATTER [1]: LOVE LEADS TO WORSHIP

So he answered and said, "'You shall love the Lord your God with all your heart, with all your soul, with all your strength, and with all your mind.'"
(Luke 10:27)

It's unbelievable what I've learned about God," Bill told me as he sat back, sipping his coffee after lunch in a tastefully decorated restaurant. Tall, slim, and soft-spoken, he had twinkling gray eyes. But the lines etched around the edges of his eyes gave just a hint of the pain through which he had come.

"Relationships, those are what really matter," he said, his voice firm. "Relationship with God. Relationships with people. I thought I had a handle on both of them till I realized I didn't really understand either one."

The successful sales manager of a well-known marketing firm whose name had garnered respect literally worldwide, Bill gave every appearance of having a handle on life. But as he was quick to put it, "There came a time when life had picked me up and slammed me down."

I had been discussing with Bill these principles of loving God wholeheartedly and loving people unconditionally. With characteristic enthusiasm, he had seized on these two important principles, applying them to his own life. This was the focus of our conversation that warm spring day as we fellowshiped over soup and salad, passed on dessert, but enjoyed a second cup of steaming coffee. Even though both of us had a lengthy list of things to do for the afternoon, we had by mutual agreement decided our fellowship across the lunch table needed to be our priority.

"The funny thing was," Bill said, running his hand through his thinning hair, "I really thought I loved God and people. In fact, I actually thought I was earning God's love by doing the usual things— you know, attending church every weekend, dropping my tithes in the offering plate. Oh, I was giving God a few things all right, but not my heart. My heart was in my work, my career. I was investing the majority of my time there. And my family was suffering from it as well."

Pausing to take a sip of his coffee, Bill continued. "And that's where I began to get off track with my relationships with people. My wife, my children—I figured I loved them quite a bit as well. After all, I was providing them with a lot of money, and more house than we'd ever had. My wife had several credit cards, we drove nice cars. In short, we had it all."

The catch in Bill's voice indicated just how difficult it was for him to talk about what happened.

"You see, the harder and harder I worked, the more and more I just gave God and my family the crumbs from my life. I was driven. I was really into this performance thing. I could get things done. I was successful. My boss respected me. My fellow workers looked up to me."

PAIN AND PERFORMANCE

I waited as he paused, took a sip of his coffee, then continued. "To be honest, on the inside I was hurting. There was a lot of pain left over from my childhood. You see, I came from a broken home. I always felt I had to perform. Somehow, if I could just get things right, maybe it would help our family get back together.

"I understand a lot about that now. Back then, I didn't have a clue. I'd always vowed I would never become an alcoholic like my dad. But then I started drinking. My boss and a number of the guys would stop to have a drink after work, and it seemed like the best way to keep in touch with what was going on—to be a part of the team."

It seemed that I saw a glint of moisture in Bill's eyes. "First thing you know, I began drinking alone. More and more. It was just to relax, I told myself. But it got out of hand. My marriage fell apart. I lost my job. Worst of all, I felt so isolated from God."

Shifting in his seat, Bill suddenly smiled. The tears at this point overflowed his eyes. "But I have to tell you, Don. It's different today. I've really learned what you're talking about. Even though my wife and I aren't back together, that's where I hope things are headed. You see, God's been teaching me the same lessons He's been teaching you: lessons about loving God and loving people. It's a whole different ball game from the kind of performance trap I've been caught in for most of my life."

Wholehearted Love

As I examined the statement of the religious lawyer in Luke 10:27 as he quoted from the Old Testament, noting how Jesus affirmed the accuracy of his observation, it dawned on me that I need look no further than this statement to see the shape and form of a loving relationship between a person and his God. Because even though the religious leader and his contemporaries had so changed the basic shape and substance of a relationship to God, turning it into a legalistic, hypocritical farce, God's mandate was still there, to be seen and applied by anyone who really cared to do so.

THE LORD . . . MUST CAPTURE MY HEART, AND WITH IT MY THOUGHTS, MY FEELINGS, AND MY CHOICES.

Love the Lord. In the previous chapter, we talked about what that means. Now, what about the descriptive word "wholehearted"? The term was used most commonly in Scripture of the immaterial part of man, the part of us that thinks, that feels, that chooses. In Psalm 16:7, the psalmist speaks of his heart "instructing him," and later of hiding God's Word in his heart to keep himself from sinning (Psalm 119:11).

The heart was also considered the center of feeling. Job spoke of the encouragement he gave to others, recalling how he had caused the widow's heart to sing for joy (29:13).

The heart also has the ability to choose, as King Solomon indicated when he prayed early in his career for an understanding heart (1 Kings 3:9, 12). His father, David, had prayed before him for God to search and know his heart in order to prevent him from wandering into wicked ways (Psalm 139:23–24). Solomon later wrote to his own son, warning him, "Keep your heart with all diligence, for out of it spring the issues of life" (Proverbs 4:23).

Heart and Soul

So what then does it mean to love God wholeheartedly? The more I reflected on this concept, the more evident it became. The Lord is to become the priority focus of my immaterial being. He must capture my heart, and with it my thoughts, my feelings, and my choices. That's the reason for the three qualifying statements that follow the phrase "with all your heart"—as the three terms that follow "heart" in Luke 10:27 can be commonly taken to refer to these three areas of human personality.

The soul or *psuche* is the basic term for breath, or breath of life.[1] Specifically, this word is used of the invisible or immaterial part of man which is the seat of his feelings, that by which he perceives, reflects, feels, and desires. Luke records Mary using the term in this way as she expressed her feelings of elation and exultation to her cousin Elizabeth. In what we commonly refer to as the Magnificat, she began, "My soul magnifies the Lord, and my spirit has rejoiced in God my Savior" (Luke 1:46–47). Two things are impossible to overlook here. The first is Mary's strong emotional response to the miraculous event in which she is to participate, the second how her emotions are focused on exalting the Lord—precisely the response we are to have.

Luke uses this word in similar fashion later in the Christmas narrative, quoting from the lips of the patriarch Simeon who predicted the sorrow Mary would experience at the death of her Son, "A sword will pierce through your own soul also" (Luke 2:35). Thirty-three years later, a long spike pierced the side of the Lord Jesus Christ. His mother was obviously pierced in her emotions as Jesus entrusted her to the care of His friend and follower John the Evangelist.

What are the implications of loving Him with all our soul or emotions? Does this mean I can have no feeling for anyone else? Clearly, this is not the point. However, two observations follow. First, the Lord should be the priority of my emotional life. My feelings, my emotions in their full range, should be connected to Him. Second, I should carefully identify, deal with, and weed out any feelings that surface in my heart which are inconsistent with the priority of my relationship with Him. Feelings for things, for people, for activities, must all ultimately be subservient to my relationship with the Savior. This kind of emotional life will be not only extremely healthy but will enable me to be prepared to respond as a Good Samaritan.

The second term found in this pointed statement is the word *strength,* which comes from a Greek word meaning to have or to hold. The word in its use denoted ability, force, or physical strength.[2] Again the implications for personal living are clear. If my love for Him is wholehearted, not only will my emotions be consistent with Him, but my physical activities, my pursuits in life—whether jogging, swimming, sailing a boat on a leisurely afternoon on the lake, shoveling snow on a frigid morning, repairing a broken lawn mower, or carrying baskets of laundry to the basement to be washed—the things I do to care for my body and the pursuits I use it for must all be consistent with my love for God.

The third term used, mind, is *dianoein,* not *noos,*[3] the more common word used for the faculty of knowing or the seat of understanding. The intensive *dianoein,* employed here as well as in the parallel passages of Matthew 22:37 and Mark 12:30, could be literally translated "the ability to think through, to meditate, to reflect." Often it was used of the faculty of knowing, understanding or morally reflecting. Our mental processes can be darkened as the result of Satan's influence and the impact of sin and the fall (Ephesians 2:3; 4:18), or they can be energized and given new capability under the New Covenant through the indwelling Spirit (Hebrews 8:10; 10:16; 1 Peter 1:13).

These are practical implications that grow from the term used here. How do I choose to use my mind? With what do I sharpen it?

Many years ago, when I was a teenager, my Aunt Dorothy—a brilliant yet bitter atheist at the time—gave me a copy of a book on astronomy written by an atheist. She was convinced that if I were mentally and intellectually challenged, she could convince me to give up my faith in Jesus Christ. A few days ago, while looking for another book, I came across the volume she had given me. I smiled as I glanced through it. It had challenged my thinking, to a degree. But it never fulfilled the purpose for which she had intended it—of convincing me to give up my faith. Ironically, just a few years ago, on her deathbed, my aunt turned from her atheism, trusting Christ as her Savior. Certainly a Savior who could love an atheist who bitterly rejected Him for so many years deserves the focus of our minds, our physical beings, our emotions, indeed our total hearts.

Now this doesn't mean that as Christians we are to check our mental processes at the door when we trust the Savior. We're not called upon to exercise blind faith. Thank God for men like Josh McDowell, Ravi Zacharias, and others who have plowed the ground intellectually to motivate us to use our minds to challenge our culture and our society for Him. Thank God for those of physical stature and athletic excellence who are willing to use their exploits on the gridiron, the basketball court, or the baseball diamond for Christ. And thanks to Him for those who can touch us emotionally with poems or songs, and for those who provide counsel and encouragement to heal damaged emotions.

What we have seen is that the person who loves God fully will make the relationship with God the priority focus of all his faculties —physical, emotional, and mental as well as spiritual.

WHOLEHEARTED LOVE FOR GOD PRODUCES WORSHIP. UNCONDITIONAL LOVE FOR PEOPLE PRODUCES ENCOURAGEMENT.

Of course this doesn't mean that the individual who has a physical affliction or disability, or has suffered great emotional pain or has some learning disability, cannot love God wholeheartedly. I am convinced that the point the passage makes is that our love for God is to use every bit of the capacity we have. The issue is not how great our capacity is or how little. It is how much of our capacity we use in loving Him.

An All-Out Approach

In other words, our approach to loving God should be the approach Bill Bates takes toward football. He goes all out all the time, giving 100 percent of his energies on every play, in games and in practice. Some people love him. Others hate him. But nobody disagrees on the all-out way Bill Bates approaches his career in the NFL.

His career has been terminated almost every year before the season begins. Summer after summer Bill Bates has been told,

"You're too old now. You're too slow. You have no place on a championship-caliber NFL team. Maybe you should try to catch on somewhere other than the Dallas Cowboys." But he has persisted, putting in long hours of training, giving every ounce of his body, his mind, and his enthusiastic emotions.

In each year he has been cut, Bill Bates has been invited to rejoin the Cowboys. And each year he has contributed significantly through his leadership, his influence on younger players, his determination, commitment, and obvious love for the game. On more than one occasion, former Cowboys coach Jimmy Johnson made it clear that Bates was one of the key factors behind the Dallas Cowboys' back-to-back Super Bowl victories.

When we come to love God with our total being the way Bill Bates loves football, we'll be making an impact on His team as one of the designated Good Samaritans.

Now if that's what love for God looks like, what does it lead to? For that matter, what will love for people produce?

As I reflected, I kept coming up with two major biblical products or concepts. Both are pervasively mandated in both the Old and New Testaments. One is an appropriate response to a Sovereign God, the other for our human peers.

Wholehearted love for God produces worship.

Unconditional love for people produces encouragement.

In short, these two processes or activities are the products that flow from loving God and loving people. And they are crucial in making me the kind of person God wants me to be, the kind of person who can become an authentic Good Samaritan.

WORSHIP AND ENCOURAGEMENT

Let me put it another way. If I really love God, I will worship Him. In fact, worship will become the characteristic of my life. In similar fashion, if I love people—assuming that such love flows from and is motivated by wholehearted love for God—then the product of this process will be encouragement.

To understand how this process works in life presupposes that we know exactly what worship is and what it isn't.

It was actually the Puritans who started me thinking about this concept. During the seventeenth century, the Puritans used a catechism, a form of learning based on questions and answers, to develop and teach their theology. Perhaps the best-known is one we refer to as the Shorter Catechism. It poses a question: "What is the chief end of man?"

Its answer: "Man's chief end is to glorify God and enjoy Him forever."

As I thought through that concept, the one word I kept coming back to was worship. Based on the English word "worth," the term underscores the fact that the individual worshiped is absolutely worthy, or has the intrinsic value that demands our allegiance. Certainly nothing could be more true than that God is worthy of our worship. He is totally deserving because of who He is, because of the perfection of His character, because of His sovereignty as Creator. We know He is worthy because of all those other truths about Him that we like to file away in our minds and occasionally dust off for consideration during seminars, Bible conferences, or Sunday school classes—truths that tell us God is unique, totally deserving. Yet how can we give Him glory? After all, He has it all.

In one sense, we can no more give God additional glory than we can take our hand-held flashlight, powered by a couple of D-cell batteries—bunny optional—point it toward the sun, and expect to somehow increase the sun's brilliance, power, or glory.

Reflecting and Declaring Glory

Yet worship in Scripture involves two important aspects. The first is reflecting His glory in a manner that draws attention to Him. The second, declaring His glory in a manner that lets others know that He is the ultimate component of our lives. Thus, worship involves giving Him the glory due Him. That's precisely what David had in mind in Psalm 29:2: "Give unto the Lord the glory due to His name; worship the Lord in the beauty of holiness."

One of our problems is that we have distorted our perspective on worship, pigeonholing it to a specific day, a specific time, a specific place, a style of music, and even a specific order of "worship service." This is not to take away from the fact that we are to worship Him corporately, investing time each week with others of His children, lifting our voices, and listening to others as we worship Him together.

But there's much more to it than that. Some of my best times of worship have been on crowded freeways during morning rush hour gridlock, when the alternative was frustration, anger, or despair. Clearly the best option is to use the time to worship Him. You can worship Him in the joy of holding grandchildren, communicating with your spouse, sitting in solitude on a park bench, or standing on the shore of a lake or ocean or before a mountain panorama. You can worship Him at work.

We can see how this works if we keep in mind the two key components that flow from wholehearted love for God: a commitment to reflect His holy, righteous glory in our lives and a willingness to use our voices and our talents to call attention to Him.

This seems to be how life worked for many of the saints in Scripture. Abraham, for example, was described as a friend of God. He was able to worship God even while facing one of the ultimate tests of life. His challenge came when God called on him to sacrifice his only son, Isaac. Trusting God to provide by raising his son from the dead, he told his servants, "Stay here with the donkey; the lad and I will go yonder and worship, and we will come back to you" (Genesis 22:5). Abraham's implicit trust, demonstrated in his unhesitating action, reflected God's glory. His words, spoken to his servants, called attention to the God he expected to come through for him at his most trying point in life.

In short, Abraham was a man who, though he deeply loved his son, Isaac, proved that he loved his God most of all. His love for God demonstrated itself in worship, giving God the glory He deserved by declaring and worshiping Him.

Endurance

Moses, another patriarch, lived through incredibly trying times. First, there were forty years of trial by advantage, living in Pharaoh's palace. Then he faced forty years of trial by isolation as a shepherd, followed by forty years of trial in the loneliness of leadership. A summary statement on the important choices that led through these phases of Moses' life, written by the author of Hebrews, tells us Moses "endured as seeing Him who is invisible" (Hebrews 11:27). In short, he lived his life day by day, hour by hour, as though God were walking right beside him. He wasn't crazy. He wasn't delusional. His conviction was riveted in reality. He knew God was with him, and God was. And though Moses stumbled and fell at times, the overall tenor of his life was that of a man whose life was marked by worship, a man who lived to call attention to God by his life and his works, to reflect the glory of God.

Although many incidents in Moses' life demonstrated this, one in particular stands out. The Israelites had fled Egypt and were encamped beside the Red Sea, relieved to be free from the bondage of Egypt. Suddenly they were terrified to discover the Egyptian army in hot pursuit. In great fear they cried out, voicing intense anger toward Moses because of the hopeless situation they perceived themselves to be in.

At this point Moses could have panicked or become dismayed. Instead, he instructed them to stop their panic, stand firm, and watch God deliver them from the Egyptians (Exodus 14:13). That evening God explained to Moses what he and the Israelites were to do (vv. 15–16) and how their actions would glorify God over Pharaoh and his chariots and horsemen (vv. 17–18).

The following morning Moses did exactly what God told him to do. After stretching his hand over the sea, he led the Israelites across the path of dry ground God provided through the water. By these actions, Moses reflected the glory and power of God. Then, after the Lord caused the waters to overwhelm the Egyptian army, Moses led the Israelites in singing praise to the Lord their strength, song, and salvation (Exodus 15:1–19). In this account it is easy to observe the two identifying marks of Moses' wholehearted love for God: actions that reflected God's glory and words that called attention to His magnificence.

These same marks can be seen in the life of David, who was branded a man after God's own heart by the apostle Paul during a sermon in Antioch (Acts 13:22). How did David come to exemplify a life of wholehearted love for God, a life of worship?

The psalmist himself explains, "I have set the Lord always before me; because He is at my right hand I shall not be moved. Therefore my heart is glad, and my glory rejoices; my flesh also will rest in hope" (Psalm 16:8–9). In short, David, throughout his life, kept his attention and his focus directed toward God. When pursued by King Saul, while enjoying the friendship of his comrade Jonathan, when consolidating his power or ruling his kingdom, David's focus remained on God. Like the Puritans, David's chief end was to glorify God, and the result was that he enjoyed Him. His many psalms of praise, recorded in Scripture, provide ample record of his commitment to lift the Lord up verbally.

Sure there were exceptions, times when David forgot God, allowed his relationship with God to drift, and failed to reflect God's glory. But the overall tenor of this man's life showed him to be an individual who loved God wholeheartedly and whose life therefore reflected worship.

CAUSE-AND-EFFECT PATTERN

We see this in the New Testament as well. The apostle Paul was a living example, modeling the principle of which he spoke in Colossians 1:18: "that in all things He may have the preeminence."

Peter wrote to urge those to whom he had ministered to live life in God-like holiness, quoting Moses (1 Peter 1:15–16, cf. Leviticus 11:44). As he called on his readers to be holy, as God is, he encouraged them to live in worshipful awe and fear at every turn of the road of life (1 Peter 1:17).

John the apostle professed no greater joy than to hear that those who were his spiritual children were walking in truth (3 John 4). Earlier John made it clear that loving worship flows from the intimate personal knowledge of the One who was from the beginning (1 John 2:13–14).

Perhaps this is a good point for me to take inventory of my life. Is worship a real part of everything I do? Of all I'm about? Or has it simply become one category, perhaps even a small one, among the many aspects of life, such as my work, my favorite professional sports team, my hobby or avocation, my physical exercise, or my family?

Does the Lord permeate all my other pursuits to the point where, to a significant degree, each of them reflects glory to Him? If not, love for God is probably not leading to worship in my experience.

The Horizontal Dimension

The statement growing out of the discussion of Jesus with the religious leader just before the story of the Good Samaritan described a vertical dimension of life, wholehearted love for God, leading to worship. But it also presented a horizontal dimension, unconditional love for people. So what happens when I love my neighbor as myself? Although we will see more of this in the following chapter, it's important to note the parallel between the vertical process and the horizontal. Unconditional love for people, flowing from a love for God, should lead to the process of encouragement. If I love my neighbor as myself, I will become involved in his life, just as I allow God's involvement in my life when I truly love Him.

The parallels between these two processes are remarkable. Worship involves a response to God. He has reached out to me through creation and most of all through Christ His Son; therefore I respond to Him with trusting worship. Encouragement is likewise a response to people, of getting involved, of touching their lives.

Worship involves communicating God's glory, making Him known. Likewise, encouragement involves the process of communicating verbally and personally with people.

Both are heartfelt motivations. Neither is to be faked, put on, or generated out of obligation or necessity.

This concept of encouragement—a major focus in the area of relationships in the New Testament—comes from a fascinating word with a wide range of meanings. It is the compound of two Greek words, *para* (beside) and *kaléo* (to call). *Parakaléo* was used in a court of justice to describe a counsel for the defense, an attorney, a legal assistant, or an advocate. From that specific use the word came to generally mean one who pleads the cause of another. In its broadest sense, it carries the significance of one who comforts or who gives encouragement or exhortation.[4]

In the following chapter we will explore how the concept originated with God and how the ultimate role model for this process is the Holy Spirit (John 14:16). At its essence encouragement is personal involvement, involvement for the good in the lives of those with whom we come in contact. And encouragement is the natural outgrowth of unconditional love for people and the fuel which drives acts of Good Samaritanism.

However, each of these two processes can be distorted, with devastating results.

Too Much of a Good Thing

Years ago, when I was teaching broadcasting, one of the most basic lessons involved instructing students to "run the board." A control console or board for radio or production is an electronic device designed to take the signals from various tape recorders, microphones, and turntables (today, more likely compact discs) and mix them together in order to feed them into the transmitter at the proper audio level. If the sound signal is too low, the radio transmission can be noisy and unclear. On the other hand, if the signal entering the transmitter is too loud—the term used by engineering types is "overdriven"—the sound will become distorted and almost impossible to recognize or understand. If you've ever tried to make a home recording and wound up feeding a tape recorder or other device designed for a "line level" input into a microphone input, the results you heard were the unpleasant distortion of sounds that were far too loud or "hot" to be reproduced clearly.

Unfortunately, human nature being what it is, we have developed a high capacity for distorting God's truth. Let me explain two of the most common ways I have seen such distortion work.

We have just observed how loving God leads to worship. Worship involves giving God glory, surrendering control to Him. Our most common way of distorting this process is by something often called perfectionism, which involves seizing control ourselves. We see it exemplified in the paragraph that follows the story of the Good Samaritan, in the life of a woman named Martha—but more about her in another chapter.

First, what about unconditional love for people and its product of biblical encouragement? We can distort this process and its product also, again by seizing control. This may involve my attempting to pull the strings in the lives of other people, to manipulate or control them, or even my allowing them to control me. One term in common use today to describe this process is codependency. It's a deadly, unhealthy distortion of the unconditional love for people which should lead to encouragement and Christlike service. Later in the book we'll talk more about what it is and how to deal with it.

But first let's look closer at the distortion of God's number one demand—wholehearted love for Him which results in worship—the distortion we commonly call perfectionism.

EQUAL OPPORTUNITY PROBLEM

While we frequently think of the classic perfectionist as a male accountant or executive type, perhaps even a military officer, perfectionism is an equal opportunity kind of problem, affecting men and women alike. I'm convinced it is not by accident that Luke the physician records the account of Jesus' visit with Martha and Mary immediately following the question of the Jewish lawyer and the parable of the Good Samaritan. For in Martha, we discover the classic perfectionist.

Obviously, a perfectionist is not someone who is perfect. Scripture makes it clear there's not a just man upon earth who does not sin (Ecclesiastes 7:20). And Paul tells us plainly that the entire human race has been affected by sin and its deadly pollution (Romans 5:12).

No, a perfectionist is someone who is driven from within to be perfect himself—or herself—and to try to produce perfection in the lives of others. Control is a major issue in the perfectionistic life—often because things were out of control in childhood. Control over everyone and everything—from relatives to the budget, children to employees (or bosses)—becomes the perfectionist's driving passion.

My friend Dick was a pastor for many years. He built a large church in a Midwestern city. His ministry was, by his own admission, built on perfectionism. Dick was committed to seeing to it that people performed up to what he believed to be God's standards. He later saw that they were really his standards. For example, he told me how he kept a pair of scissors on the Communion table, so that if a man came forward to confess faith or rededicate his life to Christ and his hair was longer than Dick believed it should be, he could immediately have the problem locks taken care of. With a chuckle, he said, "I suppose Christ and most of the apostles wouldn't have been welcome in the church I pastored."

At a pastors' conference, Dick talked with the pastors. He said, "We so often have a tendency to want to pull our Junior God badge out of a Crackerjack™ box, pin it on, and try to run the universe."

Friend, do you ever find yourself seizing control? Trying to run things? Wearing that Junior God badge?

Several years ago, while serving in a parachurch ministry, I kept a sign in my office with the initials P-A-M-I-T-P. Frequently, individuals who dropped by my office would ask its meaning. Most of them nodded in agreement when I explained what it meant:

People Are More Important Than Projects

Once we brought in a skilled executive to fill a key role in the organization. Since he and I would be working closely together and he would be taking over one area of responsibility that had been mine, I was concerned that he be a "people" person, not just a "get it done" person. But his response to the plaque on my wall gave me cause for concern. "I don't agree," he asserted. "I think it's most important that we get the job done."

Some months later, he returned to my office, a smile on his face. Pointing to the plaque, he said, "Now I see what you're getting at. You're not saying don't get the job done, you're just saying make people a priority."

The perfectionist, by placing projects over people, tends often to find his stress level building when others do not perform up to his expectations, budget as well as he does, or maintain his own strict adherence to a schedule. He is usually in a hurry, and he frequently struggles with underlying anger, anger which occasionally rises to the surface to affect those around him.

Let's take a look at ourselves. Are there not instances when we remind the Lord that He didn't act in as timely a fashion as we would like to meet a need? Have we not at times been guilty of saying, "Lord, don't You understand? I need help—and I need it now"? And haven't we occasionally warned the Lord against working out a situation a certain way, not realizing that He has far more data at His disposal for making a decision about the situation than we do?

TWO TRUTHS APPLIED

As I sat in the restaurant that spring afternoon, enjoying post-lunch coffee with my friend Bill, whose story began this chapter, I discovered he had, by his own admission, been a perfectionist. He had lived the lifestyle, partaken of the struggles.

BEFORE WE CAN REALLY BECOME EFFECTIVE AS GOOD SAMARITANS, WE MUST LEARN THE DISCIPLINE OF WHOLEHEARTED LOVE FOR GOD WHICH LEADS TO A LIFE OF WORSHIP AND WHICH AVOIDS THE DISTORTION OF PERFECTIONISM.

Interestingly, although Bill had sought to help people and be a Good Samaritan, his own drivenness—his perfectionism—which had devastated his family and work relationships, also hindered his effectiveness in serving others. As he put it, "I was involved in all sorts of charitable activities. I ran committees, became involved in fund drives, even collected things to give to the poor.

"But, Don, the motive was all wrong. I wasn't doing it because I loved God or people. It just seemed the thing to do. I was driven to get it done. And I was into control as well. I was good at taking charge of people's lives. For all the wrong reasons."

Pausing for a bit, Bill smiled. "Then through the pain of coming to grips with my addiction, breaking through the denial that was so firmly entrenched in my life, I finally admitted what I needed most of all. And Don, it's the very thing you were just talking about. I needed to love God with all my heart. I needed to worship Him. And when I admitted my need, and really trusted Him, at that point I began to learn, ever so slowly, how to worship Him, how to make Him the priority of my life, even how to enjoy Him.

"In the process, I came in contact with a caring group of Christians who reached out to encourage and nurture me, who taught me and built me up in the faith, who put up with my lack of understanding and my personal pain, who helped me learn how to sit at Jesus' feet the way Mary did.

"Out of that background, I began to learn what it really meant to serve people. So I guess that's how I learned to apply those two basic truths."

Today Bill is actively involved in a small group ministry in his local church. He has personally reached out to many who are hurting because of addiction or abuse. He's been there for others whose lives, marriages, and families have been broken. He has lovingly confronted individuals whose addictions to substance, people, or even work were cloaked by denial. And he has trained others in the art of leading and ministering through support groups and growth groups.

As we left the restaurant that afternoon, Bill summarized what he had been saying: "I was a doer, Don. I could do with the best of them. What I really needed to learn was to sit and worship at His feet. That's made all the difference in my doing."

I'm convinced he was right. Before we can really become effective as Good Samaritans, we must learn the discipline of wholehearted love for God which leads to a life of worship and which avoids the distortion of perfectionism.

NOTES

1. W. E. Vine, Jr., Merrill F. Unger and William White, Jr., *An Expository Dictionary of Biblical Words* (Nashville: Nelson, 1983), 1067.

2. Ibid., 4.

3. Ibid., 741.

4. Ibid., 200.

CHAPTER FOUR

THE HEART OF THE MATTER [2]: COMPASSIONATE ENCOURAGEMENT

So he answered and said, "'You shall love the Lord your God with all your heart, with all your soul, with all your strength, and with all your mind,' and 'your neighbor as yourself.'" And He said to him, "You have answered rightly; do this and you will live." But he, wanting to justify himself, said to Jesus, "And who is my neighbor?"
(Luke 10:27–29)

For centuries men have been told to live by the Golden Rule, which is the title frequently given to Jesus' statement in Luke 6:31: "And just as you want men to do to you, you also do to them likewise."

Unfortunately in our day, both the statement and substance of the Golden Rule have been corrupted. The statement itself has degenerated into a caricature which goes something like this: *Do unto others before they do unto you.*

Unfortunately, such a "look out for number one" philosophy has made this almost the era of the preemptive action, where in human relationships the best defense is a good offense.

Even the title of the Golden Rule has been corrupted with another commonly used phrase: *The one who holds the gold makes the rules.*

Such a view has fed the selfish and materialistic components of our society which, sad to say, have infected too many of us today, including Christians.

However, many of us aren't so inherently selfish that we have adopted a cutthroat approach to life, running roughshod over others in the desire to exalt our persons or agendas. Nor are most of us so infected by greed that it has become the totally dominant driving force that fuels our approach to life.

What seems to affect far too many of us is an approach to life that combines just enough greed and just enough selfishness with a third ingredient, which leaves us sadly deficient in loving our neighbors.

That ingredient is indifference.

So if we pose the question "Where are the Good Samaritans in our day?" we might be inclined to reply, "They have been paralyzed by indifference, slowed down by selfishness, and sidetracked by greed."

A LOOK IN THE MIRROR

One of the things I discover when I look in the mirror is that, at times, I tend to be quite able to spot the specks of greed, selfishness, and indifference in the eyes of others. Unfortunately, I find myself peering around proverbial beams in my own eyes to spot them.

At the heart of this matter of Good Samaritanism is authentic, unconditional love for people. This love manifests itself in an unusual word found in the New Testament, used primarily of Christ, but employed by Luke in quoting three of our Lord's parables that deal with human behavior, including the Good Samaritan: the word *compassion.*

But before we examine this concept of compassion, let's go back to the discussion between the Lord and the theologian over the question, "What must I do to inherit eternal life?"

The man who was interrogating Jesus was the equivalent of a professor in a theological seminary today. His area of expertise was not civil law but the religious law of the Old Testament. Seeking to discredit Jesus, probably because of the Savior's growing popularity among the multitudes, the man raised a question undoubtedly debated frequently among the religious leaders of the day. What does one do to inherit eternal life?

Graciously, the Savior bypassed the opportunity to expose the error of the man's assumptions—after all, even in human terms, inheritance is based not on activity or accomplishment, but on personal relationship. Instead Christ directed the man back to the area he considered his strength, Old Testament law, asking for both legal content and the man's personal interpretation.

The man must have salivated at what he considered to be the verbal equivalent of a hanging curveball down the middle of the plate. Indeed the Lord commends him for hitting a theological homerun with his answer, as he combined Moses' demand for wholehearted love for God (Deuteronomy 6:4–5) with a summary statement of the Mosaic code on holiness (Leviticus 19:18).

*J*ESUS CLEARLY IDENTIFIES LOVE AS THE ULTIMATE BADGE OF DISCIPLESHIP, THE ESSENCE OF HIS NEW COMMANDMENT, WHICH BOTH SUPERSEDES AND SUMMARIZES THE OLD TESTAMENT LAW.

The second of these two great statements became the subject of focus at this point, the "love your neighbor as yourself" command.

The original imperative had been given by Moses in the context of a discussion about making the right decisions, decisions that conform to God's righteous character, and day-to-day relationships with those around us (Leviticus 19:15). The two Hebrew terms Moses employed for righteousness and justice meant to conform to the norm—God's righteous standard of holiness based on the surrounding passage—and making an appropriate or right decision.

Far from being dusty Old Testament proclamations, his statements carry tremendous significance for us today. For as Jesus pointed out, the right standard for relating to our neighbor is *agape,* the kind of love of which He spoke and which He modeled by giving His life on the cross as a sacrifice to pay for our sins. It was the kind of love of which John spoke as the essence of God's person and the reflection of the way He wants us to operate toward each other.

In fact, this approach to relating to other people is foundational to the entire thrust of the New Testament. Fifteen times we are instructed to love one another, including four times by Jesus in the upper room discourse (John 13:34; 15:12, 17). Here Jesus clearly identifies love as the ultimate badge of discipleship, the essence of

His new commandment, which both supersedes and summarizes the Old Testament law.

THE MANDATE AND THE EXAMPLE

Reclining in a borrowed upper room the night before His crucifixion, Christ expounded on the new commandment "that you love one another as I have loved you." Driving home His lesson by repetition He made it clear that the kind of selfless, choice-motivated, sacrificial love shown by the Father in sending Him and by Himself in laying down His life must become the guideline and mandate for relating to each other.

Later the apostle Paul, explaining our responsibilities in light of the mercy of God extended to us, pointed out how our ultimate obligation is fulfilled in love (Romans 13:8). To practice love is to fulfill the law. In short, Paul pointed out, every legal commandment in Scripture comes under the umbrella of loving your neighbor as yourself (v. 9). Furthermore, as Paul noted, authentic love never harms another, so it fulfills both the letter and the spirit of the law (v. 10).

In his Galatian epistle, Paul further underscored how love provides the ultimate expression of the liberty to which we have been called (Galatians 5:13). Recognizing our human tendency to use both things and people for selfish reasons, Paul called on us to "through love, serve one another." As Paul reminded the Corinthian Christians, knowledge puffs up but love builds up or edifies (1 Corinthians 8:1). Paul's heartbeat was that those who read his epistles become what he had become: a loving servant of people, with that love flowing out of loving service to God.

Probably no one, including the Old Testament theological expert who confronted Jesus, knew the law any better than Paul did. Writing under the direction of the Holy Spirit and from his background in the law, Paul summarized the law in what is, in the original, a single word of instruction: "Love your neighbor as yourself" (Galatians 5:14). He reminded the Corinthians that love is the more excellent way, the superior abiding virtue that must govern and permeate every human relationship (1 Corinthians 12:31–13:13).

Earlier Paul had written to the novice Christians of Thessalonica, expressing his prayer that God would cause them to increase and flourish in love to each other and to all (1 Thessalonians 3:12), reminding them that even as young as they were in the faith, they did not need to be exhorted to love one another, but that God had taught them, through His indwelling Spirit, to love each other

(1 Thessalonians 4:9). Paul rejoiced that they were doing so and urged them to continue to abound in love.

Just what does unconditional *agape* love mean to the apostle Paul? Even a cursory examination of these passages shows that he was not talking about some dusty theological principle. Rather, such love affects relationships at a very practical level. For the Thessalonians, practicing love meant minding your own business, not getting involved in gossip, and not trying to manipulate the lives of others (v. 11). To the Galatian Christians, love meant not using others for one's own selfish ends (Galatians 5:13) or bitterly attacking each other the way angry dogs bite and devour each other (v. 15). Authentic love would avoid the works of the flesh, such as immorality, hatred and strife, selfish ambition, and self-indulgent revelries (vv. 19–21). Instead it would lead to joy, peace, long-suffering, kindness, goodness, faithfulness, gentleness, and self-control, which are all products of the indwelling Spirit (vv. 22–23). In short, one who genuinely loves will "esteem others better than himself" (Philippians 2:3).

FOR THE PASSIONATE PETER, JUST AS FOR THE ANALYTICAL PAUL, LOVE WAS THE ULTIMATE EXPRESSION OF HUMAN RELATIONSHIPS.

Clearly for Paul, loving your neighbor as yourself was not some abstract theological concept to be debated or discussed. You wouldn't find the Pharisee of the Pharisees who had met the risen Savior on the road to Damascus debating a question like "who is my neighbor?" Rather, for Paul, love had become the fabric of life that drove a person not simply to heroic acts of self-sacrifice, but to the practice of Good Samaritanism in every area of daily living.

That Paul practiced Good Samaritanism can easily be seen in several events described in the Book of Acts. He willingly cast out the demon that tortured a young maid in Philippi (Acts 16:16)—an action which cost Paul his freedom and brought a painful beating. Later he graciously healed the father of Publius and others after being shipwrecked on the Island of Malta (Acts 28:7–10).

The Apostles' Teaching

For the passionate Peter, just as for the analytical Paul, love was the ultimate expression of human relationships. For Peter, the man whose love for his Savior had been examined and challenged by the Lord before his peers (John 21:15–17), love for each other was the natural outgrowth of obeying the gospel in response to His love (1 Peter 1:8, 22). Since brotherly love was God's ultimate design, Peter used a present imperative to call for *agape* love, passionately felt, genuinely experienced, and expressed by a willingness to stretch out to others. That's the essence of what he called for in his brief statement of 1 Peter 1:22 (NIV), "Have sincere love for your brothers."

Peter had seen this kind of love exemplified by the Lord Jesus Christ. Ironically, he had also seen a Good Samaritan kind of love modeled by a woman who lived in Joppa, where he ministered for a time after persecution broke out in Jerusalem. During his stay in Joppa, Peter had come in contact with a woman named Tabitha, or Dorcas, who was "full of good works and charitable deeds which she did" (Acts 9:36). When she died, Peter, who was in nearby Lydda, was invited to return, perhaps to conduct an appropriate funeral service for one who had gained so much respect among the Christians in her community.

When Peter was brought into the upper chamber where her body lay, all the widows of the church were present. Grieving, they showed Peter the coats and garments Dorcas had made for them. What a stirring example of a first-century Good Samaritan—one who had worked behind the scenes, not to seek credit or for selfish motive, but showing a willingness to serve, even in such thankless tasks as sewing clothing to give to those who were poor and could not care for themselves. Certainly there could not have been a more appropriate person upon whom Peter could perform the miracle of restoration to life than Dorcas. Perhaps he was thinking of her chronic, infectious case of *agape* love and its fervent expression in charitable deeds when he penned that passionate exhortation to love near the beginning of his first epistle and his follow-up call to "Honor all people. Love the brotherhood" (1 Peter 2:17).

The apostle John is the New Testament writer who gives fullest expression to the mandate to love one another. Ironically, it was this disciple, known along with his brother James as a son of thunder, who expressed the desire to call down fire from heaven on a

Samaritan village that rejected Jesus' message. As an old man, John finally came to understand not only that God is light and in Him is no darkness at all (1 John 1:5), but that God is love and that the one who lives in love as an abiding characteristic is in fellowship with God (1 John 4:8, 16). He even connected the concepts of light and love, pointing out that the one who loves his brother abides in the light and does not cause others to stumble. John was quick to remind his readers that he and the other apostles were simply passing on the authoritative word from the lips of the Lord Himself, a message that demanded that they love one another (1 John 3:11). According to John, authentic love never responds in hostile or aggressive fashion, like Cain who killed his brother (v. 12) or in the way typical of a selfish, dispassionate world (v. 13). Rather, we as believers are to show the authenticity of our life in Christ by the reality of our love for each other (v. 14).

However, for John, as for Paul and Peter, such love was not simply an ethereal or emotional quality. Like God's love for us, it is sacrificial, willing to follow the example modeled by Christ by laying down our lives for each other (v. 16). Whereas many of us today live in comfortable societies where the idea of putting our life on the line for someone else is almost a foreign concept, such sacrificial expressions of love were certainly not unusual in a first-century society where Christians were frequently pressured by a hostile government to betray each other, at the risk of their own lives if they refused.

However, John took loving one another a step further than the dramatic and sacrificial, pointing out that genuine love reaches out with compassion to those in need, never refusing to meet the needs of those we are able to help (v. 17). As he went on to point out, such love doesn't simply express the right words, it takes the right action (v. 18).

This authentic love, the biblical kind, the kind Christ, Paul, Peter, and John modeled and wrote about, moves into action rather than simply analyzing or discussing its limits. It demonstrates a willingness to sacrifice rather than a desire to remain uninvolved. It will put its very life as well as its resources on the line rather than being motivated by selfish personal interest.

From our examination of how these biblical writers described this kind of love, two questions surface. First, what is the motivation at the heart of such love? Second, how does it express itself?

Heartfelt Motivation

As we read through the narrative of Jesus' conversation with the lawyer, it is almost as though the phrase "and your neighbor as yourself" becomes the jumping-off point for an attempt on the part of this theological authority to justify his own approach to life. After all, his question—"Who is my neighbor?"—had been raised and debated often in learned Jewish circles. Similarly, certain questions become the focal point for intense theological discussion in our day, questions such as whether the Rapture of the church precedes all, part, or none of the Tribulation; what spiritual gifts should be emphasized today; or at what point we should draw the lines of doctrinal cooperation or separation (this was one that also frequently came up in Jesus' day).

None of these questions is unimportant. The problem comes when they deflect us from taking action on biblical mandates. After all, it's much easier to call a symposium, bring in several authorities (perhaps in a talk show format), and try to define our terms. That's precisely what the lawyer was saying to Jesus. He was calling for definition and discussion, while Jesus called for passion that leads to action.

Warren Wiersbe tells the story of how Dwight Moody and Ira Sankey stood on a street corner in Indianapolis, Indiana. After Sankey's singing and Moody's encouragement gathered a crowd,[1] the evangelist stood on a soapbox and began preaching a sermon to an interested audience of men who were headed home from work. As the crowd grew larger, Moody led them down the street to an opera house and preached to them again. Following his sermon, he looked at his watch and announced, "I must now close the meeting. There's going to be a convention in here in a few minutes to discuss the subject 'How to Reach the Masses.'"

Some people like to discuss and analyze the truth to death. Others, like Moody and Sankey, just prefer to act on the truth they know.

But is there some factor that can make the difference, that can move us from dispassionate discussion to passionate action? There is, and it's reflected in a term found only twelve times in the New Testament. Nine are in the first two gospels, where it is used exclusively of the Lord. Three are used of individuals in parables recorded by Matthew and Luke, showing how this outgrowth of *agape* love is to be applied in our personal experience. The word used is *splagchnizomai,* or compassion.

This is not one of those words with a rich history from the Old Testament, from early Jewish writers such as Josephus or Philo, or even from the contemporary Greek of the day. In early Greek the term had been used of the inward parts of a sacrifice, such as the heart, liver, lungs, and kidneys, which were separated from the sacrificed animal and often consumed by pagan participants at a sacrificial meal. Eventually the term came to be used in much the same way we would use the term "heart" or "guts." Most nonbiblical uses of this word were of a rather crass nature, bearing no resemblance to the heartfelt mercy of which the Lord spoke when He used the term.

One New Testament linguistic authority notes that, with the exception of the Good Samaritan, the father in the prodigal son story, and the forgiving master in Matthew 18, "there is no instance of the word being used of men. It is always used to describe the attitude of Jesus, and it characterizes the divine nature of His acts."[2] This word for compassion describes the underlying attitude of a caring God for people whose emotional response to Him ranged from careless indifference to outright hostility.

Christ's Compassion

The first use of this term is in Matthew 9:36 when Jesus was engaged in an intensely active ministry in Galilee. Surveying the multitudes, He was moved with compassion toward them because they fainted and were scattered like sheep without shepherds. But such compassion doesn't exist in isolation. It always leads to action. Jesus' response was to call on His disciples to pray for laborers in the harvest field (vv. 37–38), a prayer the Lord ultimately answered by sending the twelve on a mission of preaching and healing (Matthew 10:1–8).

Later, shortly after the beheading of John the Baptizer, and following a brief withdrawal into a private place, Jesus spotted a great crowd of people coming to Him (Matthew 14:14). Again moved with compassion, He began healing their sick.

Later, near the Sea of Galilee in a mountainous area, Jesus voiced His compassion toward the multitude, observing that they did not have enough energy to go home without fainting on the way (Matthew 15:32). In response to their need, Jesus took seven loaves and a few fish and fed four thousand men plus women and children who had gathered nearby (vv. 33–39). Mark records Jesus using the same word to express His compassion in the same setting (Mark 8:1–9).

Luke's gospel includes an incident in the city of Nain, where Jesus, because He had compassion on a widow whose only son had died, interrupted a funeral procession (Luke 7:11–13). Again the order of the Lord's response is significant. He saw the woman, responded emotionally with compassion, then took action. His action must have appeared shocking to the people in the funeral procession, for He urged the woman to stop weeping. Perhaps some in the crowd even resented His intrusion. But before anyone had an opportunity to express themselves, He walked over, touched the open coffin, and called on the young man to arise. Luke, writing from his background as a physician, noted that, "And he who was dead sat up and began to speak" (v. 15).

While this miracle was clearly designed to demonstrate Christ's deity and messiahship (v. 16), the Savior's immediate action flowed out of a heart of compassion, an inner emotional response to data received by the senses, indicating that someone nearby was hurting and in need. It was a need He was capable of meeting—and He did.

Two other incidents demonstrate the incredible compassion with which Christ responded when faced with the needs and hurts of people. One is the incident following the Transfiguration, recorded by Mark, in which the nine disciples who did not accompany Jesus into the mountain attempted unsuccessfully to cast a demon from a self-destructive young man. Expressing His frustration at the faithlessness of the entire generation (Mark 9:19), Jesus engaged the father in conversation while the young man writhed in convulsions before them.

In response to the Savior's gentle question, the father unloaded a torrent of emotion, describing the young man's self-destructive, demonically-induced actions. "But if You can do anything," he begged, "have compassion on us and help us." The word the father used is the same one we have been discussing. It is followed by an unusually vivid word for help, one which, translated literally, means to run to someone in response to a cry. What the father seems to be saying is, "We need help desperately and right now. If you can, please care enough to do something."

Jesus' response was to motivate the father to faith (v. 23), "If you can believe, all things are possible to him who believes." His words provided a remarkable contrast to what the disciples had been unable to do. With tears in his eyes, the father cried out, "Lord, I believe. Help my unbelief." The word for help was the same vivid word he had used to request help for his son.

The rest of the story is familiar. Jesus rebuked the evil spirit, charging him to come out and never enter again (v. 25). When the demon convulsed him, the young man appeared dead. But Jesus lifted him, restoring him to vitality and to his grateful father.

What a remarkable scene; though frustrated with the unbelief of an entire generation, Jesus cared enough for the father to respond, and did so in such a way as to meet an even more basic need, his need for a working faith. In the process, He provided strength, insight, and motivation to faith for the disciples, who must have watched in stunned dismay as the Lord did what they had been totally incapable of doing.

The final incident in which this word is used of Jesus occurs ironically enough on the very road between Jericho and Jerusalem where the Good Samaritan helped the fallen victim. Two blind men sat beside the road begging, just outside of Jericho. When they heard that Jesus was passing by, they cried out, "Have mercy on us, O Lord, Son of David" (Matthew 20:30). Told by the multitude to shut up, they kept appealing for pity as they acknowledged the Lord's claim to be the Messiah (v. 31).

> WE MUST COMMIT OURSELVES TO FOLLOWING HIS EXAMPLE. THIS INCLUDES ALLOWING OURSELVES TO BE TOUCHED WITH FEELING BY THE HURTS AND NEEDS OF OTHERS; PERMITTING OUR SCHEDULES TO BE INTERRUPTED; REFUSING TO REMAIN INSULATED, FOCUSED, AND IMPERVIOUS.

Pausing before them, Jesus asked, "What do you want Me to do for you?"

Their immediate reply, "Open our eyes," touched both their need and His heart. Matthew gives the four-step sequence: Jesus felt compassion and touched their eyes. They immediately received sight then followed Him. The sequence is consistent with the other incidents. Awareness of need—hearing their vocal appeals for help

—prompts compassion which leads to action that meets their need. And the outcome? They gratefully followed Him.

THE ULTIMATE GOOD SAMARITAN

Taken together, these passages drive home an inescapable truth—that the ultimate Good Samaritan is none other than Jesus Himself. Coming into this world as God's perfect Son and without sin or personal need, He responded in love. Even though He was on the most important mission of all time—to provide forgiveness of sins by dying on the cross—He still allowed Himself to be interrupted by hurting people, individuals with temporal as well as spiritual needs.

From this characterization of Christ, we can draw four important applications. First, as the rejected Good Samaritan, He died to meet our greatest need, thereby providing in His person and work the ultimate answer for the inquiry of the Jewish legal authority, "What must I do to inherit eternal life?" To that question the answer is clear. We can do nothing to rescue ourselves from the moral and spiritual dilemma caused by sin and the estrangement it produces between us and God.

However, God so loved the world that He gave. As Jesus explained to His disciples, "Greater love has no man than this, than a man lay down his life for his friends." That's precisely what Jesus went on to do, lay down His life for them and for us.

So the point is clear. Inheriting eternal life happens only one way. That is to become rightly related with God by trusting His Son Jesus, who died for us and was raised from the dead to secure our inheritance of eternal life.

A second implication is clear; we should not only study the pattern Jesus established as He exemplified Good Samaritan behavior throughout His life, we must commit ourselves to following His example. This includes allowing ourselves to be touched with feeling by the hurts and needs of others; permitting our schedules to be interrupted; refusing to remain insulated, focused, and impervious. In short, we must become willing to reach out and touch others at their point of need in order to communicate to them that we really do care.

We can see these traits clearly in the life of Jesus Christ. When they become visible in us, we will be ready to serve as the Good Samaritans of our generation.

A third important implication, the answer to the question "Who is my neighbor?" can be seen both from the life of Christ and the Good Samaritan narrative. A neighbor is simply one who is near enough for me to be aware of his or her need and who has a need I am capable of meeting.

It is not without irony that Jesus took the opportunity to describe a Samaritan meeting the needs of a Jew. After all, every morning, religious Pharisees voiced prayers expressing thanks that they had not been born a woman, a Gentile, or a Samaritan.

Such racial and religious bigotry were totally foreign to what Jesus sought to communicate, through His life and in the parable of the Good Samaritan. His point is crystal clear. Being a member of the human race means I must care about every other member of the human race the same way I care about myself.

Ironically, the phrase "as yourself" has been used both to justify an inordinate emphasis on self-love and to attempt to deny any valid self-concept, self-esteem, or even godly self-respect. It seems what we need here, just as in the case of many biblical principles that appear a bit cryptic, is to take a balanced approach.

No Self-Love Command

As we shall see in a later chapter, it is often helpful to understand the passage by observing what it *doesn't* say. Jesus issues no command here to love ourselves. He simply assumes a certain degree of self-love, and He calls on us to love our neighbor in similar fashion. Now the Lord is the ultimate realist. He knows the truth about us better than anyone else. After all, it was He who told Jeremiah that "The heart is deceitful above all things, and desperately wicked" (Jeremiah 17:9). And it was He who instructed Paul to write to remind us "not to think of [ourselves] more highly than [we] ought to think, but to think soberly, as God has dealt to each one a measure of faith" (Romans 12:3). In a sense, the Lord just pointed to the reality of the inherent selfishness of human nature to teach His lesson on supernatural selflessness. He both assumes and reminds us that, to a certain degree, we all love ourselves. After all, self-preservation is one of the strongest of human drives.

On the other hand, a proper understanding of the concept of love helps us see that the more appropriately and biblically we think of ourselves, the better able we become to love our neighbor.

So how does this principle work out in life? Some time ago, my wife and I planned to have lunch and spend time with a friend and his wife. We wanted to get to know them better, but we were also concerned with extending love and encouragement, since she had just been diagnosed with a very serious form of cancer. The day before we were to meet them, I developed what might be called a "24-hour virus." I felt feverish and achy—in short, on a scale of one to ten, about a minus two. For much of the day I languished in bed, thinking little of my friend, his wife, or our concern for her cancer. My pain and discomfort caused me to focus on myself rather than on them.

However, after prayer, a large bowl of chicken soup, many glasses of orange juice, several aspirin, and a few hours of extra rest, I was feeling much better the next day. Since it was the Lord's Day, we attended worship with our friends, then drove out to a beautiful restaurant in a small town in the countryside. I was able to concentrate on my friend and his wife, talking with them, enjoying their fellowship, and communicating love, concern, and encouragement. You see, I was no longer focused on myself and my pain. Had we been scheduled to eat with them the day before, I would probably have been so aware of my pain that I would have been little encouragement to them.

The lesson seems obvious. The more we have appropriately resolved the bitterness, hurt, and pain in our own lives, the more we come to understand who we are in Christ, that we are loved, accepted, and related to Him, the more effectively we will be freed up to serve one another in love.

The apostle Paul modeled this truth in his writings to the Corinthians. In the church at Corinth there were individuals who had challenged Paul's right to serve, and whose opposition could have easily undermined his feelings about himself and God's calling in his life. However, as the apostle was quick to point out, his identity was wrapped up in his calling as a servant who had been assigned to a specific ministry (1 Corinthians 3:5). Furthermore, the same God who called him also equipped him with adequate ability to serve (2 Corinthians 3:5–6). Paul didn't have to reach into some "self-help bag of tricks" to come up with positive feelings in the face of the negative attacks of his enemies in Corinth. God's indwelling Spirit had empowered him to serve.

Furthermore, Paul didn't have any illusions about what really made the difference in his life. He was being constantly transformed into a more effective servant by a daily process through his contact with the Lord (v. 18).

Called to serve, equipped to serve, transformed in service. By understanding who he was in relationship to Christ, Paul could understand and become all God wanted him to be in relationship to other people.

Rejecting Bitterness

Furthermore, instead of becoming bitter toward God or other people because of the pain he endured, Paul was able to recognize that God was working in the pain and pressure he experienced on a regular basis.

Let's go back in our thinking to the original statement, "Love your neighbor as yourself" (Leviticus 19:18). In the context, Moses not only called for a righteous response to the poor and the wealthy, he also instructed the Israelites not to allow bitter feelings to build up against those who lived near them, whether relatives, proselytes, or even Samaritans.

Recently my wife and I moved from the Southwest to the Midwest. During this transition to our second stint of living in an area with significant winter snow, we soon became reminded of an important principle. When several inches of snow falls, the more quickly you shovel your drive and walkway after the snowfall, the less chance there is of the snow becoming packed, turning to ice, and causing a great deal of trouble later on. Conversely, once you allow the snow to become packed and turn into ice, you will have no end of grief trying to remove it. So it is with the hurts and bitternesses of life.

Barry had a deep longing to serve God, a genuine love for God and a desire to love people, yet he frequently found himself struggling in relationships. After a session with a Christian counselor, it became clear that Barry was gripped with a deep desire for unconditional love from his parents, and particularly for his father's approval.

Although Barry idolized his father, who was a respected pastor, he also felt a great deal of anger and bitterness toward his dad. It seems that through the years the father had communicated conditional love to his son. The message Barry received was, "Act like a good Christian, cut your hair to the appropriate length, make good grades in school, and meet all my other expectations, then I'll love you and accept you unconditionally." For all his knowledge, Barry's father somehow missed the fact that expectations of performance have no place in unconditional love.

Barry had never brought up his feelings with his father, never discussed them with anyone. Yet as he talked with his counselor, he began to admit to feeling intensely angry with his dad and even thinking of ways to get even for the lack of love he had received. It's no wonder that Barry not only struggled with his relationship to God but had been unable to genuinely reach out in love to other people.

Finally, under the direction of his counselor, Barry developed the courage to go to his father, discuss his feelings honestly, and confront the lack of love he felt he had received. Remarkably, God had prepared his father for this confrontation. Though initially defensive, Barry's dad finally broke down and wept as the blind spots in his own life and relationships were exposed. Both men grew stronger, and ultimately the two wound up serving together as part of a ministry team, affecting lives and exhibiting compassionate, authentic love in a way neither had been able to do before.

We have begun to see *agape* love in action. Motivated by authentic compassion, it recognizes that a neighbor is anyone nearby with a need we can meet, and it accepts who we are in Christ as the basis for loving our neighbor as ourselves. Now we come to a final question. What does the process of loving my neighbor as myself actually look like? I believe the answer, in a word, is encouragement.

Called Alongside to Help

The process of encouragement permeates the epistles. Yet the initial concept was presented by the Lord Jesus to His disciples in the same setting in which He instructed them to love one another as He loved them. Addressing their concerns over His announced departure (John 14:1–11), He promised that those who trusted in Him would be able to do the same kind of works He had done, and even greater works (v. 12). Obviously He was not speaking of a greater work than His sacrificial death on the cross. Rather, I believe He was speaking of those compassionate acts toward other people that model His love for us.

After explaining the incredible resource of prayer (vv. 13–14) and reminding them of the importance of obedient love for one another (v. 15), He explained His request for the Father to give them another Comforter, the Spirit of truth, who would come to indwell each of them and empower them to do loving works (vv. 16–17).

The more I look at the statements Jesus made about the Holy Spirit, the more convinced I am that the third Person of the Trinity is our ultimate role model for encouragement. After all, the precise term Jesus used, Comforter, was the word for one called alongside to help.[3] It was used in a court of justice to describe a legal assistant, a defense counsel or an advocate. In general use, it referred to one who pleads the cause of another, who intercedes for another, or who serves as an advocate or on behalf of someone else. In its broadest sense, it describes anyone who reaches out to help, encourage, or comfort another person. In describing the Holy Spirit as "another" comforter, Jesus used a word that meant another of the same kind, underscoring the continuity between His own compassionate ministry and that of the Holy Spirit.

> THE ENGLISH WORD ENCOURAGEMENT, IF BROKEN DOWN INTO ITS COMPONENTS, DESCRIBES THE PROCESS OF REMOVING INTERNAL FEAR BY INFUSING COURAGE AND INSIGHT.

As we observe several of the key facets of the Spirit's ministry, we can see how they apply to our role as encouragers today. The Lord promised that He would dwell within us and abide with us forever (vv. 16–17). We can encourage by loyally staying with those we encourage, maintaining contact with them. The Holy Spirit teaches us the truths of Jesus, reminding us of principles we need to apply (v. 26). We too have the opportunity to communicate God's encouraging and enlightening truth to others, urging its application. His primary objective is to focus His testimony on Christ (John 15:26). We encourage most effectively to the degree that we point others toward the Savior. The Spirit was to guide believers into all the truth, not focusing on Himself or speaking on His own authority, but on applying the truth in the lives of those to whom He ministers (John 16:13). Likewise, we have the privilege of encouraging others by applying God's Word in a growth process in their lives. Furthermore, we encourage most to the degree that we focus least on ourselves, like the Holy Spirit whose ultimate goal is to glorify

Christ (v. 14). And finally, the Spirit was to encourage by showing the disciples things to come (v. 13). We too can help alleviate anxiety and fear of the future through the process of encouragement.

Ironically the English word encouragement, if broken down into its components, describes the process of removing internal fear by infusing courage and insight.[4] Fear was the negative emotion Adam first admitted (Genesis 3:10). Furthermore, fear lies at the heart of almost every other negative emotion. Think how you would react if you were walking down a dark hallway in a deserted office and a playful fellow worker jumped out with a resounding "boo!" What would be your immediate response? For about two seconds you would probably feel scared to death. That's fear, the underlying emotion. Then, fairly quickly, you would shift to another emotion—you'd feel like punching the guy's lights out. Your fear would have been replaced by anger.

In the chapter to come, we'll talk more of how encouragement can be used by God to deal with fears, and how this ties into Good Samaritanism.

A WORLD-CLASS ENCOURAGER

I'd like to give an example of a friend who has become part of a group I consider world-class encouragers. His name was John, and early in life he suffered a great deal of discouragement and rejection. John's father was an alcoholic, and he and his brother experienced a wide range of painful abuse.

Yet as John became a man, several friends reached out to this deeply hurt individual, extending authentic love and encouragement to him. Consequently, he received a taste of God's unconditional love as he came to faith in Christ. Then he experienced a measure of healing as a result of looking at the pain he had suffered. This motivated John to invest his life in serving others.

I've personally observed him, despite the pressure of a hectic speaking and writing schedule, going out of his way to speak words of encouragement to disillusioned pastors, sharing hours of counsel behind the scenes with troubled couples on the verge of seeing their marriage disintegrate. He has invested countless hours in the laborious process of writing books to communicate principles to help others experience the kind of unconditional love and blessing John himself never received as a child.

I'll never forget one night that seems to epitomize John's commitment to the ministry of encouragement. He was scheduled to be the guest on my radio talk show, but he and his wife had also committed to spend time with another couple they had been working with. So the two couples went to dinner together, and after dinner, John found a telephone booth outside the restaurant. He stood outside for fifty-five minutes, answering radio questions over the phone, in forty-degree weather. He never called attention to the selfless nature of this act. In fact, few people, including the thousands to whom he ministered encouragement that evening on the broadcast, ever knew the chilly circumstances in which he ministered. But I considered his actions the epitome of the self-giving, encouraging love of a modern-day Good Samaritan.

NOTES

1. Warren Wiersbe, *Meet Yourself in the Parables* (Wheaton, Ill.: Victor, 1979), 59.
2. Gerhard Kittel, *Theological Dictionary of the New Testament* (Grand Rapids: Eerdmans, 1971), 7:553.
3. W. E. Vine, Jr., Merrill F. Unger, and William White, Jr., *An Expository Dictionary of Biblical Words* (Nashville: Nelson, 1983), 199–200.
4. For an expanded discussion of this concept of encouragement, see Larry Crabb, Jr., and Dan Allender, *Encouragement: The Key to Caring* (Grand Rapids: Zondervan, 1984), 71–81.

CHAPTER FIVE

—■———————■—

THE NEED FOR ENCOURAGEMENT: THE PAIN OF LIFE

Then Jesus answered and said: "A certain man went down from Jerusalem to Jericho, and fell among thieves, who stripped him of his clothing, wounded him, and departed, leaving him half dead."
(Luke 10:30)

Recently I came across a Chinese word that intrigued me. It's the word for crisis. Like all Chinese words, it's composed of a complex, intricately formed character. But this word is actually made up of two different characters connected to each other. One means danger, the other opportunity.

There's a sense in which that Chinese word is a microcosm of life today. One thing I've learned from my involvement in vocational ministry, first as a pastor and then as a Christian radio call-in program host, is that many people these days are living in crisis, close to the proverbial end of their rope.

One recent evening I decided to jot down some of the problem situations described by those who phoned in to my live late-evening call-in talk show, "Life Perspectives." One caller from Mississippi explained, "I recently lost my job. I'm a single mom with two children. Should I go back to school and study nursing?"

A man from Illinois had moved his family to the Midwest to become involved in a vocational ministry. As he explained it, "My wife left me because I had been abusing her. I've since come to understand that a lot of my abusive actions were rooted in the abuse I suffered as a child. I've dealt with it spiritually and emotion-ally, but at this point, she's not interested in reconciling. She has moved back to California and hopes to relocate there for a job. Should I give up on the relationship or keep trying to reconcile?"

Then there was the woman from an eastern state whose father had sexually abused her, leaving her self-image shattered and her life filled with bouts of suicidal depression. "In recent days I've started dealing with my depression," she explained. "Now I've just gotten engaged, and I've told my fiancé about the abuse. He's ready to kill my dad. It's a volatile situation. How should I handle it?"

Another caller explained, "Just a few months ago I graduated from seminary. It had taken several rough years with a wife and two young children. The day I graduated, my wife told me she was leav-ing me for another man, actually another student at the seminary. I felt devastated. I've relocated to Louisiana, where I had planned to pastor a church. Now here I am with my two children, and my wife has left me. How can I ever possibly be a pastor?"

The week before, I learned that a friend and colleague in minis-try had just received the devastating news that his wife has a very serious form of cancer. They went through the surgery; now she faces radiation treatments and chemotherapy. As he explained, "It's just like a roller coaster. One day what the doctors tell us is that things are looking great. The next, it sounds grim."

None of what I've just described to you is fiction. If I tried, I couldn't begin to make up the kind of catastrophic things that seem to be happening to so many people these days. Perhaps some of these particular crises have paralleled yours. Perhaps your crises have been different.

I've discovered, however, that the common denominator in all of these situations is sudden, unexpected, devastating pain.

ATTACK ON THE ROAD

That's exactly what happened to the unnamed Jewish individual who started down the seventeen-mile road that wound its way be-tween Jerusalem and the ancient city of Jericho, 3,300 feet lower, on the Jordan River just above the Dead Sea. Traveled by individuals on donkey, horseback, camels, and afoot, this road was extremely dangerous because of the barren, isolated terrain through which it wound, which provided many hiding places for the robbers who often took advantage of those who traversed it. In fact, the road had been the scene of so many criminal acts that some people called it the "way of blood." I'm sure if there had been newspapers and television during the first century, the letters to the editor column probably would have called on local officials to clean up the Jericho road. It might even have become the subject of "60 Minutes" or "20/20."

We don't know whether the Jewish traveler was fearful or whether he even thought about the danger when he left his home, or if his wife warned him to be careful, or even if he had a wife. All we know is, he was somewhere on the downhill slope between Jerusalem and Jericho when suddenly, without warning, disaster struck. One minute he was walking along the road, minding his own business. The next, he was in the hands of robbers.

In calm, dispassionate style, Jesus described the terrible sequence of events that happened during those next minutes. We don't know the number of robbers. There were at least two, likely more. Jesus noted that in the process of robbing him, they stripped him of his clothing, wounded him, and left him half-dead.

The Lord didn't go into detail, the way many of our news reports do, to show the horror, shock, and outrage of the criminal attack this man suffered.

You almost have to have been a victim of some crime to identify with the events Jesus described in the series of simple statements in Luke 10:30. If you've never been there, it's hard to imagine the kind of anger you feel; the kind of outrage; the shock; the underlying, undeniable fear; the overwhelming, pervasive question, "Why? Why did this have to happen? Why did this have to happen to me?"

And under it all, the pain.

In the case of this Jewish traveler, it was the physical pain of being beaten—whether with hands, clubs, or other weapons—plus the emotional pain of being stripped of his clothing, left in the indignity of undress on a public road, all combined with the pain and uncertainty of not knowing whether he would live or die, or whether someone would come along who would care enough to help him.

SUDDEN, UNEXPECTED PAIN

Some time ago, while calling my wife from a motel room in Abilene, Texas, where I had traveled to speak, a sharp copper wire protruding from the touchtone pad next to the number nine punctured my finger. The pain was sudden and sharp and certainly unexpected—have you ever been wounded by a touchtone telephone?

But sudden, unexpected painful things seem to be happening to more and more of us more and more of the time. Such pain can be seemingly minor, or it can have major, life-changing impact. Always, it disrupts and it hurts.

People who've been through painful circumstances of a greater magnitude, including those who have been victims of crimes, tell me that's exactly what happens to them. In fact, as I've talked with numerous Christian counselors, psychiatrists, psychologists, and therapists, I've discovered two things happen as a result of pain.

First, at a certain level, the memory of the pain and the painful event is burned into our minds in such a way that it simply cannot be forgotten. It winds up playing itself over and over, like one of the old thirty-three-and-a-third vinyl "long play" record albums we used to listen to back in the pre-CD era. Remember how they would get stuck in a certain groove, and you'd hear the same phrase over and over again? During my early days in radio, it was a frequently recurring hazard for those who played records to have them become stuck in a groove while we had stepped away to the coffeepot or the restroom.

But there's a second way the human mind copes with pain. When the pain level and its devastating effect passes a certain threshold, God has somehow designed our minds in such a way that we literally protect ourselves from it by blocking out the conscious memory of both the pain and the event which produced it.

The Pain of Trauma

That's what often happens to those who have been traumatized sexually, physically, or emotionally during early childhood years. Frequently, such individuals have significant "memory gaps." They may remember very little about their early childhood, or they may have vivid memories of grades one and two, yet remember little or nothing about grades three, four, and five, or, for that matter, all the way to junior high or high school. Most commonly this occurs as a result of some form of traumatic abuse, perhaps by a parent or other close relative, a day care worker, a neighbor, a scout or club leader, or possibly even someone from church. In fact, it may be that the individuals who produced the abuse and pain were seemingly loving, moral people, active in church. It may be that they had been victims as children, since statistics indicate that most perpetrators of childhood sexual abuse and other forms of abuse were victims themselves. Perhaps they were even involved in the occult, carrying on elaborate, unspeakable rituals of abuse which left those exposed to them with long-term emotional and even physical scars.

Whenever violent trauma of this kind occurs, the vivid, painful memories—memories that bring up all the attendant fears and feelings—are present. Sometimes they are covered by that merciful defense mechanism that takes away the memory. Always they are there. Ultimately—perhaps years later—they will need to be faced.

Steve Palermo suffered such a violent event one summer evening in 1991 near a popular Egyptian restaurant in North Dallas. He had traveled to Texas from his home in suburban Kansas City to ply his trade as a major league umpire. Following the evening's ball game, Palermo and several friends were finishing their meal. Suddenly a commotion broke out. Two waitresses were accosted by two robbers in the parking lot next to the restaurant. Reacting instinctively, Palermo and another man decided to become Good Samaritans.

Rushing to the aid of the two women, the men forced the would-be robbers to flee. As Palermo, who was in excellent physical shape because of his career, chased one of the robbers, the young man suddenly stopped, pulled a pistol, and fired a bullet which struck Palermo, causing permanent damage to his spinal column. In an instant, life for Steve Palermo had been invaded by incredible pain: the physical pain of an injury that would require multiple surgeries and would likely keep him from walking, the emotional trauma of becoming a crime victim, the loss of his career, and the inability to earn a living in the way he had before the incident.

Two years after the shooting, Palermo was still undergoing surgeries in the hope that he would eventually recover the use of his limbs and perhaps even be able to return to the major leagues.

Steve Palermo's experience should serve as a warning against getting involved in Good Samaritan activities for the wrong reasons. Ask yourself: Am I doing this so people will think of me as caring? Is my primary motivation the praise of men? Or do I genuinely care about reaching out to others without regard for the effect my actions may have on my personal comfort or welfare? After all, being a real friend can be risky, even painful.

Incredible pain. It often comes suddenly. Unexpectedly. Pain caused by the untimely death of a child. Chronic, long-term pain, brought on by the ravages of cancer. The pain of a decade of depressive personal lethargy caused by chronic fatigue syndrome.

Emotional pain when, after thirty-four years of marriage, a spouse says, "I wasn't happy when we married, and I haven't been happy a day since then. I want out." The pain of two sets of parents who receive phone calls telling them their fifteen-year-olds have been involved in a serious traffic accident and have been rushed to the hospital in critical condition. One child doesn't survive. The other faces months, perhaps years, of incredible effort in an attempt to regain health.

Then there was Cindy's pain.

Chronicles of Abuse

For Cindy the abuse started at a very early age. For years she just blocked the horrible memories from her mind, refusing even to look at the pain of her childhood. Finally the trauma of being the victim of a brutal rape at the hands of someone she knew forced Cindy to look at the reality of her incredibly painful past.

The abuse had started when she was just a little girl, and it continued well into her teenage years. As she began to look at her pain, Cindy finally realized that at least twelve people had abused her. These perpetrators ranged from family members to friends of her mother to people in her community. Each victimization brought its own layer of pain and destruction. Feeling rejected and abandoned by her mother, suffering abuse by virtually every significant male in her life, Cindy seemed like an individual who would never be able to recover.

In her own words Cindy told how "when I was quite young, I began to isolate myself from others because of sexual abuse. . . . Even when I was a very young child, I felt I could tell absolutely no one what was happening to me. . . . I never played with children in the neighborhood. It just seemed safer to stay away from everyone. Trying to figure out if there were 'good' persons around me kept me too confused. I also remember always feeling sad, dirty, and completely alone. . . . Most of all, I just felt emptiness, emptiness bigger than me.

"When I actually recognized that I had been a victim of child molestation, I was devastated. I felt more shame than ever. My flashbacks became more frequent, and I felt despicable and worthless. As God's restorative power began to take hold of me, however, I not only saw myself as a victim, but also that it was possible to become a survivor."[1]

It took years, but Cindy recovered through the influence of the story of Joseph in Scripture and the compassion of friends who reached out to her in love, modeling and expressing the care and concern of the Lord Jesus Christ, and helping her ultimately to the place where she experienced emotional healing.

Lynne also began encountering pain at an early age. Although she grew up in a loving home, her parents frequently left her with a neighbor family, unaware of the neighbors' involvement in unspeakably horrible ceremonies as a part of their ritualistic worship of Satan. Although the parents would not discover what had happened to Lynne until years later, they soon began seeing the results of the pain Lynne acted out in an increasingly rebellious lifestyle during her teenage years.

Although she had blocked most of the memories of her abuse from her conscious mind, Lynne began having flashbacks. Left with a little baby and a broken marriage, struggling to hold a job, her life began disintegrating. More and more depressed, she found herself cutting and burning herself because of her intense emotional pain. Eventually she lost touch with reality and was almost committed permanently to a state mental hospital.

One factor that prevented this compounding of tragedy in Lynne's painful life was the loving intervention of a pair of Good Samaritans: Brian, her therapist, and his wife, Laura. Even though other clinical professionals had become convinced that Lynne was the victim of some hopeless mental disorder such as schizophrenia, Brian was sure, based on his professional counseling experience and the research he had been involved in, that Lynne's combination of debilitating symptoms was caused by multiple personality disorder. The memories had been indelibly ingrained in her subconscious mind, then buried as her mind had dissociated from the trauma her body experienced. She had literally created a series of personalities into which she retreated in order to remain unaware of her trauma and pain.

Brian and Laura were sure Lynne would only recover if she were helped to uncover the painfully buried memories, process them, and thereby experience healing and renewed hope. They also realized the process would take a great deal of time and energy. Were they willing to become the Good Samaritans Lynne needed?

After talking it over together, consulting with friends, and praying about it, they decided they were willing.

For almost two years they invested their lives in helping Lynne put together the shattered pieces of hers. Their efforts were not without trauma, setback, and rejection. Frequently things seemed hopeless. Even though Lynne worked hard and responded to their love, there were times when she would revert into an angry or hostile personality. Yet they prayed, they cared, and they persisted in reaching out to Lynne with the love of the Lord Jesus Christ.

THE QUESTION SOMETIMES ARISES, DO WE ALL REALLY NEED THE ENCOURAGEMENT OF OTHERS?

Finally, responding to individual therapy and a support group that included others who had been through similar trauma, Lynne began to turn the corner. Brian and Laura saw significant improvement. The frantic phone calls in the middle of the night, the suicidal thinking, the occasional episodes of bizarre behavior in response to a specific pain coming to the surface—these became farther and farther apart.

Years later, a new marriage, a new child, and preparation for a new career became milestones in a new life for Lynne. Brian and Laura could look back on countless hours of Good Samaritan involvement in the life of someone who ultimately experienced God's healing and regained His hope.

What made the difference in Cindy's life and in Lynne's?

One key factor was significant people who entered each of their lives, demonstrating unconditional love for them and showing that love in the form of encouragement. In short, they had been called alongside to help.

THE NEED FOR HUMAN ENCOURAGEMENT

But the question sometimes arises, Do we all really need the encouragement of others? After all, if God is our sufficiency, if we have everything we need in Christ, why should we need human encouragement?

Perhaps the best place to see the importance of encouragement in the midst of pain is through the lens of an event, described by three of the four gospels, just before Jesus' arrest in the Garden of Gethsemane. As He entered this garden just outside the walls of Jerusalem, Jesus must have felt the painful weight of approaching the point of separation from His Father. He was about to bear the sins of the world. Two of the gospels record how deeply distressed, even depressed, He felt in His human spirit (Matthew 26:37; Mark 14:33–34). It was at this point, feeling "exceedingly sorrowful, even to death," that Jesus reached out to the three men who had been closest to Him throughout His years of ministry. He invited Peter, James, and John to come with Him, to stay and watch with Him. Even though their eyes became heavy and they fell asleep—and He lovingly confronted them for that failure—the event nonetheless demonstrated an important principle: Painful circumstances and traumatic events cry out for human encouragers to come alongside to help us.

The same principle surfaced in the life of the apostle Paul. Writing to the church in Corinth—where his ministry and integrity had been severely questioned—he told them about a time of trouble that occurred during a visit to Asia Minor when, as he put it, "we were burdened beyond measure, above strength, so that we despaired even of life" (2 Corinthians 1:8). After explaining how that event reminded him of the importance of trusting the Lord rather than himself and affirming continued trust in Him (vv. 9–10), Paul underscored the valuable personal encouragement he received from knowing they were praying and that they had given, along with others, to help meet his need (v. 11). "You helped," Paul told them, "by your praying, your giving to us in a tangible way, and we are grateful."

Later in the same epistle, Paul described another traumatic time. This event in Macedonia permitted the apostle and his company no rest. They were, as he described it, "troubled on every side. Outside were conflicts, inside were fears" (2 Corinthians 7:5). "Nevertheless," he continued, "God, who comforts the downcast, comforted us by the coming of Titus" (v. 6). As Paul went on to explain, the presence of this fellow servant with whom Paul had ministered earlier, coupled with his encouraging expressions conveying the earnest desire and love of the Corinthians, lifted the apostle's spirit and brought significant joy (v. 7).

Later, reaching the ebb of his life and ministry, locked away in the Mammertine prison in Rome, Paul wrote Timothy those memorable words, "Be diligent to come to me quickly. . . . Do your utmost to come before winter" (2 Timothy 4:9, 21).

If Jesus needed human encouragement the night before His crucifixion, and Paul requested it on the eve of his death as well as in earlier times of distress and difficulty, how can we pretend to think that we as believers do not need encouragement today? We do.

For just as the highest expression of love for God is seen in worship, so the ultimate expression of love for people is seen in the process of encouragement.

Replacing Fear with Courage

We've seen how the pain of life has created a desperate need for authentic encouragement from those who, like the Good Samaritan, are willing to reach out to desperately hurting individuals. Problems press in and life is incredibly busy. As a result, many feel like giving up. And often those in pain don't feel comfortable turning to people for help.

> THE PERSON WHO ENCOURAGES, WHO HELPS US REPLACE OUR FEARS WITH COURAGE, IS THE INDIVIDUAL WHO IS CALLED ALONGSIDE TO HELP.

Some time ago I sat in a coffee shop with Vincent, a successful businessman, who was facing intense pressures because of a downturn in construction coupled with an extended period of inclement weather. There was a good chance he would lose his business. He didn't know where to turn or what to do. "Don," he said to me, "you're probably the closest friend I have." His statement surprised me, because I had only known him a relatively short time, and the sum total of our contact consisted of a series of telephone conversations and a relatively small number of hours spent together.

I remember thinking afterward, with his words ringing in my ears, what a sad situation—so many of us have so few people to whom we can turn when things are difficult. How desperately we all need encouragement!

Part of the problem may be that we don't understand the true nature of encouragement or how it works. Since the process of encouragement can be broken down to being called alongside to help, the internal process that replaces a person's basic fear with courage, I believe it is accurate to describe encouragement as infusing courage to reinforce another individual internally.

That's precisely what Paul said the Lord did for him: ". . . the Father of mercies and God of all comfort, who comforts us in all our tribulation, that we may be able to comfort those who are in any trouble, with the comfort with which we ourselves are comforted by God" (2 Corinthians 1:3–4). In a sense, every crisis we face, every traumatic situation—whether caused by pressure from the present or pain from the past—seems to allow that most basic negative emotion, fear, to begin seeping into our hearts and lives. Whether fear of failure, fear of rejection, or fear of the unknown, fear can paralyze us, distract us—in short, keep us from functioning the way God wants us to.

But the person who encourages, who helps us replace our fears with courage, is the individual who is called alongside to help.

From that simple definition, let me draw several applications. First, it is important that we view the process of encouragement as a calling. There is a sense in which we have elevated such things as preaching the Word, personal evangelism, and missionary service to callings, and well we should. Each of these involves a significant form of service to the Lord and people.

But encouragement is just as important and should likewise be viewed as a calling from God. Whether the individual needing encouragement is calling for the encouragement or not, God is calling on us to encourage one another.

The church in Thessalonica was a young but fast-growing group of believers. Paul wrote his first epistle to them to teach several important principles, one of which is expressed near the end of his letter, following his discussion of the imminent return of the Lord and the impending judgment of the Day of the Lord. He writes to urge them not to live in the sweet by and by, but to continue steadfast in the nasty now and now. To do so, he summarizes, "Therefore comfort each other and edify one another, just as you also are doing" (1 Thessalonians 5:11). What Paul was doing, in short, was extending to them the biblical calling of encouragement.

An important corollary of this principle is our willingness to call on others to encourage us, to be vulnerable, and to let people know when we are hurting. During the course of hosting my live radio call-in programs, I've come in contact with a number of Christian leaders, who are often considered by some to be towers of spiritual strength and invincibility. I'm always intrigued with the openness of men like Gary Smalley and John Trent when they admit to times of discouragement, to feelings of despair, and to needing encouragement from friends.

Alongside

In fact, it was Gary Smalley, as he addressed a caller on "Life Perspectives" one evening, who came up with one of the best illustrations of the second word in our short definition of encouragement: what it means to be *alongside*. As Gary explained to the caller, he had recently been looking for a way to communicate to his wife, Norma, how he wanted to be an encourager in her life. Finally, he hit on what he considered to be a word picture that would best express what he felt. "I want to be there for you, Norma, in your boat. Imagine yourself in a boat on a stormy lake. You could be out there alone, by yourself. But you're not, because I'm there for you, right in your boat. And I'll always be there for you."

That, my friends, is the essence of encouragement. To be there for that person, if not in person, at least by telephone or letter. Even more than just physical presence, to be available, to be interruptible.

During the course of writing this chapter, I was interrupted by phone calls from my son and my parents. After each call, I paused to thank the Lord for graciously reminding me of the importance of implementing the principles I was trying to communicate.

A third component of our simple definition is to help. Now, sometimes the people who are there for us are less than helpful. Three individuals who immediately come to mind are the men we typically refer to as Job's friends. Initially they were helpful. They responded to the situation and came to Job. They spent seven silent days in his presence. They were there for him. During that time, their presence must have been a source of real encouragement and support.

But once they began opening their mouths to speak, any encouragement they may have brought immediately crumbled before their harsh, scathing words, as they called on Job to repent of sins he had never committed.

It's interesting, isn't it, how often the "help" component of encouragement involves words. The author of Proverbs was right to place such an important emphasis on the spoken word:

"A man has joy by the answer of his mouth, and a word spoken in due season, how good it is!" (Proverbs 15:23).

"A word fitly spoken is like apples of gold in settings of silver" (Proverbs 25:11).

"Death and life are in the power of the tongue, and those who love it will eat its fruit" (Proverbs 18:21).

Eight times in Proverbs the tongue is identified as a powerful instrument, able to wield incredible influence for good or bad.

As I think back over some of the toughest spots in my years of ministry, I can still hear the encouraging words of caring friends, sharing encouragement, urging me not to give up, reminding me of their concern, their prayers, that I mattered to them. Frequently these words of encouragement have been permeated with Scripture. Often they have been reinforced by tangible deeds of kindness.

For many years I've had the privilege of being friends with Christian psychiatrist Dr. Frank Minirth. Our friendship began the first day we met. I had been scheduled to interview Frank at noon for the talk show I hosted on a Christian radio station in Kansas City. I was to record the interview at his hotel room near downtown. Twice I found it necessary to phone and push the time of our scheduled interview back because of pressing responsibilities at the station. Finally, around three in the afternoon, I was able to break away, grab a cassette recorder and microphone, and rush to the hotel.

As I walked into the room, the smell of a freshly cooked hamburger, just delivered by room service, reminded my sense of smell and my empty stomach that it had been a long time since breakfast. Disciplining myself not to think about my own hunger, I said, "Frank, don't let me stand in the way of your eating your lunch. Go ahead, I'll wait to record the interview until after you eat."

Imagine my surprise—and encouragement—when he replied, "I had my lunch earlier, Don. That's for you. I took the liberty of ordering it because I figured you'd been so busy you hadn't had a chance to eat."

Talk about encouragement in a tangible way! After well over a decade of friendship, I still haven't forgotten that incident.

Nor have I forgotten many times when Frank and other good friends have shared Scriptures with me, Scriptures that have affected their lives, and which ultimately impacted mine as well. No matter how many times any of us has read through the Bible there are still principles and promises God uses others to call to our attention, ones that are particularly suited to times of special need.

Rather than citing all the encouragers by name, let me just mention some of the biblical words of encouragement that my friends have shared with me at times of difficulty and pain.

"Through the Lord's mercies we are not consumed, because His compassions fail not. They are new every morning; great is Your faithfulness. 'The Lord is my portion,' says my soul, 'Therefore I hope in Him!'" (Lamentations 3:22–24).

"For I know the thoughts that I think toward you, says the Lord, thoughts of peace and not of evil, to give you a future and a hope" (Jeremiah 29:11).

"I will both lie down in peace, and sleep; for You alone, O Lord, make me dwell in safety" (Psalm 4:8).

"As for me, I will see Your face in righteousness; I shall be satisfied when I awake in Your likeness" (Psalm 17:15).

"Wait on the Lord; be of good courage, and He shall strengthen your heart; wait, I say, on the Lord!" (Psalm 27:14).

"The Lord is my strength and my shield; my heart trusted in Him, and I am helped; therefore my heart greatly rejoices, and with my song I will praise Him" (Psalm 28:7).

"The Lord your God in your midst, the Mighty One, will save; He will rejoice over you with gladness, He will quiet you in His love, He will rejoice over you with singing" (Zephaniah 3:17).

As I put this list of verses together, I realized it could well extend through the total number of pages in the rest of the book. Suffice it to say, God has blessed me with a number of encouragers who have personally and biblically encouraged me in word and deed during life's painful circumstances.

It's important to realize what encouragement is and what it is not. It is not quick-fix advice, when all my wife wanted was a word of support and affirmation. It is not a how-to sermon, piously delivered, when all my child sought was to know I was there for him. It was not harsh, critical words—"Get your act together, son!"—or thinly veiled sarcasm—"Another burnt offering for dinner, dear? What has Chef Boyardee prepared tonight?" Nor is it surface politeness, the syrupy smooth-talking manipulative salesperson who simply pushes positive buttons for his or her own ends.

In the next chapter, we shall consider more about how to become a "world-class" encourager. Right now, however, think with me back to either the most recent major pain you experienced or perhaps that most traumatic of times of pain that hit you unexpectedly—that came crashing into your life, overwhelming you like a tidal wave following an earthquake.

Back to the Thorn

Apparently, that's what happened in the life of the apostle Paul in the event he described in the twelfth chapter of Second Corinthians. Discussing the ups and downs of his ministry career—he had just described being elevated to the third heaven where he saw and heard things normally restricted from mortals—Paul talked about being given a thorn in the flesh. Remembering the relatively small pain caused by that wire protruding from the keypad of the telephone in Abilene, Texas, I think in a very small way I can relate to what Paul was talking about. Apparently something caused him to incur sudden, unexpected, and intense pain. Whether it was an eye problem, some other kind of physical weakness or injury, I don't know. I do think the initial or primary thrust of his pain was physical—after all, he described it as a thorn in the flesh. Where there had previously not been pain, now there was, in large measure: The word he used did not describe a small briar, but a large sharp stake! It was a pain that distracted the apostle from his ministry, that demanded his attention, that, in short, made his life miserable. The intensity of his reaction to the pain is seen in his persistent plea for the Lord to remove it.

Three Agendas

From his discussion of this thorn, three agendas or purposes for his pain can be identified. All three, in my opinion, have significance for us. The immediate agenda identified by Paul in his painful suffering is Satan's, for the apostle describes his thorn as "a messenger of Satan to buffet me."

If you've ever been on an airplane during heavy turbulence and listened to some of the comments of the passengers around you, you'll understand the meaning of the term "to buffet." I believe Satan's agenda is to use pain to shake us up, to bruise us, to hurt us—with the goal of ultimately causing us to quit, to give in to evil, to become discouraged and despondent.

That was Satan's agenda behind the painful series of events that swept into the life of Job like a series of spring thunderstorms roaming the prairie. Satan's purpose, as expressed by Mrs. Job, was to get the patriarch to curse God and die.

That same agenda frequently lies at the heart of the evil circumstances Satan pushes into our lives. His message, in a word, is quit. Give it up. Stop trying to serve God. The pain is too great; it's just not worth it.

A second agenda appears in Paul's description of his thorn in the flesh. It's his own agenda, and it can be summarized in two words: pain relief.

> *[GOD] TAKES THE VERY CIRCUMSTANCES SATAN TRIES TO USE TO DERAIL US FROM EFFECTIVENESS IN OUR RELATIONSHIP WITH THE LORD, AND TO CAUSE US TO GIVE UP, AND GRACIOUSLY USES THEM TO STRENGTHEN OUR HIDDEN WEAKNESS.*

Ever notice how many pharmacies or drug stores we have in the United States? Do you wonder why? The answer is, to be frank about it, we don't enjoy pain. And we'd like to have a pill or some kind of medicine, thank you, to relieve all our pain. Like Paul, our immediate response is usually to beg the Lord to take it away.

Now it's important to note that God doesn't condemn Paul for praying this way. Nor does Paul condemn himself. He simply notes that this is his agenda—and ours—when pain is present.

But a third agenda surfaces in Paul's account of his thorn in the flesh. It's a little bit harder to pick up from the text of 2 Corinthians 12, but it is present. In fact, Paul actually repeats a phrase, apparently to make sure we don't miss it. That phrase is "lest I should be exalted above measure." It's found both at the beginning and the end of verse 7, and it's not accidental repetition or a stall for time while the apostle tries to think of what to say next. This agenda represents exactly what a loving God wants to produce in Paul's life, keeping him from an overabundance of personal exaltation. In other words, God wants to keep the apostle humble.

You see, Paul apparently had a hidden weakness, something he wasn't fully aware of. Yet he had begun to catch a glimpse of it, even as he returned from his exhilarating trip to the third heaven. God, omniscient, aware of Paul's tendency toward pride and self-reliance—his major hidden flaw or weakness—permitted this thorn in the flesh and used it to strengthen him against the devastating effects of pride and self-reliance.

And that's the amazing truth about the loving God we serve. He takes the very circumstances Satan tries to use to derail us from effectiveness in our relationship with the Lord to cause us to give up, and graciously uses them to strengthen our hidden weakness.

And if He didn't do so, the results could be devastating.

When the Hyatt Regency Hotel was built just south of downtown Kansas City, Missouri, it was the marvel of the community. The atrium of this grand hotel included several elaborate sky bridges, carefully constructed to allow people to stand one, two, or even three stories above the main floor. Soon after its opening, the hotel began hosting a popular series of Friday evening dances. Hundreds of people would crowd into the hotel, filling the lobby below and the sky bridges above.

One Friday evening in July 1981, without warning, a hidden flaw caused the seemingly secure walkways to give way. In the panic and pandemonium of that moment, more than one hundred people lost their lives. Hundreds of others were injured. Many lives were left scarred by trauma.

And all because of a hidden weakness, one not previously exposed and dealt with.

It appears from the order of 2 Corinthians 12 that Paul's hidden weakness was his tendency toward self-reliant pride. For Job, it was a persistent fear of which he was not fully aware (Job 3:25). But in their lives, and in ours, God used traumatic, painful experiences to strengthen a hidden weakness.

We don't know what was going on in the life of the man who fell victim to the robbers. We're not given even a clue of how God may have ultimately used this experience in his life.

Except for one thing.

We do know his life was infinitely better because, there on the road where he had fallen victim, a man we now refer to as the Good Samaritan reached out to him in encouraging love.

May we be that kind of Good Samaritan to those with whom we come in contact today.

NOTE

1. Cynthia A. Kubetin, *Beyond the Darkness: Healing for Victims of Sexual Abuse* (Houston and Dallas: Word and Rapha, 1992), XVII-XXI.

CHAPTER SIX

THE PSEUDO-SOLUTION: THE UNCARING PROFESSIONALS

"Now by chance a certain priest came down that road.
And when he saw him, he passed by on the other side.
Likewise a Levite, when he arrived at the place,
came and looked, and passed by on the other side."
(Luke 10:31–32)

Sports have become a major industry in our day. Part of the reason is the word *professionalism*. Although the Olympics has traditionally remained a bastion of the amateur athlete, recent developments such as the 1992 summer Olympic basketball contest in Barcelona, Spain, finally opened the door for a United States "dream team" of the world's most skilled professional basketball players—men uniquely recognized by such single name designations as Michael, Magic, Larry, and Sir Charles.

In our society today, the designation *professional* has become synonymous with one who possesses the most carefully refined, totally developed skills possible, who is—to use one of the sportscasters' favorite trivialities—"at the top of his (or her) game." Professionals can usually run faster, jump higher, change directions more rapidly, throw the ball with more precision and velocity, hit the ball farther, shoot the ball more accurately, slap the puck—or the opponent—more viciously, and slam-dunk the ball more spectacularly than anyone else.

Some professional athletes define a sport. For example, a few decades ago a young quarterback out of Alabama named Joe Willie

Namath signed for a then-unheard-of $400,000—peanuts by today's inflated athletic salary standards—and gave instant credibility to the fledgling American Football League. A few years later, he helped bring about a merger between the upstart American Football League and the established National Football League when he backed up his "guarantee" of a victory for the New York Jets over the talented NFL Baltimore Colts in Super Bowl III.

Occasionally, a professional athlete will transcend his sport, as in the case of Michael Jordan, whose product endorsements earned him ten times the millions he was paid by the Chicago Bulls to play professional basketball. Retiring from the NBA after leading his team to three consecutive world championships, Jordan decided to attempt what only a handful of athletes have succeeded at—becoming a "professional" at a second sport. Michael's choice was professional baseball.

The barrier between professional and amateur sports has been lowered in some Olympic sports, such as ice dancing. A ruling by the International Skating Union changed Olympic eligibility rules, permitting 1984 gold medalists Jayne Torvill and Christopher Dean of Great Britain to return to what is now referred to as world-class competition. Like the American basketball stars, they had turned from amateur status to professional, doing ice skating exhibition shows. But the change in rules motivated the pair to attempt to repeat their feat of a decade ago, when they received unanimous perfect scores of "six" after an innovative routine set to the music of Ravel's *Boléro*.

DOWNSIDE TO PROFESSIONALISM

But there's a downside to such professionalism, one perhaps expressed best by my father-in-law, an avid sports fan who has spent many an evening watching high school football or basketball in a dimly lit high school stadium or gym. From his perspective, the professionals are just a little bit too good, too glitzy. Often they don't even seem to care about what they're doing. They've lost the freshness, the enthusiasm, the spirit. They have all the polish and skill, but little of the fresh, enthusiastic "heart." The downside of a "professional" may be a blasé attitude, a lack of enthusiasm or caring, a retreat from personal involvement.

Some sports commentators agree. Former NBA all-star center and color analyst Bill Walton criticized twenty-two-year-old phenomenon Shaquille O'Neal for putting time into sideline pursuits, such as rap music and movie making, rather than honing his considerable basketball skills.

Former New York Yankees shortstop and baseball analyst Tony Kubek voiced his criticism of numerous current major leaguers for their rush to leave the stadium without taking the time to sign autographs for young fans because of their hurry to get to trading card shows where they can, in his words, "rip off more kids and make more money."[1]

Professionals and Samaritans

Perhaps at this point you're asking yourself what all this has to do with the Good Samaritan or his modern-day counterparts.

Quite a bit, I'd like to suggest.

As we resume our consideration of the tragedy that struck the Jewish traveler who was robbed, assaulted, and left half-dead between Jerusalem and Jericho, we discover that, ironically, the first two individuals to spot him were "professionals"—religious professionals. One was a priest, the counterpart to a vocational minister in our day. The other, whose vocation also involved religious service, was a Levite.

We are not told how skilled the priest was in fulfilling his religious duties, or the Levite, who played a key role in serving at the temple. Each of these men could have been the very best at his profession in his day. The text doesn't say. But what Luke does record Jesus telling us about them speaks volumes.

Both of these men, who were supposedly committed to loving God with all their heart and loving their neighbors as themselves, spotted the victim who had been attacked. The Levite even came over for a closer look. Yet according to Jesus, both men passed by on the other side.

Luke doesn't tell us how those who stood around listening to Jesus' conversation responded at this point. Perhaps a gasp went through the crowd. Maybe some shook their heads in shock and outrage. Perhaps even the religious authority to whom Jesus was speaking reacted in some overt fashion. After all, surely if you could count on anyone to show love for God or neighbor, it would be a priest or a Levite.

Although we don't know what was going through the minds of these two professional servants of God, there are some likely factors that affected their reactions.

Since the priest was traveling from Jerusalem to Jericho, we can assume that he had finished his current term of service among the twenty-four courses of the priesthood who served on a rotating basis in Jerusalem. Like many commuters today, including individuals who serve in state and federal government positions such as the Senate or the House of Representatives, such individuals came to the capital city, served their time, then returned home.

The Old Testament law clearly warned that contact with a dead body would cause ceremonial contamination and require a ritual of purification (Leviticus 21:1–4). What if the man the priest spotted had already died, or what if he were to expire at the very moment the priest reached out to help him? Then the priest would be required to return to Jerusalem and undergo the ritual of ceremonial purification. Not only would this be a personal hassle, it would disrupt his reunion with his family and whatever business or other plans he may have had. Perhaps he also considered the possibility that the outlaws who had attacked this man may have been waiting nearby, using the half-dead victim as bait. Who knows what personal dangers he might be subjecting himself to? As a priest, he occupied an important role in the life of the nation. He might even be a more conspicuous target than the ordinary run-of-the-mill traveler.

There's yet another rationalization he may have employed. After all, this kind of rescue operation really wasn't his "gift." His calling involved serving in the temple, taking care of important religious duties, not stopping to help people who perhaps through simple misfortune or carelessness had become victims of a crime. No, God had called him to do something more significant, to serve in the exercise of religious activities. Perhaps he even felt that he'd already fulfilled his duty to God and man, and he was now "off duty."

Whatever the priest was thinking, or the Levite who came along just after he left the scene, the Savior's description of their actions makes it clear that their hearts weren't in helping their fellow man.

Segmented Ministry

Tragically, this same kind of mentality frequently exists in those who are involved in vocational service today. During my years in ministry I've come in contact with more than one pastor who proudly told me, "I jealously guard my scheduled study time. I don't let anything or anyone interrupt it." Another man said, "Pastoral visitation is as out-of-date as a Model A. We live in the jet era."

Or, as I heard from another man, "My gift is preaching and teaching the Word. I let someone else take care of the people and their needs. I feel mine is a higher calling than getting involved in the less important activities, like hospital visitation or calling on shut-ins."

Another minister put it this way, "I feel it takes away from the gifts of other people for me to take time to visit the sick or shut-ins."

Now, I know many pastors who invest huge chunks of time in people, who balance careful study of the Word with significant people involvement, ranging from discipleship and mentoring to calling on people in hospitals or nursing homes to building friendships with those who need the Savior. My point is simply to make sure that we do not allow our involvement in tasks, ministry or otherwise—even good and important ones—to keep us from making involvement with people a priority.

We might have understood better—though leaving a man half-dead without any assistance still couldn't be justified—if the priest had been headed *toward* Jerusalem, his religious duties just ahead of him.

Whatever these two men really cared about on that occasion, the needs of a hurting, injured individual were not included.

Recently my wife, Kathy, and I were having dinner with Florence and Fred Littauer, discussing the busy speaking schedule which takes them on frequent trips across the country, as well as to many other parts of the world. We were talking about something they have adopted passionately as a policy whenever they are out speaking, and that is to spend time whenever possible, both before and after they speak, talking to the people who come to hear them. They told of the many positive comments they have received from people where they have spoken who express surprise that they make themselves accessible to talk with people.

They relayed a couple of stories from Florence's book *Silver Boxes,*[2] including the one about the night they arrived at a large Christian convention in a hotel to speak. As they were waiting outside the room where they were to present a workshop, the doors opened and the group that attended the previous workshop came streaming out. As Florence and Fred smiled and nodded to the people who walked by, not one person spoke to them. When everyone had left, as they started to walk into the room, they noticed the title on the door: "The Techniques of Personal Evangelism."

On another occasion when Florence was to speak at a major event, a professional audio man brought her a lavaliere microphone and battery pack to use. After she finished her address, when he came to retrieve the microphone, she took the time to thank him. She explained to us how she was shocked by his response. "You are the first speaker who's ever thanked me." He told her, "All I ever get are complaints. I get the blame when the mikes don't work. But I never get any credit when they're right."

As she talked further with this man, she discovered that often the more important or well-known the singer or speaker, the worse the person treated him and the other sound engineers. "In their eyes," he said, "we are non-persons."[3]

WEEKEND OF ENCOURAGEMENT

Over the past couple of years, I've become friends with former pastor, author, and conference speaker Ron Dunn. As we have presented "Weekend of Encouragement" conferences in churches together, time after time I've seen Ron, even when exhausted from an intensely rigorous schedule, take the time to talk with hurting individuals without showing impatience. To the degree that it's possible within the schedule constraints of the conference, Ron is there for those who hurt and who need encouragement.

ONE OF THE WORST THINGS WE CAN DO IS TO RUSH TO APPLY A VERSE LIKE ROMANS 8:28 IN BAND-AID™ FASHION, WITHOUT EVEN ACKNOWLEDGING THE HURT AND PAIN OF A SITUATION.

Sometimes just being there for a person can make all the difference. Frequently I've heard Ron tell the story of a middle-aged couple in Mississippi who walked up to him at the close of one conference session. He was somewhat taken aback with the wife's greeting when she said to him, "It was good to see you smile tonight." Noticing his reaction, she went on to explain, "Six months ago my seventeen-year-old daughter was killed in a car wreck. I felt so hurt and bitter; I thought I would never laugh or even smile again. One of the reasons I came out to hear you tonight was I knew you had lost your eighteen-year-old son. When I saw you smile and laugh this evening, I knew there was still hope."

The hurting people we encounter may not be physically lying injured beside the road. But many times that may be exactly where they are emotionally. A kind word, a listening ear, even a brief time of contact says to them, "You are important. Your hurts matter to God, and I consider you a person of sufficient value to at least give you as much of myself as I can."

One of the ways we can adopt that callous-professional attitude of indifference so common today is simply not to have time for people. But there's another way we can pass by on the other side. That is to paste on a smile, to pretend there is no pain. Or worse yet, to dispense pious platitudes.

I remember some years ago returning from a trip over icy roads to discover that, during an ice storm, the teenage son of a friend and ministry colleague had been killed in a traffic accident. Sadly, I was present to hear and see a number of Christians, most of whom should have known better, urge these grieving parents, "Don't be sad, now. After all, all things work together for good! Let the world see what a strong testimony this is. Make this a cause for rejoicing."

Now don't get me wrong. I'm convinced that Romans 8:28 is true. As my friend Ron Dunn likes to put it, "There are no loopholes in Romans 8:28. I haven't found a one."[4] I've personally shared this verse with many people as a form of encouragement and have seen it have its desired impact.

However, I'm convinced that one of the worst things we can do is to rush to apply a verse like Romans 8:28 in Band-Aid™ fashion, without even acknowledging the hurt and pain of a situation. In the verse I consider the "Romans 8:28 of the Old Testament," one that has meant a great deal to me, Job affirms, "But He knows the way that I take; when He has tested me, I shall come forth as gold" (Job 23:10). Significantly, the patriarch doesn't come to this conclusion until after he has expressed wave upon wave of bitter pain, using words such as:

"My days . . . are spent without hope" (Job 7:6).

"My soul loathes my life; I will give free course to my complaint, I will speak in the bitterness of my soul" (Job 10:1).

"For You write bitter things against me, and make me inherit the iniquities of my youth" (Job 13:26).

"You destroy the hope of man" (Job 14:19).

"Where then is my hope?" (Job 17:15).

"He breaks me down on every side, and I am gone; my hope He has uprooted like a tree. He has also kindled His wrath against me, and He counts me as one of His enemies" (Job 19:10–11).

And even after his great affirmation of Job 23:10, he admits, "I am terrified at His presence; when I consider this, I am afraid of Him. For God made my heart weak, and the Almighty terrifies me" (Job 23:15–16).

CLICHÉD COMPASSION

It's so easy within ourselves, and especially toward others, to paste on a smile, to voice pious platitudes, to glibly recite phrases like "count it all joy" or "all things work together."

Now it's important to acknowledge the truth of these great statements of Scripture. The problem is in the way we so often apply them. May God grant us the sensitivity to be available, to take a loving, compassionate approach with those in deep hurt. May we stand in stark contrast to the uncaring professionals of whom Jesus spoke in Luke 10 and their contemporaries of our day.

So are the only options for encouragement either professionals who no longer really care, who take a jaded approach to those who hurt, or those who may care but who lack the skills to really be of help?

I see another alternative, one I believe to be exactly where God wants us to be in a day when many have fallen in pain along the road of life. That alternative is to develop the skills and insights necessary to be a world-class encourager.

WORLD-CLASS ENCOURAGERS

This idea of a world-class encourager came to me from the Olympics. As I watched the various contests shown on nightly television from Barcelona, Spain, in 1992 and Lillehammer, Norway, in 1994, I was struck by what I've come to consider a rather important insight. Many of the people who now compete in the Olympics either are or have been professional athletes. Others are not.

The major issue concerning these athletes is not whether they hold "professional" or "amateur" status. The real issue is their level of proficiency, their commitment to excellence, their willingness to sacrifice in order to become good enough to be considered "world class" at what they do.

That's precisely what I'm contending for in this important art of encouragement. What I'm calling for is nothing less than a commitment to becoming world-class encouragers.

> # THERE IS A DESPERATE NEED FOR ENCOURAGEMENT TODAY. PEOPLE HURT. THEY ARE BUSY. AND THEY OFTEN FEEL LIKE GIVING UP.

Consider the desperate need for encouragement today. Life is so busy. People are rushing everywhere, many times carrying burdens no one knows about. For many, the pressure of the present is compounded by the pain of the past. On our live radio call-in ministry, I hear it night after night:

"We're financially overwhelmed."

"My husband is no longer interested in me. He just doesn't seem to care."

"My wife has left me for another man."

"We're just finishing seminary, and my second teenager is now rebelling just like the first did. I don't think I can handle it."

"I find myself waking up night after night having flashbacks, remembering in vivid detail the horrible sexual abuse my father inflicted on me. The shame and pain are so great, I often feel like killing myself."

From a teenager: "I've tried to witness to my parents but they just laugh at me. They make fun of me. They're not interested in spiritual things. They think I'm stupid because of my commitment to Christ."

"My wife has just been told she has breast cancer. Some days are good for us, others are terrible. The ups and downs, the uncertainty, the prospect of radiation and chemotherapy. We've heard all the horror stories. In the back of our minds, we can't seem to get rid of the thought that this is just a death sentence."

No doubt about it, friends, there is a desperate need for encouragement today. People hurt. They are busy. And they often feel like giving up.

The fact is, God has designed life so we can reach out to others, genuinely caring, giving encouragement, replacing fear with love.

We've talked about what encouragement is, from a biblical perspective. Our question now is, How can a person become a world-class encourager? Perhaps the best answer is, The same way many people become skilled at golf or tennis: by following the pattern of others who have become world class at what they do.

I'm not an avid golfer. And I'm not really very good at it. But I did have the privilege once, many years ago in Kansas City, to follow along as part of the news media while Jack Nicklaus, Lee Trevino, Arnold Palmer, and Tom Watson played an eighteen-hole exhibition. Needless to say, their approach to the game of golf was quite different from mine, and the result was equally different. I'm not sure I even qualify for the lower levels of hacker or duffer. On the other hand, each of that foursome had earned the right to be considered world class.

However, for those of us who had the opportunity to watch them that day, there were lessons to be learned about golf, from the basic "head down, eyes on the ball, follow through smoothly" to some that were much more complex.

Several friends of mine are avid duffers who have purchased golf videos. They watch these videos carefully, study them conscientiously, then work to apply them. I think taking this same approach to encouragement can help make us world-class encouragers, those who can reach out like Good Samaritans rather than passing by on the other side like callous professionals.

So how do we do it?

First, we must study and follow the biblical patterns. Scripture is filled with an impressive array of encouragers from whom we can learn, who fit the world-class profile. Let's look at a few together.

Our first example is Jonathan, son of Saul, the first king in ancient Israel. When he met a young shepherd boy of rugged appearance and ruddy complexion who was willing to take on Goliath, the hero of the Philistines, he realized he had found a kindred spirit. The initial meeting between these two men took place immediately after David had killed the Philistine giant with a sling and a stone (1 Samuel 17:50). And Jonathan, just days before, had taken on an entire garrison of the enemy, trusting God for victory as he and a servant slew more than twenty Philistines within a half-acre of land (1 Samuel 14:4–14).

Jonathan felt an immediate kinship with David. It was unconditional love, the oldest son of the king reaching out to the youngest son of a common man (1 Samuel 18:1). Undoubtedly at Jonathan's initiative, the two men struck a covenant (v. 3), which Jonathan sealed by giving David his robe, his sword, his bow, and his belt. In some parts of the world, the kind of action Jonathan took toward David by giving him these articles is still considered the highest honor one human being can bestow on another. Later, when David found himself at risk of losing his life because of Jonathan's father's paranoia, Jonathan risked his own life to warn David of the danger (1 Samuel 19:2), spoke positively about his friend to his father (v. 4), and lovingly confronted his father, reminding him that it would be a sin for Saul to persecute David, who had never sinned against the king.

When Saul again attempted to take David's life, Jonathan continued this pattern of encouraging his friend, maintaining his loyalty (1 Samuel 20:1–4), reaffirming his love for David (v. 17), risking his own life, actually dodging a spear cast at him by his father when he spoke in David's defense (vv. 32–33), and verbalizing the intensity of his love and the loyalty of his commitment to David during their final meeting (vv. 41–42).

Jonathan was not the only world-class encourager in David's life. Many years later when David, now the king, had no one around him, including his erstwhile best friend Joab, who was willing to confront him about his sinful relationship with Bathsheba or his plot to take the life of her husband Uriah, a prophet named Nathan came to the king. He cared enough for David to creatively follow God's instruction to confront the king, using a parable of a rich man who took one little lamb from his poor neighbor to meet his own selfish needs. When David responded with intense anger, saying that the man who did this thing should surely die, the prophet replied simply and pointedly with two Hebrew words, translated in English, "You are the man." You, David, are the one I'm talking about.

To expose the king's self-deceitfulness this way could have easily cost Nathan his life. Yet David responded to this courageous rebuke by confessing, "I have sinned against the Lord" (2 Samuel 12:13). After successfully confronting David, Scripture tells us Nathan departed to his own home (v. 15). Ironically, rather than marking the end of any relationship between Nathan and David, we discover that Scripture records a close ongoing relationship between the prophet and the king's entire family. Remarkably, after David and Bathsheba experienced the death of their first baby and God graciously gave them another son, it was Nathan the prophet who brought God's message of mercy, naming the baby Jedidiah, or "beloved of the Lord." This child grew up to become better known by his other given name. We might even refer to him today as J. Solomon, son of David.

And though David soon began to experience more of the consequences God had predicted through Nathan, the king's response was not to bitterly reject the prophet. Years later—after David extended loyal love to Mephibosheth, the crippled son of his friend Jonathan—it was Nathan, faithful friend of David and his family, who warned Bathsheba of the plot of Solomon's half-brother Adonijah to take the kingdom. The king had grown old and was near death, and it was both God's and David's intention for Solomon to assume the throne. But it was Nathan's courageous action that saved the lives of Solomon and Bathsheba as well as the prophet's.

Following Nathan's warning and counsel, Bathsheba entered the king's chamber, reminding David of his promise that Solomon would reign in his place, and warning him of the plot to give the kingdom to Adonijah. While she was explaining the plot, Nathan himself entered the chamber, confirming Bathsheba's words and giving David the opportunity to authorize Nathan, Zadok the priest, and Benaiah to anoint Solomon king, blow the ceremonial trumpet, issue the official proclamation "God save King Solomon," and seat the young man on David's own throne. Because of the caring involvement of a world-class encourager, lives were spared and God's purposes fulfilled.

The following chapter will tell the story of another Old Testament encourager, a relatively obscure man with the unusual name Ebed-melech.

NEW TESTAMENT ENCOURAGERS

The New Testament tells about several world-class encouragers, the most prominent of whom was a man named Joseph, a Jewish Levite from the country of Cyprus.

Joseph, you ask, from Cyprus? Never heard of him.

Perhaps, like Jedidiah of the Old Testament, his other name will be more familiar. Because of his persistent efforts at encouraging the saints in Jerusalem, the apostles gave him the name Barnabas, which means "son of encouragement."

When he chronicled the activities of the early church, Luke pointed out four characteristics of Barnabas that marked him as a world-class encourager, using four concise yet pointed collections of verbal snapshots that give us a remarkably accurate picture of what a world-class encourager might look like today.

Material Encouragement

First, a world-class encourager encourages with his means or possessions. In other words, he puts his money where his heart is.

In recent years we have heard a great deal about recession, and there are still some people around who remember how bad things were during the Great Depression. But in the early church, things were one notch worse. What was happening was not a recession or a depression, it was persecution. Christians were finding themselves stripped of their lands, houses, possessions, and jobs. Many were being thrown into prison. Yet Luke records the incredible commitment believers had to each other, a commitment that led not only to powerful witnessing, but to a virtually universal sharing of possessions, so that the needs of those who had little or nothing could be met (Acts 4:34–35).

After framing the general picture, Luke focused in with his verbal zoom lens on Joseph, who had been surnamed Barnabas by the apostles. We can see clearly that he possessed land, an inheritance, which in that society meant a great deal. Seeing the need, he took action, sold his land, and brought the entire sum of money—we know this from the contrast with Ananias and Sapphira, who exaggerated the extent of their giving—and laid it at the apostles' feet.

Later, the apostle John, one of the men at whose feet Barnabas laid this gift, would write, "Whoever has this world's goods, and sees his brother in need, and shuts up his heart from him, how does the love of God abide in him? My little children, let us not love in word or in tongue, but in deed and in truth" (1 John 3:17–18). Perhaps the aged apostle had Barnabas's selfless action in mind as he wrote.

Now we don't necessarily need to give everything we have. The point of application is obvious: When we see a need and are able to meet it, we shall move into action, to encourage with our means, with our possessions.

Consistent Loyalty

The second trait of a world-class encourager we draw from the record of Barnabas is that such an individual exercises loyalty, even when it may not be popular. In Acts 9, the church in Jerusalem was under pressure from an arrogant, militant young Pharisee named Saul of Tarsus. This individual who was having Christians imprisoned right and left was dramatically converted to Christ on the road to Damascus, baptized there, then quietly brought back to Jerusalem, where he attempted to join himself to the disciples.

Their reaction? It was pretty logical, given the circumstances. Luke carefully records both their feelings and their thinking about the idea of having "public enemy of the faith number one" join their fellowship. "They were all afraid of him, and did not believe he was a disciple" (Acts 9:26). The next two words in the text tell us something of the courage and loyalty of Barnabas, the "Son of Encouragement." They would have turned him away, "but Barnabas." Our encourager took Saul, brought him to the apostles, declared to them how Saul had seen the Lord on the roadway and how the Lord had spoken to him, and how Saul had then preached boldly in Damascus (v. 27). Barnabas's courageous combination of words and actions, at a time when no one else was apparently willing to speak up, led to the apostle's acceptance by the fellowship in Jerusalem, and undoubtedly helped motivate him to continue speaking boldly in the name of the Savior (vv. 28–29).

It would have been easy for Barnabas to simply sit silently as part of the group, perhaps nodding agreement when others expressed concern as to whether Saul was "faking it" or argued against his acceptance. Instead, Barnabas chose to verbally exercise loyalty.

Many years ago a rumor about a Dallas Seminary alumnus who was involved in a ministry in the Dallas area reached the ears of Dr. Donald Campbell, then president of Dallas Seminary. Like Barnabas, Dr. Campbell acted quickly and purposefully. Investigating what he had heard for factual basis, he determined it to be a rumor and not truth. Next he called in those from whom he had heard it, confronting them with the inappropriateness of spreading this sort of information and challenging them to go back to their "sources" with the truth.

Next Dr. Campbell phoned the alumnus in question and invited him to lunch. There he explained what he had heard and the action he had taken. He affirmed his encouragement and support for a young man who easily could have been so discouraged by the spread of this rumor that he would have quit the ministry altogether. Dr. Campbell confirmed, "I want you to know that Dallas Seminary and I, personally, stand behind you and your ministry 100 percent. We are committed to making sure that we do not accept or spread any rumors of this kind."

Like Barnabas before him, Dr. Campbell's actions earned him an Olympic gold medal in the encouragement category.

Verbal Motivation

The third snapshot of Barnabas taken by Luke shows how a world-class encourager exhorts verbally as a team player. In Acts 11 the scene has shifted to Antioch, primarily because of persecution that broke out in Jerusalem in the aftermath of Stephen's martyrdom. Antioch, the third largest city in the world of that day, was located three hundred miles north of Jerusalem. Although the apostles were still in Jerusalem, many believers had fled to Antioch. Before long, a great number of other individuals came to faith in the Lord. What was to be done with this crowd of converts?

Word of the desperate need to strengthen these new believers came to the attention of the church in Jerusalem. Their immediate response: "Let's call on Barnabas." And his response? He went, gladly. In fact, his encouragement of the believers in Antioch undoubtedly played a key role in their being the first believers to be labeled "Christians" (Acts 11:26).

Luke notes several important characteristics about Barnabas's encouragement. First, it flowed from a heart of gladness and a positive attitude. Many people struggle when they attempt to encourage others because they are persistently plagued by negativism. Barnabas could have complained about having too many people to deal with, being overworked, or having to serve under less than ideal conditions. Instead, he was glad when he saw how God's grace was operating in these new Christians' lives.

In addition, his encouragement was ongoing, not a "one shot" matter. The imperfect tense Luke used indicated that he began exhorting them all, then continued the process.

Third, his encouragement was not designed to make them disciples of Barnabas, but of the Lord. He didn't exhort them to cling to himself or even to the church in Antioch. Rather, his desire was to motivate their commitment to the Lord Himself.

Finally, Barnabas's encouragement grew out of a godly, consistent lifestyle. As Luke explained, he was a righteous or good man, filled with the Holy Spirit and a man of faith (Acts 11:24).

When, as a result of his encouragement, many additional people came to faith—evangelism is a frequent by-product of biblical encouragement—Barnabas took a time-out to recruit an additional encourager. He traveled all the way to Tarsus in pursuit of the man to whom he had been loyal back in Jerusalem, found Saul there, and brought him back to Antioch where the two men began functioning together as a ministry team (vv. 25–26). During the next year, their joint ministry of encouragement and edification laid the foundation for an incredibly strong local church, one that financially supported needy believers in Jerusalem (vv. 29–30) and sent out the first team of vocational church-planting missionaries (Acts 13:1–4), Barnabas and Saul themselves.

There's one more remarkable angle to see from this snapshot of a world-class encourager. When the team began its ministry in Antioch, it was known as "Barnabas and Saul" (Acts 11:30). Before long, that designation began to shift, and by the time they neared the end of their initial missionary journey, they had become known as "Paul and Barnabas" (Acts 13:46, 50). Barnabas is the classic example of something Zig Ziglar says, "There's no telling what one individual may be able to achieve if he doesn't care who gets the credit."

Barnabas was a classic encourager. He wasn't primarily concerned with whose name came first on the marquee or the cover of the book or in the printed literature publicizing their missionary crusades. A true encourager at heart, his major goal was to see that the work of the Lord was done.

A Second Chance

The fourth snapshot of this world-class encourager named Barnabas shows how such an individual extends a second chance. The first missionary journey had been a rousing success, and after the gospel had been defended at the Jerusalem conference, Paul suggested to his colleague that they make a return trip to the churches they planted on their first missionary trip to encourage them in the faith (Acts 15:36). Barnabas immediately expressed his determination to take John Mark along with them. Paul was equally determined not to take this individual—he had come to consider John Mark a ministry liability since the young man quit the first missionary journey at Pamphylia (vv. 37–38). Luke tactfully recorded the sharp contention between these two men that led Barnabas to take Mark and sail to Cyprus, while Paul chose Silas and left, with the commendation of the brethren, heading for Syria and Cilicia (vv. 39–41).

Many preachers have pounded the pulpit and firmly asserted that Paul was in the right not to take this quitter along with him. After all, as one preacher put it, "We don't hear another word about Barnabas or John Mark in the entire book of Acts. The whole story is devoted to Paul and Silas. So Paul must have been right, and Barnabas wrong."

WHEN IT COMES TO ENCOURAGEMENT, THE REAL ISSUE HAS NOTHING TO DO WITH WHETHER WE ARE VOCATIONALLY INVOLVED IN MINISTRY OR NOT.

For a long time that line of reasoning made sense to me. Then I discovered an interesting statement tucked away near the end of Paul's second letter to Timothy, written while the apostle was waiting to die in prison. Paul acknowledged that he was nearing the end of his course, calling on Timothy to stand firm in ministry and to visit him soon (2 Timothy 4:5–9). Then he lamented the defection of his ministry colleague Demas and the departure of another colleague, Titus (v. 10). Perhaps the memory of Mark's earlier defection passed through the apostle's mind as he wrote, "Only Luke is with me" (v. 11). But his next statement strikes me as absolutely remarkable: "Get Mark and bring him with you, for he is useful to me for ministry."

Isn't this the apostle who had no use for Mark the quitter? Or could he be talking about a different Mark?

Yes, this is the same apostle and the same Mark. So what's the difference?

In a word, Barnabas.

I'm convinced that this world-class encourager began to use his skills to reclaim young John Mark, to rebuild his flagging persistence, and to strengthen his faith. In short, to turn him into a man who was fit for spiritual warfare, or, to use Paul's words, profitable for the ministry.

After all, humanly speaking, had it not been for the encouraging ministry of Barnabas, we might not have a gospel of Mark.

ANOTHER ENCOURAGING MEDALIST

Then there's Onesiphorus, mentioned briefly by Paul in the paragraph following his reference to John Mark. Apparently he had already died by the time Paul wrote to Timothy (2 Timothy 4:19). He's not very well-known, and I can't recall hearing any messages preached about him.

But if you miss Onesiphorus, you've missed someone special. Earlier in Paul's second letter to Timothy (1:16–18), the apostle went into great detail to explain how Onesiphorus refused to "pass by on the other side." Although he is mentioned only in these two brief New Testament references, Onesiphorus deserves a special place as a gold medal winner in the Olympics of encouragement, and Paul explains why.

A Frequent Refreshment

First, Onesiphorus was a frequent source of encouragement and refreshment. To use Paul's words, "He often refreshed me" (v. 16). Seldom do we think of someone like the apostle Paul feeling down. Yet I've had the privilege of knowing several respected servants of God closely enough to see just how ministry can "take it out of you" and even leave a person at the brink of depression. Frequent ministering to others can leave one feeling drained. Compounding this was the fact that, during these latter years of his life, Paul was imprisoned. And the conditions of his imprisonment were not like some of the "country club" facilities populated by white-collar criminals in America today. Yet Onesiphorus provided a consistent source of refreshment for Paul. The word the apostle uses for having his soul lifted is only used here in the New Testament. The encouraging work of Onesiphorus was not a "one shot deal"; it was a source of ongoing joy.

Unashamed Compassion

Second, a part of Paul's joy was wrapped up in the fact that Onesiphorus was unashamed of the apostle's status as a prisoner (v. 16). For some people the idea of having personal contact with one who has been or is imprisoned comes just short of unthinkable, at best.

That wasn't how it was with Onesiphorus. He was undaunted by Paul's status as a "criminal." I have heard Chuck Colson and others speak of how individuals reached out to them when they were serving prison terms. Perhaps they took Onesiphorus as their role model.

Diligent Effort

A third facet of his encouraging ministry was the diligence with which Onesiphorus sought out Paul in the empire's capital. We are not told why this obscure servant of Christ had come to Rome, but we are told he carefully, thoroughly, sought for the apostle (v. 17). Furthermore, his mission was successful. He persisted until he found him. Now finding someone like the apostle Paul in Rome may seem relatively easy. But keep in mind that in Paul's day there were no telephone books, no pagers, not even newspapers, radio, or television. Nor is it likely that there was any form of public transit. In fact, to ask about the apostle Paul might have involved personal risk, since he was such a notorious prisoner. But none of this hindered Onesiphorus. He diligently sought out the apostle until he had found him.

Multifaceted Encouragement

One final word about this obscure yet world-class encourager. Paul reminded Timothy, "And you know very well how many ways he ministered to me at Ephesus" (v. 18). Paul and Timothy had spent an extended time serving the Lord at Ephesus. Apparently, this is where the apostle first became acquainted with Onesiphorus, and where the encourager first began to exercise his skill.

Significantly, Paul notes that he did so in a variety of ways. That opens the door for us to become world-class encouragers in a variety of ways as well, perhaps by phoning those who are discouraged, by spending the day with a cancer patient, by taking a disillusioned minister to lunch, or by writing a note to cheer up a sorrowing parent who has just lost a teenager. Perhaps even by volunteering to baby-sit for young parents who cannot afford to go out to eat. And, if you really want to go "world class," provide the cost of the meal too.

You see, when it comes to encouragement, the real issue has nothing to do with whether we are vocationally involved in ministry or not. Sure, we need more people in vocational ministry. I agree with the concerns expressed by my friend and colleague Woodrow Kroll, who has issued a call to Christians for vocational ministry.[5]

However, when it comes to encouragement, it isn't vocational versus nonvocational. Just like in modern Olympic competition, I'm convinced that, whether priest or Levite, pastor, missionary, housewife, businessman, farmer, or laborer, the real issue when it comes to encouragement is: Will I, when I see a hurting, fallen brother or sister, choose to pass by on the other side? Or, will I, like the Good Samaritan, reach out to encourage and get involved?

NOTES

1. *USA Today* (18 February 1994), 3c.
2. Florence Littauer, *Silver Boxes: The Gift of Encouragement* (Waco, Tex.: Word, 1989), 35.
3. Ibid.
4. Ron Dunn, *When Heaven Is Silent* (Nashville: Nelson, 1994), prepublication manuscript.
5. Woodrow Kroll, *The Vanishing Ministry* (Grand Rapids: Kregel, 1991).

CHAPTER SEVEN

THE REAL SOLUTION: PREJUDICE-FREE COMPASSION

"But a certain Samaritan, as he journeyed, came where he was. And when he saw him, he had compassion on him."
(Luke 10:33)

There is no such thing as a Good Samaritan."

If we were somehow able to step into a time machine, transport ourselves back into first-century Palestine, enter the marketplaces of Jerusalem or Galilee, survey pad in hand, and talk with the average Jewish individual, that's probably the response we would receive, perhaps 99 percent of the time, maybe even more often.

As we pause to consider the person on whom Jesus focused the attention of those who listened to his discussion with the theological expert, we are confronted with a shocking reality. The man Jesus selected as a hero came from a group of people who, ethnically and nationally, would never have been recognized in Israel as heroes. In fact, Jewish men who considered themselves godly thanked God daily that they were not Samaritans. The following summary vividly demonstrates the attitude toward Samaritans in Israel.

> The Samaritan was publicly cursed in their synagogues—could not be adduced as a witness in the Jewish courts—could not be admitted to any sort of proselytism, and was thus, so far as the Jew could affect his position, excluded from eternal life.[1]

What a remarkable development, that Jesus would select a member of such a despised minority as an example of demonstrating unconditional love toward one's neighbor.

And what a clear-cut statement against racial prejudice. In effect, the Savior was laying down a foundation for what Paul would express later, the truth that "God does not show favoritism" (Romans 2:11 NIV). And, "there is neither Jew nor Greek, slave nor free, male nor female, for you are all one in Christ Jesus" (Galatians 3:28 NIV).

PROLIFERATION OF PREJUDICE

Despite incredible efforts over past decades, racial prejudice in our society is as up-to-date as today's front page. The lead story in bold headlines in our local newspaper the day I sat down to work on this chapter read, "Massacre, Riots Leave 55 Dead: Jewish Settler Uses Assault Rifle, Grenades Against Muslims Worshipping at Mosque."[2] The Associated Press story went on to tell the story of Dr. Baruch Goldstein, father of four, who was part of a group of followers of the late Rabbi Meir Kahane, who believed it to be God's will that they commit violence against goyim, or non-Jews.

This act of violence took place not far from where the half-dead robbery victim was attended to by the Good Samaritan. Ironically, Dr. Goldstein, who had served as the main emergency doctor in the Jewish settlement of Kiryat Arba, had on many occasions treated victims of Arab-Israeli violence. Other physicians who worked with him said he sometimes turned away from Palestinians who needed attention. Such actions and such an attitude would have been consistent with those of Jews toward Samaritans in Jesus' day.

However, hostile attitudes and hatred between Palestinians and other Arabs and Israelis have been a broad two-way street for many years. An Associated Press sidebar to the Goldstein story identified the incident as one of fifteen major violent incidents between Palestinians and Israelis since the establishment of the state of Israel in May of 1948. These included the massacre of more than two hundred Arab men, women, and children in the village of Deir Yassin by radical underground Jewish fighters just days before the establishment of the state of Israel; the May 1972 attack by Japanese terrorists hired by the Popular Front for the Liberation of Palestine who killed passengers and tourists at Lod Airport near Tel Aviv; the grisly murder of eleven members of Israel's Olympic team by PLO terrorists in September of 1972 during the Munich games; and the bloody incident in which seventeen Palestinians were killed and more than one hundred and fifty wounded in a melee involving Israeli police and a Palestinian mob on Jerusalem's Temple Mount.

Although the roots of this hostility go back as deeply into human history as almost any such conflict, this kind of racial violence, prejudice, and hatred has not been limited to Jew and Arab.

The cover of a recent issue of *Time* magazine featured the face of bow-tie-clad Louis Farrakhan under the title "Ministry of Rage: Louis Farrakhan Spews Racist Venom at Jews and All of White America."[3] In its cover story, *Time* labeled Farrakhan "America's most controversial minister," noting that to some he is poison, to others an antidote. Anti-Semitic and otherwise racist rhetoric by Farrakhan, and notably by his aide Khallid Muhammad in a speech at Kean College in New Jersey, drew shocked negative reaction, even from mainstream civil rights leaders in the black community. Controversy boiled over Khallid's intensely racist remarks and Farrakhan's semi-disavowal of them. A wide range of leaders, including Abraham Foxman of the Jewish Antidefamation League, and a broad range of American blacks expressed their fears that such anti-Semitic rhetoric would erode the moral authority of Farrakhan's appeals against racism. As *Time* magazine put it, "His success underscores two ugly truths of American life. A great many black Americans view their fellow white citizens with anger. And a great many white Americans view their black fellow citizens with fear."[4]

The Fuel

Anger and fear. Two volatile emotional ingredients which fuel racial prejudice. Ironically, the *Time*/CNN poll cited by the magazine noted that over half of the more than five hundred African-Americans polled considered Farrakhan a good role model for black youths, and almost 10 percent identified him as "the most important black leader today"—three times as many as those identifying Nelson Mandela, who led the fight against apartheid in South Africa, and a higher percentage than for anyone except for the Reverend Jesse Jackson.

Yet racial violence and hatred is not limited to either the Middle East or America, nor to the apartheid conflict in South Africa.

Violence in Somalia, launched in an effort to end conflict involving Somali warlords such as Mohammed Farrah Aidid, drew American soldiers into what was labeled the longest sustained firefight since the Vietnam War, costing eighteen American lives and seventeen additional casualties.

Then there was Sarajevo. A decade ago this beautiful capital of Bosnia, in the former Yugoslavia, was the center of world attention. The 1984 Winter Olympics were underway, and the city was putting on its best face as Bosnians, Serbs, Croats, and other ethnic groups worked together to host an event watched by virtually the entire rest of the world.

A decade later, as civil war and ethnic purging "nears its second anniversary . . . the death toll far exceeds 140,000—some 17,000 of them children."[5] As war correspondent Michael Nicholson described it, "I had spent 25 years reporting on wars; this was my 14th. I had been witness to murder in Nigeria, genocide in Biafra, rape in the Congo. I had been among the last out of Phnom Penh and Saigon. Yet I was not prepared for the savagery of Bosnia."[6]

While the world watched the 1994 Winter Olympics from Lillehammer, Norway, news reports from Sarajevo provided a counterpoint of gruesome violence, as scores of people were killed by shelling and automatic rifle fire during this struggle of racial violence and ethnic cleansing.

And while we sit in our living rooms and dens, comfortably viewing the violence from other parts of the globe, feeling safely insulated, racial prejudice and even violence, fueled by anger and fear, continue to push themselves into our lives.

To some degree or another, we all struggle with prejudice. I saw this clearly as I grew up in a part of the south where blacks and whites drank from different water fountains and rode different buses to school, where blacks were forced to ride in the rear of transit buses and attend supposedly "separate but equal" educational facilities and were often referred to by racial slurs and nicknames that aren't worth repeating.

After I finished college and went off to Dallas, Texas, to seminary, I began working at a Christian radio station, initially to support my wife and twin daughters, but in what ultimately would become a key component of my ministry.

My programming segment, from midnight to 6:00 A.M., was called "Night Flight," a mix of traditional and light contemporary Christian music. The programming block just before mine, called the "Hallelujah Express" and consisting primarily of black gospel music, was hosted by a young man named Bob, who soon became one of my closest friends. Bob would often sit for an hour or two, sometimes more, visiting with me during the quiet, lonely hours of all-night radio. We discussed a wide variety of topics and grew closer as we encouraged each other.

I had been raised in a white neighborhood permeated by prejudice against blacks. Bob grew up in a black ghetto in South Dallas, where whites were usually not trusted or well-liked.

On many occasions we talked about the kind of atmosphere in which we had grown up, conditioned to mistrust those of a different race, ingrained with suspicion and prejudice, fear and anger.

The two of us became remarkably close as we learned to appreciate each other's differences and similarities and as we prayed together, united in our commitment to the Lord and each other.

Many years ago I heard a story about General Robert E. Lee, the commander of the forces of the Confederate States of America. It seems one morning General Lee walked into a church to pray. The closest place to kneel at the altar was next to a black man, a recently freed slave. Without hesitation, General Lee knelt beside the man and lifted his voice to God in prayer. Later a shocked aide asked him, "How could you do that?"

General Lee is said to have replied, "Sir, the ground is always level at the foot of the Cross."[7]

That's a lesson I had seen early on from studying Scripture, and one I learned in practical experience from hours of fellowship with Bob Easley, and later from Reuben Connor, Eddie Lane, and Tony Evans.

During the years I pastored in a small town in Central Texas, a number of people who attended our church had also grown up in an atmosphere charged with prejudice. Some of them were shocked when my wife and I invited Reuben Connor and his wife to our church and to our home for dinner. Several conversations, some intense, grew out of that event.

Many months later, our church and several others decided to cooperate in a countywide evangelistic crusade. On the first night of the crusade, I stood near the north entrance to the football stadium, watching to see what would happen as an African-American family walked toward the stadium. Standing at the door ushering was one of the men with whom I had held several of those earlier discussions.

I was thrilled when this man graciously and warmly greeted the family, welcomed them to the crusade, and personally escorted them to some of the best seats near the front of the platform.

Ingrained Prejudice

Prejudice is a difficult thing to deal with. It can develop deep roots. It certainly had become deeply ingrained in the society of Jesus' day, just as it has in ours.

The name Samaritan comes from the Hebrew *shomronim,* which is associated with the geographic region of central Palestine. The city of Samaria stood on a three-hundred-foot-high hill overlooking a valley some twenty-three miles inland from the Mediterranean Sea. The city had been purchased from its owner, Shemer, for two talents of silver by Omri, one of the Northern kings of ancient Israel. Omri built a city on the hill and named it after the hill's owner (1 Kings 16:24).

During much of the Old Testament, Samaria was a hotbed of idolatry. Ahab built a temple to Baal there (vv. 32–33), and Samaria was frequently included in prophetic warnings against idolatry from such men as Isaiah, Jeremiah, Ezekiel, and Micah. Yet Ezekiel noted that Samaria had not committed half the sins of Jerusalem (Ezekiel 16:51).

Invading Syrian armies twice besieged Samaria, first in 863 B.C. (1 Kings 20:1), then about thirteen years later under Ben-Hadad (2 Kings 6:24ff.). Miraculously, in fulfillment of the prophet Elisha's prediction, God sent a loud noise to terrify the Syrians, who fled in the evening, leaving tents, horses, donkeys, and all their provisions (2 Kings 7:7). Shortly afterward, four lepers from the city of Samaria slipped into the deserted camp, began plundering it, then paused and said to each other, "We are not doing what is right. This day is a day of good news, and we remain silent" (v. 9). So they returned to Samaria and informed the king that the invaders had abandoned their camp. Then the residents of the city shared in the joy and provision of God's supernatural deliverance.

More than a century later, in 721 B.C., King Sargon of Assyria destroyed the city and the ten-tribe Northern Kingdom. Shortly after that the city was besieged and destroyed by John Hyrcanus of the Maccabees.[8] When Sargon besieged the city, he carried off almost twenty-eight thousand inhabitants, and in the following years, the region was repopulated by several bands of pagan colonists. Four centuries later, Alexander the Great invaded Samaria.

The Jewish people who were left after the deportation intermarried with those of other nations. Consequently, the Samaritans became a mixed race with a pagan heritage. Yet their worship originated primarily from the days of Jeroboam, first king of the Northern Kingdom of Israel, who established the golden calves as visible worship symbols of the invisible God, breaking the second commandment of Moses, which had prohibited any graven image (2 Kings 17:12). Later a priest was sent to "teach them the rituals of the God of the land" (v. 27). In Ezra's day, the Samaritans were considered adversaries who hindered Zerubbabel's efforts to re-build the temple (Ezra 4:1). Later Nehemiah expelled Manasseh be-cause of an unlawful marriage. It was Manasseh who ultimately built the Samaritan temple on Mount Gerizim about 409 B.C. From that time until the days of Christ, there was constant hostility between Jews and Samaritans.

> # *S*UFFERING AND ADVERSITY . . . CAN LEAVE US BITTER, SELF-CENTERED, AND INSENSITIVE TO THE NEEDS OF OTHERS. OR THEY CAN PROVIDE US WITH A GREATER DEGREE OF SENSITIVITY, AN AWARENESS OF THE NEEDS OF OTHERS.

For their part, the Samaritans rejected the entire Old Testament with the exception of their version of the Pentateuch, which they claimed was older and more accurate than the one followed in Je-rusalem. By the time of Jesus, the comment of the woman of Sa-maria at the well—that Jews do not drink from the same cup as the Samaritans—had come to be symbolic for refusal to have any more than the minimum business or social contact possible. Even though the center of worship on Mount Gerizim had been destroyed by John Hyrcanus more than a century before Christ, the Samaritans continued to insist that this was the correct place to worship, rather than Jerusalem (John 4:20).

ON THE JERICHO ROAD

By the time of Christ, the Jews and the Samaritans had had cen-turies to strengthen the walls of hostility between them. The Samar-itan who was traveling down the Jericho road in the incident described by Jesus was undoubtedly a product of his culture. As indicated by the narrative, he likely was a businessman. He had probably experienced firsthand a measure of the prejudice and hostility between Jews and Samaritans. He may at some point have been victimized by discrimination himself. Certainly he would have been conditioned by his own background to look with suspicion and hostility upon those of the Jewish nationality. And it is likely that his view of the Old Testament Scriptures and of worship did not carry the doctrinal accuracy demanded by the Pharisees and scribes and Israel.

Yet he became the centerpiece for Jesus' demonstration on what it really means to love your neighbor as yourself.

Although we are not told this in the text, it seems safe to assume that whatever adversity or discrimination he may have experienced had left him even more compassionate for the wounded man he encountered.

Adversity's Effect

Ironically, suffering and adversity of any kind can have one of two effects on our lives. It can leave us bitter, self-centered, and insensitive to the needs of others. Or they can provide us with a greater degree of sensitivity, an awareness of the needs of others, an openness to reach out to help—in short, a willingness to become a Good Samaritan, to get involved in the lives of others.

According to the apostle Paul, this second effect is how God intends it to happen. Writing during a time of great difficulty in his own personal ministry, Paul described for the Corinthian believers a troubling experience in his life which, although he does not specify its exact nature, created great pressure beyond what he could handle, so that he didn't even expect to survive (2 Corinthians 1:8). Yet, rather than leaving him bitter toward God, self-centered, and ignorant of others, this experience left him trustfully rejoicing in God, grateful for the help of others, and willing to continue serving God and people (vv. 9–11).

How could this happen? Primarily because of the encouraging nature of God Himself, according to Paul. In fact, the apostle titled God "the Father of mercies and God of all comfort" (v. 3). In other words, from the apostle's perspective, despite his troubles he was sure he worshiped a God who empathized with his adversity and whose very nature was to give encouragement.

Furthermore, Paul saw God as acting on the basis of His nature, providing encouragement for every situation that produced pressure or pain (v. 4). Such benevolent action on the part of a loving, comforting God was designed to make it possible, even desirable, for Paul and those who had suffered adversity to extend encouragement to others who faced any kind of adversity or pressure, based on the encouragement received from "the God of all comfort" (vv. 3–4).

Less than twenty-four hours ago, I saw this principle at work again. My scheduled guest for my radio program "Life Perspectives" was forced to cancel because of a sudden and serious family illness. It didn't take me long to look over my "short list" of guests who could be available to devote an hour of their time between 10:00 and 11:00 P.M., listening and responding to the hurts and pains of individuals from across the country. I phoned my friend Cindy Kubetin, director of the Houston Christian Counseling Center and author of the book *Beyond the Darkness*.

Cindy, as described in a preceding chapter, had suffered the pain of abuse. It would have been very easy for her to become hopelessly bitter and self-centered, unwilling to receive or give love.

Yet those who know her best have found Cindy to be exactly the opposite of many bitter, harsh, self-centered victims—for Cindy has experienced God's grace and love in a way that motivates her to reach out to others in need, just as Paul explained to the Corinthians.

When I asked Cindy what she would like to talk about on the radio on such short notice, she completely bypassed the opportunity to promote her excellent book *Beyond the Darkness*. "Let's talk about ways to communicate love," Cindy suggested. I was delighted because her suggestion provided a perfect complement to the program of the previous day, in which John Trent discussed the gift of the blessing.

Cindy explained how love can be communicated by meaningful touch, encouraging words, acts of service, personal gifts, and quality time. When I questioned her, she agreed with me that acts of service certainly fit the profile of what the Good Samaritan did, then she observed that she had become convinced that many victims of abuse, discrimination, or other forms of pain would be better served to shift their focus from their own hurts and pain to the hurts of others. "It's not easy," she told one caller who seemed to be stuck in the victim role. "I too was a victim for many years. It was almost as though I wore a target on my back that said, 'Abuse me.'

"But finally I came to grips with the fact that God Himself was the ultimate answer for my pain. As I came to understand how much He loved me, I learned to handle the fact that many people responded to me in less than loving fashion."

It was the same perspective voiced years earlier by Bob. Sure, he could vividly remember incidents of prejudice, times when he felt the pain and pressure of discrimination. Indirectly, it was there almost constantly. Directly, there had been occasions when he was exposed to prejudice, to harassment, to discrimination.

Yet Bob was committed to using his life and gifts to minister to others, to people of all races. "I hope I can encourage people of whatever background," he told me on more than one occasion. "White, black, Hispanic—after all, God is color-blind in the way He relates to us."

Years later I had the opportunity to become friends with Louis, who pastored a predominantly black church in the Midwest. He and I had a room together at a week-long pastors' seminar in Indiana. During that week we came to know and appreciate each other in a significant way. I particularly gained perspective as he showed how, as a child, he had experienced firsthand what it was like to grow up as a "second-class citizen." "I know a lot of people who are bitter over the kind of treatment I received," he said as we sat together on the plane, flying home from the conference. "But you really only hurt yourself by being bitter. The message of Jesus Christ is the ultimate answer. In Him we are all one, and if we do our part by demonstrating love to each other, then we're in a position to deal with prejudice right at its root."

When I asked him about the civil rights movement, he responded, "Well, it's done some good. There's no question that Dr. King and others have accomplished a great deal for all minorities." We talked about the history of the movement and its various organizations and about civil disobedience and nonviolent protests.

But Louis explained his perspective, that the most effective way to change the society was to change the individual from within. In animated fashion, he reminded me of the words of James, who called on first-century believers not to show favoritism to the richly dressed individual who attends the assembly or to discriminate against the poor man in shabby clothing (James 2:1–4). He went on to remind me how Jesus had reached out in His ministry to those who were considered to be of the lesser levels of society: the poor (Luke 4:18; 14:13), women (Mark 5:25–34; Luke 10:38–42), Gentiles

(Matthew 8:5–13; Mark 5:18–20), and other outcasts (Matthew 11:19; Mark 2:15; Luke 4:18; 7:22).

Then he summarized, "Here's how I think it should work. All of us in our old nature, whether believers or not, struggle with feelings of prejudice, pride, and hatred. The gospel changes our whole outlook because we respond to God's love for us. And as we respond to His love, we learn to love others. That kind of love leads to serving others—the opposite of prejudice."

We aren't told what the Good Samaritan's motivation was. Yet he certainly provided a shocking example to motivate those individuals who listened to Jesus as He held this man up as an example of loving humanitarian service.

Old Testament "Samaritan"

Recently I came across an Old Testament counterpart to the Good Samaritan. He was a man from a disadvantaged racial minority, whose basic role in life was that of a slave. Yet he responded selflessly when he spotted another human being in need, reached out to help at personal risk, and provided us with a great example of selfless loving service. This man lived during the days of the prophet Jeremiah, a time of spiritual indifference and political and economic instability. His name, Ebed-melech, graphically described his occupation. It literally meant "servant of the king."

The events recorded in chapters 37 through 39 of Jeremiah trace the prophet's ministry during the final siege and fall of Jerusalem. King Zedekiah had asked Jeremiah to pray to the Lord for Jerusalem (Jeremiah 37:3). The prophet prayed, and God answered, but not in the way the king had hoped. Nebuchadnezzar's army would burn the city of Jerusalem, leaving it destroyed (v. 8). "Don't fool yourselves," the prophet warned. As he finished delivering his grim message, the captain of the king's guard seized him, arrested him, and charged him with treason. The prophet was beaten and imprisoned.

Some time later, Jeremiah was granted a private audience with King Zedekiah, who asked if he had a further word from the Lord. The prophet replied that God had not changed His word. Probably in his sixties by now, Jeremiah pleaded with the king not to return him to prison because of the risk to his life (v. 20). King Zedekiah responded favorably to the prophet's plea, ordering him moved from the underground dungeon where he had been imprisoned to the courtyard of the guard, and arranging for him to receive bread each day as long as food remained in the city (v. 21).

However, during Jeremiah's confinement in the courtyard of the guard, four high-ranking officials overheard him discussing God's message of doom. Shephatiah, Gedaliah, Jucal, and Pashhur sought an audience with King Zedekiah. Before the king they accused Jeremiah of sowing gloom and doom to seek the ruin of his people, even though his purpose had in fact been to motivate them to repentance. Weak and vacillating, King Zedekiah handed Jeremiah over to these four men, who had him thrown into a cistern, a large pit used to gather rainwater in the winter for later use during the dry months of summer.

Earlier, Jeremiah had written accusing Israel of forsaking God's cistern of living water and hewing out broken cisterns that could not hold water (2:13). Perhaps due to the extended drought spoken of in Jeremiah 14, the cistern wasn't filled with water. There was only the mud and mire into which the prophet sank. At this point, his life was in serious danger.

Ebed-melech the slave heard of Jeremiah's plight. We know little about this man except that he was a slave of the king and he came from Cush, the area currently represented by southern Egypt, northern Ethiopia, and the Sudan. Like many African-Americans of earlier generations in our country, he had been deported from the land of his nativity and forced to serve as a slave in a foreign country. He could be considered a classic victim of prejudice. As such he might have easily focused on himself and the injustices he had faced, even though, as a servant of the king, he enjoyed privileges others of his race might not have had.

However, what is outstanding about this obscure Old Testament slave was his response to the plight of the prophet. He immediately left the king's palace, went to the Benjamin Gate where the king was seated, and delivered word of the urgency of Jeremiah's situation. It seems from Jeremiah's narrative that Zedekiah had paid very little attention to the plea given by the four enemies of the prophet. Apparently, he simply gave his approval without considering the implications for the life of the prophet he had earlier ordered removed from a similar dungeon.

It is quite likely that Ebed-melech made his appeal at no little risk to himself. Like Esther pleading to King Ahasuerus for the well-being of her people, Ebed-melech could well have found himself facing a summary death order from the king. Such responses were not rare in those days.

However, Zedekiah responded positively to the courageous action of this Old Testament Samaritan, instructing him to take thirty men and immediately remove Jeremiah from the dungeon in order to save his life (38:10). Quickly following instructions, Ebed-melech and the soldiers took old rags and worn-out clothes and passed them down to Jeremiah to put under his armpits. Then the contingent of soldiers pulled the prophet up out of the sticky mire at the bottom of the cistern with the ropes. Perhaps some of the soldiers also stood guard to protect against any who might oppose the rescue of the prophet.

While Luke's Good Samaritan has rightly received a great deal of attention, based on Jesus' description of his actions, few have noticed or called attention to the courageous heroics of this man Ebed-melech on behalf of God's prophet Jeremiah.

Good Samaritans of the Holocaust

Similarly, until 1993, few people noticed the efforts of an industrialist named Oskar Schindler, a German member of the Nazi party who became personally involved in the risky business of employing Jews in defiance of the Third Reich. While the courageous stands taken by individuals such as Dietrich Bonhoeffer and Martin Niemöller had been chronicled,[9] I had personally seen very little on the subject of Oskar Schindler. Apparently, neither had very many others, until a film produced and directed by Steven Spielberg, himself Jewish, documented the actions of this man, garnering a great deal of press attention and eleven Oscar nominations in the process.

In the book describing Schindler's actions,[10] Thomas Keneally, one of the individuals whose life was saved because he was employed by Schindler, describes how the businessman initially was motivated more by making money than by the plight of the Jews and the Holocaust.

However, before long, Schindler was touched by the atrocities suffered at the hands of the Nazi soldiers, and he began to look for ways to preserve as many Jewish lives as possible. At one point, Schindler found himself jailed just because he had kissed a young Jewish girl at a birthday celebration held in his honor. Still he persisted, at risk of his own well-being and safety, ultimately saving more than twelve hundred Polish Jews from death in the ovens of

Auschwitz. By the end of the war, profits no longer mattered, and he was spending vast sums of money to be able to keep the Jews he employed alive. Certainly Oskar Schindler, though he was not a Christian, provided a classic example of modern-day Good Samaritanism in the face of human prejudice and atrocity.

*Y*OU MIGHT ASK, BUT CAN ONE PERSON'S ACTION MAKE A DIFFERENCE? ABSOLUTELY. NO QUESTION ABOUT IT.

Martin Niemöller was one of a small minority of pastors of the Confessing Church in Nazi Germany who attempted to attack the laws against non-Aryans as a violation of the convictions of the church. Although he fought for the rights of Hebrew Christian pastors, Niemöller later recognized that he actually could have done more to stand against the Third Reich. While serving as pastor of Berlin's Dahlem Church, he circulated a letter to other ministers inviting them to join a "pastor's emergency alliance" in response to widespread actions taken against individual pastors.[11] Arrested in 1937, Niemöller was sent to the Sachsenhausen concentration camp, from which he was transferred in 1941 to Dachau. Efforts by leaders from around the world to free him had no effect.

"Never Again"

Some years ago my wife and I visited the site of the Dachau concentration camp on the outskirts of Munich with a Christian tour group. As our bus drove up in the later afternoon and we spotted the wooden barracks and other buildings, one thing stood out to us more than anything else: a sign containing just two words in four languages, "Never again."

Even now, years later, it is almost impossible to describe the horror of what happened in that camp and others like it. Pictures in the museum area showed indescribable indignities suffered by human beings—and the gaunt, emaciated appearance of many of the victims. We walked through the stark barracks where prisoners were kept, then saw the ovens where political prisoners had been murdered *en masse*. The scene brought home vividly the sheer horror of the evil of the human heart.

WHAT CAN WE DO TODAY?

What can we do to stand against such prejudice, such hatred, such incredibly evil results?

Like Martin Niemöller and Ebed-melech, we can take a stand, even at the risk of our lives. Like Oskar Schindler, and like the unnamed Samaritan of the New Testament, we can put our resources at risk by getting involved in the lives of others. Like my friend Bob, we can refuse to allow the prejudices we have suffered to become an obstacle in our showing compassion to others of all backgrounds. Like Cindy, we can reach out in compassion and concern to others who have been hurt, empowered by the grace of God which has provided healing for our hurts.

You might ask, But can one person's action make a difference? Absolutely. No question about it. That's why Jesus would ultimately challenge the religious leader to whom He recounted the story of the Good Samaritan to go and do likewise.

That's exactly what my friend Bob did. He became involved in the lives of many of the young people who lived in the ghetto in which he had grown up. He also took the time to provide encouragement and ministry to poor individuals of other races, including whites and Hispanics. He devoted a great deal of his time and energy to demonstrating genuine love and concern for others, just like the Good Samaritan did.

NOTES

1. The International Standard Bible Society, *International Standard Bible Encyclopedia,* ed. James Orr, (Grand Rapids: Eerdmans, 1939), 5:960.

2. *Lincoln Journal Star* (26 February 1994).

3. *Time* 143, no. 9 (28 February 1994).

4. Ibid., 21.

5. Michael Nicholson, "Escape from Sarajevo," *Reader's Digest* 144, no. 863 (March 1994), 120–21.

6. Ibid., 120.

7. Derric Johnson, writer and producer, "America Is" radio feature, Impact Records.

8. *Encyclopedia,* 5:957.

9. For an excellent treatment of this subject, see David A. Rouch, *A Legacy of Hatred* (Chicago: Moody, 1984).

10. Thomas Keneally, *Schindler's List* (New York: Simon and Schuster, 1982).

11. David A. Rouch, *A Legacy of Hatred* (Chicago: Moody, 1984), 164–66.

CHAPTER EIGHT

THE GOOD SAMARITAN'S RESPONSE: COMPASSIONATE SIGHT

*"But a certain Samaritan, as he journeyed, came where he was.
And when he saw him, he had compassion on him,
and went to him and bandaged his wounds."*
(Luke 10:33–34)

There is no more recognizable symbol of the United States than the bald eagle. It is a beautiful and graceful creature with a wingspan of several feet and a beautiful white head in which are set piercing eyes with incredible visual acuity. The bald eagle's feathers have long been coveted by Native Americans. Long ago the bald eagle was placed on the endangered species list.

Several years ago, while on a trip to Alaska, I had the opportunity to see bald eagles in their natural habitat. As we flew from a remote location near the southeast Alaskan coast toward Anchorage in a small private plane, our pilot pointed out several bald eagles, some flying close enough to our plane to be able to be seen clearly. Others were resting on poles in a remote, marshy area. Our host lamented how close these birds had come to extinction, but he expressed a positive feeling that, due to government protection, the bald eagle was making a comeback.

Sadly, in our world today, Good Samaritans have been about as rare as bald eagles. While there have been some recent evidences that these individuals are making a comeback, there is a significant need for an even greater number of Good Samaritans in the world in which we live.

Without question, those of us who are Christians, who have tasted of the love of God, who have benefited from His grace by receiving the eternal gift of His life, should be taking the lead in becoming Good Samaritans, or friends in deed.

But how can you spot a Good Samaritan? Does he wear a certain kind of clothing? Does he spend money on a certain item?

Some years ago, a number of individuals banded together in New York City to help protect those who rode the subways from muggers, rapists, and others who preyed on subway passengers. Distinctive red berets marked these individuals who were referred to as Guardian Angels.

Unfortunately, Good Samaritans aren't as distinctive in appearance as bald eagles or Guardian Angels.

During the week preceding my work on this chapter, two major snowstorms dumped several inches of snow on our home in Nebraska. The first had been predicted; the second seemed to catch even the National Weather Service by surprise.

The storm surprised me as well. A few random flakes fell as I left my car for the studio to produce "Life Perspectives" at a quarter before ten on a Thursday evening. The show ended just after eleven, and my producer and I stepped outside, surprised to see our vehicles covered with two inches of fresh snow.

Later that evening, blowing snow was whipped by winds of almost fifty miles an hour into drifts that reached five feet deep in places. A Red Cross spokesman in Hastings, Nebraska, told the Associated Press, "We had a lot of Good Samaritans out there last night. A lot of people who were in the ditch caught rides with people passing by." A photo printed in the Lincoln paper was captioned, "Two Good Samaritans Push Car in Norfolk, Where Wind Chill Was Minus 37 Degrees."

The weekend before, I had been in southwestern Virginia speaking at a conference in a church near Roanoke. Although temperatures were in the fifties and sixties, piles of snow and ice were left on sidewalks and parking lots—mute evidence to the latest in a series of vicious winter storms that had battered the east coast during the preceding weeks.

Residents of Roanoke and Rocky Mount, Virginia, told me of numerous Good Samaritan activities that took place during and after the storms. We've all heard similar descriptions in the aftermath of hurricanes, tornadoes, major flooding, and earthquakes, as well as during wars, riots, and other times.

It seems like both natural and manmade disasters tend to bring out Good Samaritans.

SPOTTING GOOD SAMARITANS

But it doesn't take this kind of dramatic event for us to be able to spot a Good Samaritan. In fact, as He told the story of the original Good Samaritan, Jesus gave important clues that can help us identify others who are authentic Good Samaritans and let us know whether we ourselves fit the profile.

After describing the condition of the half-dead victim lying by the side of the road, noting the disinterest and uninvolvement of the priest and the Levite, and introducing the Samaritan traveler, Jesus explained the three components that mark the true Good Samaritan. Two of these we will consider in this chapter, the third in the one to follow.

These three characteristics are vision or awareness, compassion, and involved action. Or, as the Lord put it, he saw him, he had compassion, and he went to him and bound up his wounds (Luke 10:33–34).

In contrast to the Roman general Julius Caesar, who described his approach as, "I came, I saw, I conquered," the Good Samaritan came, saw, and caringly got involved.

It's easy in our time to develop what we might refer to as "tunnel vision." After all, there are so many needy people around us, we can actually develop what we might call compassion overload. Furthermore, most of us are extremely busy, pursuing things we consider to be of some importance. If they aren't actually important, they are at least urgent and cry out to demand our attention. Each of us has bills to pay, automobiles to have repaired, income tax forms to fill out, expense reports at work to complete and turn in, rented movies to return to the local video shop, correspondence to keep up with (or at least sporadic long-distance calls to family in far-flung areas), groceries to purchase, clothes to launder, and an endless ongoing list of the activities of life. How can we possibly find the time to develop a successful "Good Samaritan" approach to life?

We can borrow a page from Emmitt Smith, perhaps the most successful running back in recent years in the National Football League. Designated by the sports media as the Most Valuable Player for the Super Bowl champion Dallas Cowboys, Emmitt was recently asked about the key to his success in running the football. After all, as the interviewer observed, he was neither the fastest nor the biggest nor the strongest running back in the league.

DEVELOPING GOOD SAMARITAN-LIKE VISION

Like many great running backs before him, Smith attributed much of his success to his ability to see a great deal of the field at the same time. As he lined up in his spot seven or eight yards behind the quarterback, he was able to observe almost the entire defensive team without moving his eyes. He could take note of where defensive ends, linebackers, and safeties were stationed, and even get an idea of what angles his blockers might take to open holes through which he could run for extra yardage.

Just as incredible peripheral vision set apart superior NFL running backs such as Emmitt Smith, and Tony Dorsett of an earlier Cowboys Super Bowl championship team, so it is with Good Samaritans. The first characteristic is awareness, or vision.

This kind of awareness was visibly demonstrated one Saturday afternoon during an extended luncheon, where my wife and I spent time with a couple we had come to know well and an internationally known Christian leader named Charles.

I've had the privilege of eating lunch or dinner with quite a number of well-known Christian leaders, authors, and Bible teachers. Getting them to talk about themselves proves enjoyable because I find their experiences fascinating, and I learn as I listen to them. In addition, it's usually not very difficult to get people, especially well-known people, to talk about themselves.

That's why I was surprised at the direction our conversation took that particular day. From the beginning of our time together, it was evident that Charles was more interested in us, and more determined to learn about us, than he was in impressing us with his latest exploits for the cause of Christ.

Now he didn't engage in false humility or refuse to say anything at all about himself. To do so would have been unrealistic. But he did focus in on talking with the two couples with whom he was having lunch.

The other couple who had joined us for the meal had recently suffered a terrible trauma, one which was extremely difficult to discuss. Just months before, their daughter, who had lived in an apartment in California, had been viciously raped and murdered. These friends of ours were still processing their grief over their tragic loss.

It didn't take Charles long to spot the fact that he was with people who had been deeply wounded. Without prying, he graciously encouraged this man and woman, both involved in vocational ministry, to tell what they had been through. Without glossing over the pain or expressing pious platitudes, he gently encouraged them to uncover their grief, to share their hurt. He didn't exhibit the least sign of boredom, something I have seen people do at times when exposed to the hurts of others. Nor was he uncomfortable with their pain and hurt or even their anger. He didn't minimize their tragedy by telling them about a lot of other people who had been through the same thing, nor play the frequently engaged-in game of one-upmanship that so often shows itself in "Let me tell you about a *worse* tragedy that happened to me or someone I know."

Instead, Charles kept steering the conversation back to their circumstances in such a way that I was left with the overwhelming conviction that I was in the presence of a master encourager.

At an earlier strategy session, several people, including the ministry colleague who was with us at lunch, had expressed the opinion that Charles would be the ideal speaker for the important event we were planning. "After all," as one member of the committee had put it, "there's nobody who sounds any more compassionate or caring than he does on the radio." While literally millions of people undoubtedly shared that opinion about Charles, I had seen firsthand his self-imposed awareness of those around him. He was *observant*.

*T*HE LINKING OF SEEING WITH CARING, RATHER THAN SIMPLY THE CULTIVATION OF POWERS OF OBSERVATION, IS WHAT MAKES THIS PROCESS SO UNIQUE IN PROVIDING THE HALLMARK OF GOOD SAMARITANISM.

Try an experiment to see how observant you are. The next time you drive between your home and work or your favorite store, see how many things you can notice that you've never actually observed before. Make a list of them. You may be amazed at how unused your powers of observation really are.

Then take the process a step further. Start with the people you work with, or those in your church or Bible study. Try looking for clues as to who is really happy and, conversely, who may be struggling, burdened, or feeling down. You might, if married, enlist the help of your spouse in this little project. Perhaps the two of you could work on the area of observation together, sharpening the observational powers of both of you. And then, next time you are in a conversation with one of those people, make a point to find out more about the person—without prying, but just allowing and encouraging him to talk about himself.

CHRIST THE OBSERVANT ONE

As I thought about the trait of observation, the Person who immediately came to mind was the Lord Jesus Himself. Over and over the four evangelists noted that "He saw." Two words commonly used by the New Testament writers, *blepo* and *horao,* are used by Jesus of the priest who saw and then passed by and of the Samaritan who saw and responded with concern. The two words have a lot in common, though some scholars give more prominence to mental discernment and perception when *horao* is used.[1] This is Matthew's word to describe Jesus observing Peter, Andrew, James, and John before calling them to become fishers of men (Matthew 4:18, 21) and of His observation of large multitudes with great needs (Matthew 8:18; 9:36; 14:14). Matthew and his colleague Mark both use *horao* of Jesus spotting Matthew (Matthew 9:9; Mark 2:14). Mark uses it of Jesus spotting the disciples as they desperately rowed against a storm one night on the Sea of Galilee (Mark 6:48), of Christ observing the crowds as they ran to see a young demon-possessed adolescent just before the Savior delivered him (Mark 9:25), and of the Savior's perception of the disciples' rebuke of those who brought children to Jesus (Mark 10:14).

Yet the linking of seeing with caring, rather than simply the cultivation of powers of observation, is what makes this process so unique in providing the hallmark of Good Samaritanism. Time and again the New Testament writers said of Jesus that He saw and He cared, He saw and He had compassion. It's one thing to see a hurting individual such as a street person as an obstacle or a nuisance to avoid, as a problem to analyze or discuss;[2] it is yet another to see and be prompted to care.

SEEING AND CARING

Jesus inextricably links these two concepts in two of His most remarkable parables, the description of the Good Samaritan and the father of the prodigal son (Luke 15:20). In both instances it is worth noting that one might not observe, or might observe and not care. However, in both these instances, the Lord's hero both observed and cared.

To continue the analogy from the world of sports, it is not sufficient for a running back of Emmitt Smith's stature and skill to simply be able to spot the relative positions of offensive and defensive players on the field. He must also care enough about the sport to discipline himself to endure pain, to condition his body so he can act on his observations for the good of his team.

And that's exactly what Emmitt Smith did. On at least two occasions during the 1993–94 season, he cared enough to keep playing despite a great deal of pain. In one instance, because of a separated shoulder, he played with, as he later told a sports interviewer, "more pain than I've ever had in my life." Because of his injury, he wasn't even expected to appear in that game at all, and if he did, it was thought he would only put in a token appearance or two. However, his team was about to play two crucial games: one against NFL East rival New York Giants, the other with the San Francisco 49ers, the team most sports experts gave the best chance of defeating the Cowboys. It was clear that, if the Cowboys were to win, they would need Emmitt Smith's running skills. And he cared enough about his team's performance to compete, even when getting involved in the conflict would certainly not be comfortable.

That's precisely the kind of activity, in an entirely different arena, that should characterize a Good Samaritan.

What are we learning here about the characteristic marks of a Good Samaritan? First, he sees the need. He observes what's going on. Second, he is moved to care. He is not simply a dispassionate observer. His emotions are sensitive, just like Christ, the Great High Priest who can be touched with the feeling of our infirmities (Hebrews 4:15) and therefore makes available His grace and mercy to help us in our time of need.

That brings us to the third trait of the Good Samaritan. He acts on his feelings.

COMPASSION IN ACTION

How are we to apply such compassion? How does it operate in our lives?

Three New Testament epistles drive home to us just how this word should operate in our day-to-day experience. Understanding it and applying it can help make us recognizable as Good Samaritans.

First, the apostle Paul used the term in Ephesians 4:32 in the context of resolving bitterness by extending forgiveness. As Paul put it, all bitterness, anger, and feelings of retribution toward others need to be put aside; furthermore, we are to adopt attitudes of kindness, tenderheartedness—compassion—and forgiveness toward one another, based on the fact that God has for Christ's sake forgiven us.

What are the implications of this in my life?

What Paul recommends—whether we have been victims of discrimination, as my friend Bob had been; suffered abuse, like my friend Cindy; or whatever—God's instruction is clear. Based on Christ's forgiveness extended to me, I am to choose to forgive, releasing the right to take vengeance for every wrong committed against me. Part of what we need in order to do this is a tenderness of heart. Unfortunately, when we have been hurt deeply, it is quite common for us to develop a callousness, a hardheartedness. I often describe this as a "hard edge" toward life. It involves a harshness in our approach to others, a frequent use of sarcasm, and a tendency to put others down. All these give evidence to a lack of compassion, or a "hard edge." Just as in the physical realm where scar tissue or calluses can build up to protect against further wounding, so a callused indifference—a "hard edge"—can become an emotional or spiritual mechanism by which we try to avoid being hurt again.

However, Paul makes clear that tenderheartedness is an essential component, along with Christ-like kindness and the choice to forgive those who have wronged us.

In other words, we can't really become Good Samaritans without cultivating tenderheartedness.

Peter made the same observation as he called on the suffering individuals to whom he was writing to exercise tenderhearted compassion toward each other as brothers and sisters in the family of God (1 Peter 3:8). The apostle had just concluded his discussion of domestic life—submission by wives; compassionate, understanding honor by husbands—and he followed by reminding all believers, married or single, to be like-minded, to demonstrate compassion and brotherly love, to take pity, to practice courtesy, and to refuse to take vengeance or repay evil for evil.

It's impossible for us to know exactly what was in the apostle's mind when he wrote this, yet his use of the verb we are discussing suggests at least one instance when he saw the Lord's displeasure at a lack of compassion. It happened at a time when Jesus had been even more busy than usual as He presented His gospel of the kingdom. A short time before, He had revealed His glory to Peter and two of his colleagues on the Mount of Transfiguration. Over and over during those days they had seen His compassion extended to the multitudes. On the day in question, Peter apparently passed the word along to Mark (who recorded it in his gospel) that individuals from the far side of the Jordan were bringing young children to Him so He could touch them—an element of the Hebrew blessing which is so much a part of the Old Testament. That the children were of various ages is indicated by the general term for children employed by Mark and Matthew and by Luke's use of the word for nursing children.

[GOOD SAMARITANS] ARE INDIVIDUALS OF INCREDIBLE VISION—VISION THAT ALLOWS THEM TO SPOT, AMONG THE HUMANS AROUND THEM, THOSE WHO ARE SUFFERING, HURTING, AND IN NEED.

All three evangelists recorded how the disciples sternly rebuked the adults who brought their children. You could almost hear Peter boldly and with not a little anger in his voice saying, "Get those brats out of here! We don't have time for this!"

Only Mark notes the emotional response of Jesus, though the other evangelists record His words. Christ was greatly displeased—literally, indignant. In effect, He felt pain Himself over the rejection of these little children, and the efforts by those He had sought to disciple as His own children to remove these little ones from His touch left Him hurt and angry. So He spoke, "Let the little children come to Me, and do not forbid them; for of such is the kingdom of

God" (Mark 10:14). Explaining how these little children modeled the faith that was necessary to enter God's kingdom, the Savior then took the children into His arms, placed His hand on them, and blessed them—just as a father would. One by one He took the time to reach out to each of these little ones, even though, like the Samaritan, they ranked near the bottom of the chain of respect in the society of that day.

The final use of this word in the New Testament can be found near the end of the letter written by James, the half-brother of the Lord (James 5:11). Rather than employing the word as an exhortation to Christians, James uses it in a two-part Old Testament illustration he presents to reinforce his call for steadfast endurance in the face of adversity. Alluding to Psalm 103:8 and the steadfastness of Job, he reminds his readers that the Lord is "multi-merciful." That is the literal rendering of the compound term James uses to demonstrate the intensity of God's unfailing tender compassions and His loyal love—traits described by the prophet Jeremiah in Lamentations 3:22–23. James uses the word as part of his motivational call to suffering Christians to endure steadfastly. I think it doesn't do violence to the intended application of the text to suggest that such steadfast endurance includes showing the kind of tender compassions that are characteristic of our long-suffering Lord.

So what have we learned about spotting Good Samaritans?

First, they are individuals of incredible vision—vision that allows them to spot, among the humans around them, those who are suffering, hurting, and in need, like Charles did. They are individuals who respond to that need by becoming involved, who open themselves up to be moved, who genuinely care, who refuse to allow a "hard edge" to develop that may blunt or hinder compassion.

The term for compassion was used in the extra-biblical literature of the day to describe the process of surgery.[3] Perhaps there is a carryover meaning, in that surgery entails opening a person up, while compassion involves opening ourselves up to others with genuine concern.

OPPORTUNITIES TO CARE

Many years ago Sir Winston Churchill described certain individuals as people who have the ability, after stumbling over incredible opportunity, to pick themselves up and keep going without bothering to look at what they stumbled over. Tragically, some of us—as we frantically dash through life—find ourselves stumbling over great opportunities to help without ever observing the opportunity to care or being moved by the kind of compassion that leads to action.

It is this kind of compassion that is so closely related to *agape,* the kind of love that is "Christianity's own original basic conception."[4] This is the love that looks beyond the worth or lack of worth in the object, the word that described that which is freely given to all, that which contrasts with the warm liking implied by *philos* or the physical attraction described by *eros.*

To exercise *agape* is to choose to consider as valuable and to convey value. While Peter urged both compassion and brotherly love (1 Peter 3:8), it is in John's first epistle that we find an extensive emphasis on the kind of love that gets involved, that moves into action.

As John wrote his letter, his mind may have gone back to the evening before the Lord's crucifixion, when the Savior gave His disciples a new commandment, a badge of discipleship (John 13:34–35; 15:12). This new commandment, as John made clear, was simply that we practice *agape* love to one another (1 John 2:7–11). Furthermore, one way we can spot those who are children of God, as opposed to those who are children of the devil, is by whether or not they practice love for their brothers (1 John 3:10–14).

In the following paragraph, John points out two specific, tangible ways we can demonstrate such love. The first is a willingness to lay down our lives for others (v. 16). It's the kind of courageous care exhibited by Ebed-melech in the Old Testament and the Good Samaritan in the New.

The second, also demonstrated by the actions of the Good Samaritan, involves reaching out materially to meet the needs of others (v. 17).

After listing these basic ways to show love for each other, John issues a clear call for action with the words, "Beloved, let us love one another, for love is of God; and everyone who loves is born of God and knows God" (1 John 4:7). The apostle's motivation is clear: "If God so loved us, we also ought to love one another" (v. 11). We will remain in fellowship with the God who abides in us, and experience growth toward maturity through His love operating in us, as we love one another (v. 12). Furthermore, we cannot claim to love God, who cannot be seen, and refuse or fail to love our brother whom we can see (v. 20).

John's message, and that of James, Peter, and Paul, is crystal clear. In light of a loving God, in view of a compassionate Savior, in the face of the example of the Good Samaritan, the father of the prodigal son, and the graciously forgiving king, we must exhibit compassion and love for others.

There are complicated ways to do this, and there are simple ones. Taking time for people. Giving or helping. Even praying. Especially praying.

Some time ago a lady with the rather unusual name of "Happy" phoned our radio call-in program. As I would later learn, her real name is Lois, and she is a professional fishing guide. I was especially surprised to learn that she stayed up nearly every night to listen to our program, "Life Perspectives," since fishing guides usually start work very early in the day.

Her reason was even more surprising—and delightful. Happy explained to me one evening in a phone conversation, "Your program has really ministered to me. I've been personally encouraged by the things you and your guests have shared. I've sensed that the people you have on the program really care, and I've come to care about hurting people too.

"That's why I stay up late every night to listen to your program. I make a list of first names of those who phone in. Then I continue praying for them by name, based on the needs and problems they share on the broadcast."

When I talked further with Happy, I discovered that she had been through a lot of pain and hurt in her life. Rather than focusing on her pain and hurt, she had chosen to observe others in need, to reach out to them by praying for them, and to look for ways to offer tangible help to the hurting people with whom she comes in personal contact.

So we can spot Good Samaritans by their vision for the needs of others, by their compassion and authentic care, and by their willingness to move into action to get involved.

But the real question is not how many Good Samaritans we can spot in the crowded church on Sunday, or in the marketplace, or at work during the week. Rather, do you see a Good Samaritan when you look in the mirror?

NOTES

1. W. E. Vine, Jr., Merrill F. Unger and William White, Jr., *An Expository Dictionary of Biblical Words* (Nashville: Nelson, 1983), 1009.

2. Warren Wiersbe, *Meet Yourself in the Parables* (Wheaton, Ill.: Victor, 1979), 57–58.
3. Nigel Turner, *Christian Words* (Nashville: Nelson, 1981), 79.
4. Ibid., 262.

CHAPTER NINE

LOVING ACTION: THE SAMARITAN MAKES CONTACT

*"[He] went to him and bandaged his wounds,
pouring on oil and wine; and he set him on his own animal,
brought him to an inn, and took care of him."*
(Luke 10:34)

Patients today seldom feel the touch of the hand of a doctor, a nurse, or a dentist. In our AIDS era, modern medical care is almost always insulated by at least one layer of latex. Or, as one medical professional expressed it, "First the gloves, then the procedure—no matter what the procedure."

A nurse was forced to retire from her chosen profession due to an allergic reaction to latex. She was well-trained, she enjoyed her work, she was good with patients, she knew the medical field well, and she worked competently with the doctors and other professionals on her treatment team. But she simply was unable to continue nursing because every time she put on latex gloves she began to experience a serious physical reaction.

Rob, a friend of mine, has been an EMT (emergency medical technician) for a number of years. In his chosen vocation, he has been confronted with the reality of sudden, violent death on the highway; he has treated the unpleasant effects of coronary occlusions, myocardial infarctions, and other forms of serious heart attack; he has tended to senior citizens and children, men and women, healthy and unhealthy people, those in the prime of life and those at the point of death. For Rob, rubber gloves have become a way of life. "No matter how much we may be in a hurry to treat the patient, we always put on the gloves first. It's standard procedure today."

For Dr. Edward Rozer, wearing rubber gloves wasn't standard procedure when he became a cardio-thoracic surgeon in the early eighties. When he was a guest on my radio call-in program, he described coronary surgery in a graphic way I had never imagined. "In the process of open-heart surgery, we often found ourselves digging around with both hands in the chest cavity. There were all kinds of ways to cut yourself, especially on bone tissue. Even if we had worn rubber gloves—and we didn't back then—I'm not sure they would have protected us."

Surgical procedures have changed today, and so has Dr. Rozer's life. Several years ago he tested HIV positive after cutting himself while doing surgery on an HIV-infected patient. Although he died of AIDS in 1993 shortly after I interviewed him, his book, *Laughing in the Face of AIDS,*[1] has provided a great deal of insight from a medical, spiritual, and personal perspective into this dreaded disease.

PHYSICAL CONTACT, AIDS STYLE

So we are living in the AIDS era today. Does this mean we can no longer make contact with hurting people? Must we and our relationships with others follow the model of these "high-tech" medical procedures that often seem to guard against any kind of personal contact?

Quite the contrary. I'm convinced that when we love people unconditionally, when we are moved with compassion, we'll follow the old telephone commercial and "reach out and touch someone." I'm not suggesting we should never exercise caution, or that the procedures Rob and others in medicine use are inappropriate. I'm just saying there are still ways we can reach out to those who hurt.

That's precisely what the Good Samaritan did. As the Lord described his actions on the road between Jerusalem and Jericho, he reached out to a hurting, half-dead individual he encountered, expressed his compassion, and made contact that demonstrated his personal care for this wounded man.

Sadly, we live in a society which often doesn't want to get involved in the lives of others. About a year ago, I found myself on the streets of downtown Los Angeles, surrounded at one point by scores of homeless individuals. I had seen pictures on television of homeless people roaming the streets of our major cities, looking for either work or a handout, or perhaps a place to stay. I had spotted them from my car, standing on street corners, holding signs saying "Will work for food."

But it was a different thing entirely to come in contact with so many of them, up close and personal. There was the sight of their makeshift attire and the sound of their demands for food, money, or help—often insistent and intrusive, to the point where one member of the group I was with finally sighed in exasperation, "Why can't the police get these people out of here?!" Then there was their smell—about what you'd expect from people for whom a nightly bath is as foreign as a seven-course meal in an upscale restaurant.

That scene reminded me of another experience I had some years before. I had been invited to speak to the medical staff of the AIDS treatment unit of a major Chicago hospital, and the topic was burnout.

When I flew into a snowy Chicago the evening before and had dinner with the medical director and other members of the staff, I soon discovered I was about to experience a unique opportunity to demonstrate the love of Jesus to individuals who not only were not Christians, but who held a different view than I did on many issues. I discovered as well that many of the staff were confessed homosexuals who bristled at the thought that God would frown on such relationships.

After a dinner at which I was questioned thoroughly about both the nature of Christian faith and the attitude of Christians toward those with AIDS—particularly homosexuals—I was convinced I would face quite a challenge when I spoke to the entire staff the next day.

The following morning I left my hotel, praying as I took a cab the fifteen or so blocks to the hospital. I was to discover quickly that these individuals were far more interested in knowing how much I *cared* than how much I *knew.*

In preparation for my visit to the AIDS unit and my workshops on burnout, I had talked with a number of medical authorities on the subject of AIDS. Everyone agreed with the current research: You couldn't contract AIDS by casual contact.

However, as I walked through the double doors into the unit that morning with two members of the medical staff, I couldn't help recalling all the horror stories I had heard—stories about catching the AIDS virus from breathing the air around those who were HIV positive or contracting AIDS from tears or perspiration from HIV-positive food preparers. I faced a great opportunity to turn my fears and concerns over to the Lord.

The Personal Touch

The first thing I spotted as we rounded the corner and entered the unit was a huge sign asking, "Have you hugged an AIDS patient today?" It didn't take long to figure out how they planned to find out how much I really cared.

Sure enough, the two medical professionals who were with me took me in to meet several of the AIDS patients. I could see the relief on both their faces when I shook hands with one, then hugged another.

Now, don't get me wrong. I'm not setting myself up as a paragon of Good Samaritan virtue. There are times—and this was one—when I have felt at least some measure of hesitation.

However, I was convinced that now was the time and this was the place to do what God had called me to do—to exhibit the love of Jesus Christ to hurting individuals—and to leave my ultimate physical protection in the hands of the God who is more than capable of taking care of such things.

After shaking hands, hugging, and talking with several of the patients, I was taken to the conference room where I was to speak. Despite the fact that most of those who had come to hear me were not Christians, the atmosphere was decidedly warm. The medical director made it a point during his introduction to speak of my contact with the people they were involved in treating on a daily basis. My credibility was enhanced not so much by any books I had written, degrees I had earned, radio programs I had hosted, or research on burnout I had conducted or reviewed. Rather, they cared to find out what I knew because they knew I cared enough to come in contact with the same people they cared for.

So the door was opened for an amazing opportunity to present the gospel. A member of the nursing staff, a young man in his mid-twenties, raised his hand during a question-and-answer period. "I just don't get it," he sighed. "I feel so guilty treating these people. I've been gay for many years, and I haven't contracted AIDS. Yet I deal with people every day who have, and here they are dying. After all, 100 percent of the patients who come to us are terminal. Can you share anything with me that would help me deal with this?"

Thanking the Lord silently for an incredible opportunity and the grace to take advantage of it, I answered his question. Calling the young man by name, I said, "You know, you've just hit on something very important—feeling guilty. You see, our guilt really has nothing to do with being HIV positive or negative, or even our sexual orientation.

"The truth is, every single one of us is guilty. I'm straight, and I'm guilty. You are gay and guilty. Why? Because no matter who we are or how we may have lived, none of us has perfectly lived up to God's standards. That's why, no matter what we have done in life, no matter how we live or by what moral code, none of us will ever be good enough to make it on our own."

I went on to explain how God had provided for our guilt by allowing His Son, Jesus Christ, to die in our place to pay the penalty for our sins, and how He offered us hope beyond death through His resurrection.

I talked at length with this young man and with others afterward, and although he did not choose to trust Christ at that time, he did agree to give the matter serious consideration.

Mandate to Reach Out

I am convinced that we have been given a mandate to demonstrate Christ's love, not simply by giving or by praying for those who are hurting. We fulfill that mandate best as we get involved in the lives of others, as we make contact.

In his manual on Christian counseling, Gary Collins quotes from a chapel address delivered by one of his students at Trinity Evangelical Divinity School, who talked about ministering to the gay community.

> Come to one of the dozens and dozens of gay bars in Chicago with me tonight, and at 3 A.M. I will show you . . . people . . . who are crying out to be loved—hundreds of them—and where are we who know the love of Christ? Surely the search for love often takes on twisted and sinful expressions. But the hunger, the heart's cry, the vacuum—seeking to be filled with the love of God—is there, and it is the same as yours and mine. Christian friends need to be there, not tract-wielding preachers, but listening, compassionate friends. . . . We have Christ in us and we know the love of Christ—the redeeming, sanctifying, healing power of God's incarnate love. Our whole world has a desperate need to see this love of Christ and to feel it, to touch it, to experience it personally, and we are His instruments.[2]

Whether we're talking about the homeless, homosexuals, the victims of pain and abuse, or any of a wide range of other disadvantaged individuals lying wounded alongside the highway of life, the Lord's bottom line, based on the story He told about the Good Samaritan, is quite simple.

Make contact.

Get involved.

Dan Griffin's pastoral ministry in Dallas spanned many years. A caring pastor, Dan's pattern of getting involved in the lives of people rubbed off on others in his church.

One excellent example of his contagious compassion can be seen in the life of a physician, Dr. James Boyd, into whose life Dan had built. James discovered another physician, Robert Gehring, in his office after hours one day in a drug-induced stupor.[3] He not only moved quickly to get Robert to a hospital for treatment—he was near the point of death—Jim also enlisted his pastor's assistance, and for a number of months Jim and Dan poured time and personal energy into Bob's life.

Bob finally came to Christ after years of drug abuse, family collapse, multiple hospitalizations, and suicide attempts. Bob Gehring's life turned around when two Christians were willing to spend the time and energy to get involved in serving him at his point of desperate need.

MARK OF AUTHENTICITY

The first-century church to which the author of Hebrews wrote was filled with hurting people. These individuals faced intense persecution. A large number had lost their jobs, their way of living. Many had been alienated from family and friends because of their commitment to Christ. Their lives were at risk, and some had already lost relatives who had become martyrs because of their faith.

The temptation must have been great to turn back, to bail out, to quit. That's why the author of Hebrews spends so much time talking about encouragement—urging them to "encourage each other daily" (Hebrews 3:13 NIV), not abandoning contact with each other but encouraging even more as the day of Christ approached (10:25).

Sandwiched between these two notable calls to encouragement in Hebrews is a significant word of commendation and exhortation to Christ-like service, the kind of service that constitutes a prime mark of authenticity in an often inauthentic world.

We are all familiar with image-building advertising. It's done by everybody from insurance companies who want us to know they are not part of the cause for escalating medical costs to oil conglo-merates who wish to convince us that, despite major tanker disas-ters, they are part of the solution for protecting the environment rather than defiling it.

The American Plastics Council has recently been spending ma-jor dollars on image ads to let us know what a marvelous substance plastic is. Their ads are catchy and rather impressive. Still I can't help thinking these people have a long way to go before they con-vince us that plastic, when used as an adjective, isn't a synonym for something false or phony. After all, most of us have been guilty of negative comments about plastic flowers at a wedding or funeral, plastic silverware at a sit-down dinner—even a picnic—or the plas-tic bumper that has replaced its metal predecessor on many late-model cars—as well as "plastic money" for those who are short of the real thing.

If, as some cynics tell us, we are living in what might be termed a plastic world, one where much is not what it appears to be, the author of Hebrews seems to be reminding us that Christ-like serv-ice is a mark of genuineness, of authenticity, in such a culture. Or, as he puts it, "For God is not unjust to forget your work and labor of love which you have shown toward His name, in that you have ministered to the saints, and do minister" (Hebrews 6:10).

Throughout his letter, the author of Hebrews presents several warning passages, solemn words of caution against defecting. Often controversial and subject to multiple interpretations, these warn-ings served as a practical motivation to believers to stay on course. The encouragement of Hebrews 6:1 to press on toward maturity gives us the practical point of the solemn warning found in verses 4 through 8.

In verse 9, the author of Hebrews points to the Christ-like serv-ice of his readers as evidence that they are continuing on the right track, and in verse 10 and following he encourages them—and us—to continue in such service.

The Benefits of Christ-like Service

First, he explains the "why" or benefits of such Christ-like serv-ice. Such efforts extended to others on behalf of God will not go unrewarded. God will remember them.

Have you ever had your birthday or wedding anniversary for-gotten? It's not a very pleasant experience, especially when the one who forgets is a spouse or parent. The encouraging word to those individuals who may be growing weary of serving each other is simple. God will never forget a single thing they have done to serve Him. His character is righteous, and His memory is tied to His omniscience. So they, and we, can count on His remembering.

We have a classic illustration of this principle in an event which occurred near the end of the earthly life of the Lord Jesus Christ.

> ALL THE DEEDS WE DO TO SERVE THE LORD AND OTHERS MAY NOT BE TOLD THROUGHOUT THE WORLD, BUT GOD WILL NEVER FORGET ANY OF THEM.

The Savior was spending the evenings in Bethany during the week preceding His crucifixion. He had come to the home of Simon the leper for a special dinner in His honor. Three of the four gospels, Matthew, Mark, and John, provide extensive details. A woman bought a pound of incredibly expensive perfume, worth a year's wages, and poured the ointment on His head, then used the rest of it to wash His feet as she wiped them with her hair. In response to Judas and the other disciples who indignantly questioned what they considered gross waste, Jesus reminded them that they would always have opportunities to reach out and minister to the poor, yet this woman had seized a golden opportunity to lovingly serve the Lord. And because she had done so, the Lord asserted that her deed would never be forgotten. In fact, His specific promise was that, wherever the gospel would be preached throughout the world, the story of her labor of love would be told (Matthew 26:13).

All the deeds we do to serve the Lord and others may not be told throughout the world, but God will never forget any of them. That's what Hebrews has promised.

The Nature of Christ-like Service

But what does it mean to reach out to others in service to God? What do such activities look like? Do they involve lighting candles, placing money in offering plates, or what?

Hebrews 6:10 uses several words to describe these activities. First, such service was hard. The author does not use the normal word for service or work, but a synonym which actually carries the idea of hard, difficult toil—the kind that isn't necessarily pleasant or enjoyable.

For several of my teenage years, I served as part of the kitchen team for a Christian camp in central Alabama. I had never enjoyed such household chores as washing dishes, even though as a child I learned early the value of doing them. But I was able to earn a free week at camp by working on the kitchen crew. The work wasn't particularly easy, since this was before air-conditioned camping facilities. The kitchen was hot and humid, and cleaning the dishes was nasty work. Looking back on it today, it probably wasn't as hard as it seemed then, but it was worthwhile.

Not only was the service of his readers difficult, the author of Hebrews hastened to add that it was motivated by love. Frequently in Scripture we see love and work linked together. Again we are reminded that true *agape* love is not simply a sentiment or emotion. It involves a choice, a decision, which expresses itself in action. After all, God so loved that He gave, providing our salvation. When we love, we work.

Third, such work was "shown toward His name." In other words, it glorified God.

Some years ago, a rather cantankerous older lady lived in the community where I pastored. She had little use for God or people. The death of her husband years before, plus other adversities in life—including some unpleasant experiences at the hands of Christians—had left her bitter.

One day, following a severe storm, our youth group showed up to help her remove fallen leaves and debris. Some of the individuals volunteered to come back later and nail shingles onto her roof as soon as she could work out the details with her insurance company to get them.

She couldn't believe these teenagers could actually care enough about her to help in these ways. Her comment, a tribute to the God they served and toward whom she felt so bitter, "Maybe He's not so bad after all, if this is the way some of the people who follow Him act."

What a practical reminder for us all! Others may not always notice our acts of service on behalf of others, but they do ultimately glorify God.

Such Christ-like service also serves people. During crisis times when many were suffering losses and facing intense adversity, serving one another was absolutely essential. The author of Hebrews had learned this lesson from the apostles, who had seen the Lord firsthand (Hebrews 2:3). One of that number, Paul, had written, "Through love serve one another" (Galatians 5:13). When we serve the saints, we follow the example of the Savior who came not to be served, but to serve and give His life for others (Matthew 20:28).

There's one final characteristic of such Christ-like service: It's not a "one-shot" thing, but a continuing process: "You have ministered to the saints, and do minister" (Hebrews 6:10b).

Some years ago a fairly young Christian observed, "I can't wait till I get older when I don't have to serve others and they can serve me." The truth is, there is no such point in the Christian life. Serving others never goes out of style, and we will not reach a point where we only receive service and don't give it.

How Christ-like Service Works

Having explained the "why" or benefits, and the "what" or characteristics of Christ-like service, the author of Hebrews next points out the operational essentials, or the "how," in Hebrews 6:11–12. "This is what we want you to do," he explains. "We want each of you to show diligence in serving, rather than be lazy or sluggish. Instead, we want you to diligently imitate those who modeled faith and steadfastness in serving God in generations past."

During the 1994 Winter Olympics, a great deal of attention was focused on Nancy Kerrigan, who was favored to win the gold medal in figure skating and who ultimately wound up with the silver.

One evening prior to her competition, CBS aired a special featuring several previous American women's figure skating gold medal winners. An earlier winner, Dorothy Hamill, described what it took to be able to compete successfully in an international forum like the Olympics. Kristi Yamaguchi, who received her gold medal at the 1992 games in Albertville, offered thoughts on the kind of concentration, determination, and intensity it would take for Nancy to win the gold.

That's the picture being painted by the author of Hebrews as he points to Abraham and other heroes of faith from an earlier era in order to encourage and motivate his readers toward authentic Christ-like service. The bottom line for his discussion was the idea that we will ultimately harvest a reward if we refuse to give up in serving others. Or, as the apostle Paul expressed it, we should seize the opportunity to do good to everyone, especially those who are part of the household of faith (Galatians 6:9–10).

PRINCIPLES OF INVOLVEMENT

The Good Samaritan wasn't afraid to get involved. He could have rationalized. After all, he was not a trained medical technician; what could he do to help this wounded, half-dead man he had found? Perhaps he would do more harm than good. In our day we can worry that helping might subject ourselves to a lawsuit.

Or he could have been subjecting himself to danger. What if the victim's assailants were still nearby, waiting to see what other potential victims might come along? Or what if he attempted to take this man to a place where he could receive treatment and encountered a group of Jews traveling along the road? What would it look like, after all, for a Samaritan to be carrying a wounded Jewish citizen? He might very likely find himself under suspicion as the one who had perpetrated the attack in the first place!

> WHEN A CRITICAL NEED IS PRESENT, WE DON'T SPEND A GREAT DEAL OF TIME STUDYING THE SITUATION, CALLING A COMMITTEE TOGETHER, OR HOPING SOME OTHER SOURCE OF HELP WILL COME ALONG. RATHER, WE GET INVOLVED OURSELVES.

However, he didn't allow himself to be hindered by any of these concerns. Luke spelled out the specific actions of this compassionate man in a series of descriptive verbs. He went to him. He bound up his wounds, pouring in oil and wine. He set him on his own beast. He brought him to an inn. He took care of him. Then, as we shall see later, he invested his own money to provide for this victim's needs, since the robbers had clearly taken everything the man possessed.

Luke 10:34 emphasizes personal contact and involvement. As I have reflected on these actions of the Good Samaritan and how they should affect our lives, several principles have come to mind.

Spontaneous Contact

First, such personal contact is typically spontaneous. In other words, when a critical need is present, we don't spend a great deal of time studying the situation, calling a committee together, or hoping some other source of help will come along. Rather, we get involved ourselves.

The Good Samaritan acted spontaneously without giving things a lot of thought. Seeing the need, he was moved to care. And he acted.

Now I'm not saying there isn't a place for planning or an appropriate use of committees, studies, or research. I'm just observing that we need to respond in a manner appropriate to the need. If we're talking about a long-term plan to deal with homelessness or to provide for the elderly who do not have families to care for them in a local church, then appointing a committee, conducting a study, and coming up with a proposal might be the best approach.

On the other hand, if, while I'm driving home from church, I spot someone whose automobile has slid off an icy road into a telephone pole, that's clearly not the time to conduct a study. I need to find a safe place to pull over, stop, button up my coat, then get out and render aid to the best of my ability.

I have discovered two major sources of Good Samaritan stories in the modern media. One, the *Reader's Digest,* has been around for a long time. The other, the television series *Rescue 911,* is a fairly recent addition to the growing "docu-drama" program genre.

The August 1991 issue of *Reader's Digest* told the story of a tragic collision between a thirty-nine-ton tanker truck carrying eighty-seven hundred gallons of gasoline and a passenger car near a suburban shopping mall in south Auckland, New Zealand.[4] The collision occurred just as twelve-year-old Shirley Young was getting out of the car as her mother dropped her off to shop.

After the collision, Shirley's mother, Gaylene, was pulled to safety by a bystander, David Petera—a Good Samaritan. Shirley remained trapped between the rear wheel of her mother's wrecked car and the chassis of the burning trailer. It seemed there was no hope of rescuing her.

Yet firefighter Royd Kennedy, who was wearing heavy protective gear, heard young Shirley's cry for help and crawled to her side. The trailer shielded them from most of the flames. Then an explosion rocked the trailer, and flames began to lick around both of them. The truck driver sprayed the area around the trapped girl with a fire extinguisher from the cab of his truck. Kennedy placed his firefighter's helmet over the twelve-year-old girl's head and face. Finally, after more than half an hour, the rescue team was able to use airbags to move the trailer just enough to disentangle the girl's crushed legs and free her.

The lives of both mother and daughter had been saved thanks to the spontaneous efforts of a truck driver, a bystander, and a fire-fighter, all of whom were willing to get involved when seconds counted.

Risk

The rescue of Shirley and Gaylene Young illustrates a second important principle of personal contact drawn from the story of the Good Samaritan. Such contact requires a willingness to take risks. During the long minutes while Royd Kennedy stayed with Shirley Young in the vortex of flames that surrounded the spot where she was trapped beneath the tanker, there were several opportunities when he could have left her. Both their lives were at incredible risk—she remained trapped, but he was free to save himself.

Yet even when a member of the rescue team offered to relieve the exhausted firefighter, Kennedy refused. "I must stay with her. I promised."

The danger was ice rather than fire in Romney, West Virginia, when a car carrying two teenage girls plunged into a partially-frozen branch of the Potomac River. Associated Press news reports told how sixteen-year-old Jason Canon had been driving behind the two teenage girls when he saw their car skid on the ice and mud, then sink into the river. Jason ran three hundred yards to call for help, then rushed to the riverbank. The girls had managed to free them-selves from the car. As he raced toward the water's edge, he spotted the girls as they came to the surface, jumped into the icy water, and pulled them both to safety. Sixteen-year-old Christine Malcolm, who was driving the car, told news reporters, "If he wasn't there, we probably would be dead." According to Jim Mills, chief of Rom-ney's volunteer fire department, Jason's action, putting his own life at risk to jump into the freezing waters, "was not something that ordinary people would do."[5]

Twice during a recent two-week period, I have flown into the nation's capital, once to attend a convention, the other to make a connection for a speaking engagement at a church in Virginia.

Whenever I fly into Washington's National Airport, I remember the dramatic television pictures when an Air Florida Boeing 737 crashed into the Memorial Bridge while on takeoff from National during a snowstorm some years ago. Few of us who saw them can forget the pictures of a young man leaping into the icy Potomac waters and swimming out to rescue a flight attendant—or of the man who kept giving his turn to be rescued to others but finally lost his grip, slipped beneath the surface, and drowned.

When I commented on my memories of that crash and the rescue efforts during a coffee break at my Virginia speaking engagement, one of the men quietly commented, "I was there that day."

Dan Kirk, now retired, was a captain for what was then Piedmont Airlines. His aircraft had been second in line for takeoff when that Air Florida 737–300 began rolling down the runway on its ill-fated attempt to become airborne. "It was snowing so heavily, none of us could see what happened. We heard the Tower calling him, and there was no response. An incoming flight landed next, and they asked him to roll to the end of the runway to see if the cockpit crew could tell whether or not Air Florida had aborted takeoff and run off the end of the runway. Just a minute or so later, they apparently received notice that the plane was in the water. They immediately closed the airport and ordered our aircraft and the others who were in line for takeoff back to the gates.

"I didn't go out to the site," he told me later, when there was time for me to ask him for more detail, "but I stood inside the airport and watched on the television monitors. I couldn't believe that guy on the bank who jumped into the water. He swam with such vigor and strength that it seemed like his body was halfway out of the water.

"A few days later I ran into the crew of a Delta flight down in Raleigh-Durham. The captain of that crew was the father of the flight attendant who was pulled out of the water. Was he ever grateful for that rescue!"

These are just two of an incredible number of rescues in which individuals have put their lives on the line, demonstrating a willingness to take risks on behalf of someone else.

Vulnerability

Yet not every situation that demands personal contact involves risk. Sometimes contact simply requires vulnerability.

During my return flight from that weekend conference in Virginia to my home in Lincoln, I was delayed by an aircraft malfunction and found myself stranded for several hours, first in Washington, D.C., then in Chicago. Browsing through the current issue of *Reader's Digest,* I came across another of those stories of personal involvement.[6] In this story, Ira and Barbara Spector were about to take off in their private aircraft from an airport in Mexico's Baja peninsula to return to their home in Calexico, California, after a week's vacation. Just before boarding their plane, they were interrupted by a man who asked for their help. "I'm an American and I got bumped from the flight to Los Angeles. I need to catch my connecting flight to Florida."[7]

Despite Barbara's reluctance, Ira felt inclined to help the man. He recalled an earlier trip he and Barbara had made to Mexico, when a group of college students had helped them back to safety after they had become stranded in the desert.

The Spectors took off with their passenger, who told them his name was Virgil. As their plane approached the U.S.-Mexican border, they encountered violent turbulence and a sandstorm. Flying visually, Ira found it impossible to see the airport. Just as he had given up hope of landing at Calexico, the sandstorm opened up and Barbara spotted the airport. As the plane descended toward the runway, a wind shear set off the stall warning alarm. Yet Ira was able to land the plane safely. After the landing, Ira turned around to look at his passenger, thinking that in all his years of flying this had been his closest call. He said, "I looked at Virgil—and I couldn't believe how calm he was. He was sitting there reading, and of all things, he was reading a Bible."[8]

Inside the airport, Virgil sat down with the Spectors to have a cup of coffee. When they asked what he had been doing in Loreto, he explained that he and his wife had been in a terrible accident in Loreto ten years before.[9] The two of them had managed to escape from a burning motor home, but the couple who accompanied them couldn't get out and had been killed. "My wife and I were burned pretty badly, and my spleen had ruptured."[10]

Virgil told how a Mexican passerby pulled over and rushed them to be cared for at the Health Center of Loreto. "They saved our lives. But the clinic was poorly equipped. . . . I vowed I would come back and give the clinic money to buy proper equipment and medical supplies."[11]

That's what Virgil had been doing in Loreto. He had felt prompted to bring a financial gift to the clinic, and had flown down from Los Angeles that morning to write them a check, but had been left stranded when the flight back to Los Angeles turned out to be full.

The story reminded me how vulnerable we can be when we help others. When the Spectors had been stranded in the desert, they were helped by strangers. They, in turn, helped Virgil when he was stranded at the Loreto airport. He was there, in need of their aid, because he had responded in kindness to the help he had received years earlier from a passerby and the staff of the Health Center of Loreto, who had saved his life and that of his wife.

Getting involved in the lives of others requires a degree of vulnerability. But God sees to it that we are ultimately rewarded for such involvement. As a wise Old Testament writer put it so many years ago, when we cast our bread on the waters, it will ultimately find its way back to us (Ecclesiastes 11:1).

Personal Openness

My friend and colleague Ron Dunn says that the one word that most clearly characterizes his ministry is encouragement—and I enthusiastically agree. Last year, at a luncheon attended by some thirteen hundred pastors, Ron discussed the ten-year battle he had fought with depression.

As we have conducted "Weekend of Encouragement" conferences, Ron and I have both become convinced of two things. First, Christians today desperately need to be encouraged, to receive help and understanding for the pain they face. As Ron put it, "The truth is, generally speaking, I have found more understanding from the world for my troubles than I have from the church."

Second, many Christians will respond when someone is willing to be vulnerable about pain and encouragement.

That's why Ron often tells a story about the time when one of his sons was battling bipolar depression, another son had broken his leg, and Ron and his wife, Kay, had just gone through a time of intense adversity at the church he pastored. Taking some time off, they went down to Galveston, Texas, to spend several days at the beach. There, as Ron put it, "I encountered an unwelcome visitor who woke up with me in the morning, who stayed with me throughout the day, and who went to bed with me at night. His name was Depression."

For several days, Ron felt more discouraged and despairing than he had ever felt before. "I just couldn't shake that black cloud," he said, "until Thursday morning. I woke up, and he wasn't there. I started to go looking for him, afraid he was just hiding and would come back to haunt me. But he was gone.

"Later, I came to understand why, when I returned home and opened a letter from a friend of mine, who had written me a note while passing through the Dallas/Fort Worth area."

The note, scribbled on motel letterhead, was from Jack Taylor, another evangelist and a close friend of Ron's who had written just a few short words of encouragement at three o'clock the previous Thursday morning, expressing his commitment to pray for Ron and his desire to take some of the burden of the pressures Ron was facing onto himself. The note had been written on the very night before Ron awoke to find his feelings of depression gone.

Ron has recounted the story to countless others who have been encouraged by it. Many of them, in turn, have been motivated to become vulnerable to others in pain. So the process of encouragement goes.

Encouraging personal contact does require vulnerability. And vulnerability about our hurts can greatly encourage others.

Involvement in the Distasteful

Encouraging personal contact also requires becoming involved in what may be distasteful. My friend Rob, the paramedic, has occasionally hinted that there are times when his job is the most distasteful in the world. Most of us shudder at the thought of broken, bleeding bodies, yet these are the kinds of situations he faces daily.

Another situation that invades the lives of so many people these days and demands this kind of caring contact is cancer. While working on the book *When Cancer Comes* (Moody Press, 1993), I interviewed a number of individuals who had been through lengthy battles with cancer. One of those, Shannon Mahoney, had lost her husband "Doc" to pancreatic cancer less than a year earlier. Dr. Jim Mahoney had been one of the original participants in my radio program, and I was grateful to have Shannon tell some ways individuals could encourage the cancer patient's family.

It turned out that one of the major encouragers for Doc and Shannon had been Ron Dunn's friend Jack Taylor. "He was really there for Jim," she told me. "They had been to seminary together. Jack would come to Houston periodically to visit Jim and Jamie

Buckingham, who was also hospitalized in Houston for cancer. Jack was an incredible encourager—he even taught us about different spiritual issues like prayer and spiritual warfare. And he taught us in such a supportive fashion."

Shannon also told of a young man named Ron Johnson, who had been discipled by Jim Mahoney. Ron had been an encourager during Shannon's day-to-day ordeal of caring for Jim during the worst days of his illness. Caring for him after the surgery involved a seemingly endless succession of chores. Shannon recalled, "There was washing towels and bed linens. Sitting with Jim while I went to the pharmacy. Allowing both of us to express our anger and frustration about the cancer, without condemning us. Jim needed round-the-clock care, but insurance wouldn't cover 24-hour care, so I learned to give him his injections for pain. Later, when he developed diabetes, I had to give him his insulin injections. Ron was willing to help with it all."

Encouraging contact involves giving of ourselves even to the point of personal sacrifice.

On a practical level, Shannon Mahoney and others have told me how friends reached out to help cook meals, clean dirty dishes, provide transportation, shop, get a car repaired, and do many other routine and sometimes distasteful chores when loved ones have been seriously ill. They have unanimously agreed on how encouraging such Good Samaritanism has been.

Dirty Hands

Some time ago I came across a story that communicates this principle with incredible clarity.

A student in a Bible school in the Philippines had become disturbed over the condition of the men's restrooms. They were usually neglected during routine cleaning of the building. When nothing was done to eliminate the filth, the student decided to take matters into his own hands. He went directly to the principal of the school with his complaint.

Some time later, the student noticed that the problem was being corrected. He was amazed when he realized that the man who was cleaning up the mess was the principal himself.

The student said later, "I thought that he would call a janitor. But he cleaned that filthy bathroom himself. It was a major lesson to me about being a servant. It also raised a question in my own mind as to why I hadn't just taken care of the problem."[12]

Somehow this story brings to mind a group of twelve men, reclining around a table in first-century Palestine eating a Passover meal, arguing over which of them was the greatest, only to discover their discussion interrupted by their Mentor, with bowl and towel in hand, washing their feet.

May we be motivated to remember the example of the Savior, who was willing to reach out to others even when it might be distasteful.

Personal Sacrifice

Finally, encouraging contact involves giving of ourselves even to the point of personal sacrifice. Luke's record of the Savior's story simply says the Samaritan bound up the hurt man's wounds. We aren't told where the Samaritan obtained the cloth to bind the wounds. Two possibilities suggest themselves: the clothing he was wearing or the clothing he was carrying on the back of his donkey. In either case, the man gave of his personal resources. The oil and wine he poured on the wounds to clean and to prevent infection and to provide relief from pain must have also come from his personal supplies. It was his own donkey, the animal that was his personal property and mode of transportation, that he used to transport the man to the inn. And it was his money he spent to have the man cared for at the inn. This Samaritan showed his care through *involvement,* as he gave of himself, making his possessions available for someone in need.

One area in which incredible needs have surfaced involves homelessness. A recent draft presidential policy memo suggests that more than seven million Americans have been homeless at some point since the mid-1980s.[13] According to this memo, on any given night, there are more than 700,000 homeless people in America. Although some are mentally ill or addicted to drugs, millions of Americans are on the street because of poverty and joblessness. The Secretary of Housing and Urban Development recently identified fighting homelessness as a top priority.

Dianne Dunne became involved firsthand in a ministry to the homeless when she was confronted by a street woman who yelled at a street-corner evangelist in lower Manhattan, "What do you know about being homeless?"[14] As a result of contact with that woman, Dianne and a friend began delivering clothing and food to the Tompkins Square Park neighborhood in lower Manhattan.

Since 1987, their ministry has grown into an outreach called "Hope for the Future," serving one thousand meals to homeless people each week, providing medical aid, directing addicts to drug and alcohol rehabilitation, furnishing job training, and witnessing to the Good News of Christ. One winter they gave out four hundred sleeping bags as gifts to homeless individuals. Dianne recalls, "We had to spray paint 'Jesus is Lord' on them so junkies wouldn't sell them on the street."

Dianne suggests that providing food for the homeless is just one way to serve this needy segment of society. "And," she adds, "experience has taught me that it's far better to serve the homeless through a local church ministry or social agency than on your own. I've seen well-meaning people hand out food and clothes to street people, unaware of the ones who turn around and sell everything for profit. Also, whenever you minister to the homeless through an existing organization or church, you have a better chance of hooking them into a Christian community."[15]

There are other tangible ways Dianne Dunne suggests individuals can minister to this segment of society, such as donating furniture, volunteering to teach reading and other important skills, and medical personnel volunteering their time and resources.

MIDDLE-CLASS HOMELESS

Some time ago a family I know well was confronted with an unusual but growing phenomenon, an opportunity to give of themselves in an extended manner to a growing segment of society: the middle-class homeless.

Wayne and Sue and their teenage son, Ed, lived in a beautiful two-story home in suburban Dallas, Texas. Ed had been friends with Steve for many years and was aware that Steve and his brother, Dell, had shifted back and forth between living with one or the other of their parents, who were divorced, and an uncle.

One Friday Ed came home from school and asked his parents if Steve could spend the following weekend with them. Wayne and

Sue quickly agreed. Since both boys had spent time with each other on previous weekends, this didn't seem out of the ordinary.

"By the way," Ed added, almost as an afterthought, "there's a chance Dell and their mother, Judy, may also need a place to stay."

"No problem," Ed's parents agreed.

That weekend Steve, Dell, and Judy arrived. What had originally been intended to be a three-day stay wound up stretching into more than three months.

Judy, who was between jobs, had placed her furniture in storage. A new job which she had planned to start the following week fell through unexpectedly.

When presented with the situation and the opportunity to open their home, Wayne, Sue, and Ed (who was included in the decision), agreed it was the thing to do.

As Ed later explained to another friend, "We have a large house with enough space to take them in, even though at least one of them had to sleep on the couch in the den most of the time. And even though at times it was uncomfortable having another family underfoot, we managed pretty well. When a new situation opened up for them, none of us was heartbroken, but it was good we could help them. They had a legitimate need, and we were able to help."

You may not be confronted with some half-dead individual lying beside a road. Your opportunity to become involved may be with a middle-class homeless family, or with someone with a long-term chronic disease like cancer. An opportunity to help may require vulnerability as you reach out to a hurting individual. It could involve personal risk or quick, spontaneous action.

Whatever the case, the subject of involvement always seems to raise one fundamental question. It's the old standby originally voiced by the very first human being born on planet Earth.

"Am I my brother's keeper?"

Rob, the EMT we met earlier in this chapter, leaned back in a folding chair, stirring a cup of hot coffee. The occasion was a break in the action as several Christian friends worked together to help with a repair project for another friend.

"Sure, I'm on duty for quite a few hours during a week—and I never know when I'll be called out, or what I'll face when I get there. My job is to be a Good Samaritan, to help others. That's sort of what an EMT does.

"But I think being a Good Samaritan extends way beyond any job, including that of a paramedic. There's a sense in which I'm on duty all the time. In fact, each of us who are Christians is on duty—I think it's part of our God-given responsibility to be available when others have needs. Just like on this project. Or, if I come upon an accident on the way home, I should stop and get involved whether I'm an EMT or not.

"I think being a Christian means we care enough about other people to get involved in their lives. After all, Christ cared enough to get involved in ours."

NOTES

1. Edward Rozer, *Laughing in the Face of AIDS* (Grand Rapids: Baker, 1992).

2. Trinity Evangelical Divinity School, unpublished student chapel address, quoted by Gary Collins, *Christian Counseling: A Comprehensive Guide,* rev. ed. (Dallas: Word, 1988), 289–90.

3. Guy Greenfield, *We Need Each Other* (Grand Rapids: Baker, 1984), 122–23.

4. James Hutchison, "Don't Leave Me," *Reader's Digest* (August 1991), 45–50.

5. *Lincoln Journal Star* (18 February 1994), 3.

6. Ira Spector, "Our Mysterious Passenger," *Reader's Digest* (March 1994), 167–72.

7. Ibid., 167.

8. Ibid., 171.

9. Ibid., 171.

10. Ibid., 172.

11. Ibid., 172.

12. *Illustrations for Biblical Preaching,* ed. Michael P. Green, (Grand Rapids: Baker, 1982), 330.

13. *USA Today* (18 February 1994).

14. Dianne Dunne with Victoria Henley, "A Heart for the Homeless," *Today's Christian Woman* (December 1993), 73ff.

15. Ibid., 129.

CHAPTER TEN

THE INVESTMENT: THE SAMARITAN'S FINANCIAL COMMITMENT

"He . . . brought him to an inn. . . . On the next day, when he departed, he took out two denarii, gave them to the innkeeper, and said to him, 'Take care of him; and whatever more you spend, when I come again, I will repay you.'"
(Luke 10:34–35)

'm sick of all those sermons about money. Money, money, money —that's all they ever talk about."

The young man's blue eyes practically flashed sparks with the intensity of his emotion. We were sitting around a circle in his nicely landscaped backyard, enjoying burgers which had been charcoaled on his grill. I had recently become the pastor of the church this man and his friends attended. It was my first opportunity to get to know them personally.

"Now the church we attended before, that's all we ever heard. Give, give, give. I think preachers ought to stick with the Word and not spend all their time trying to get a hand in somebody's billfold."

If I had the age and experience I do now—I was quite a bit younger at the time—I might have gently challenged this man's notion. The truth is, he would have been surprised at how much Jesus had to say on the subject of money. The gospels quote the Lord as saying more about money than He did about heaven and hell combined. And the bottom line, according to the Lord, is, "Where your treasure is, there your heart will be also."

The Lord made that observation at least twice in His life: once, early in His ministry, in what we refer to as the Sermon on the Mount (Matthew 6:21); the other time near the close of His ministry in the context of a warning to prepare for His second coming (Luke 12:34). In both instances, Jesus placed a premium on seeking His kingdom rather than pursuing material things, which we are to trust God to provide.

TREASURE IN HEAVEN

The Savior's perspective was that His true followers would demonstrate themselves by lovingly giving to meet the needs of others (Luke 12:33; Matthew 6:20). To do so is to lay up treasure in heaven.

My friend who was so adamant in his opposition to preaching about money would probably have resented the ministry of Jesus, for the Lord spoke to many people who were like him. They enjoyed a comfortable living, they had been able to set aside money for retirement, they enjoyed many of the amenities and pleasures of life. And they did, on a regular basis, give to the temple, and to help meet the needs of others less fortunate than they.

It wasn't that they didn't want to give at all. It's just that, as my friend put it, "You know, things are getting tough these days. A lot of people have been laid off from their jobs. [He hadn't been one of them.] And it costs more to live. I'm doing just about all I can right now. I don't need somebody guilt-tripping me, or trying to tell me what I need to do with my money."

Maybe the last part of his statement was part of the problem. Not only his problem, but my problem, your problem, the problem we all have.

After all, the Scriptures make it clear: Stewardship doesn't mean what my friend thought, that God owns 10 percent of my income, and the other 90 percent belongs to me to do with as I please. Stewardship entails a 100 percent ownership by the Lord, who has put me in trust to use all of it—including what I give, what I invest for the future, and what I spend in the present—in a way that pleases Him. Or, as another friend would put it years later, "God expects us to hold everything we have loosely."

The Good Samaritan, the man whose story Jesus was using to shock one of the religious leaders in Israel, not to mention those standing around listening, was an individual who held his possessions loosely. His generosity jumps off the pages of Luke's gospel and confronts our attitudes about money, giving, and meeting the needs of those who are our neighbors.

We have already seen the extent to which this man became personally involved in rescuing the half-dead traveler, cleansing and bandaging his wounds, using his own garments, pouring on his own oil and wine, placing the wounded man on his own beast of burden, and bringing him to a nearby inn where he personally took care of the man for that first critical evening, perhaps even sitting up all night to attend to the man's wounds.

Where His Heart Was

The following day the man resumed his journey, but before doing so, he made a significant financial investment of his personal resources for the well-being of the robbery victim, giving an additional generous commitment to the innkeeper, "Take care of him; and whatever more you spend, when I come again, I will repay you" (Luke 10:35).

In other words, this man put his money where his heart was. He demonstrated the genuineness of his commitment and his concern by investing financially in the well-being of the man who had become his neighbor, without considering any possibility of a return on his investment.

I don't know how the religious leaders may have responded to Jesus' words. Perhaps they felt as intensely about having some rogue rabbi or preacher talk about money and giving as did my twentieth-century friend at the church cookout. Yet the truth is evident. By including this as the climactic and final portion of the narrative, Jesus makes clear that one essential part of what we are to do as Good Samaritans is to invest in the needs of others. For the Good Samaritan did more than just refuse to pass by on the other side. He even did more than getting involved in helping the man deal with his pain. When the need presented itself, he became involved financially. He didn't claim that there was a recession going on, or say that Jews typically make more money than Samaritans, or use any of the arguments he might have marshaled to justify uninvolvement on his part.

He simply acted out of a heart of compassion to meet the need of his neighbor. In doing so, he left us a legacy, an example, a pattern of genuine compassion.

Dropping Contributions

Today contributions seem to be falling off across the board, whether you're talking about churches, parachurch ministries, or charities to help the homeless, feed the hungry, or reach out to others in need. Perhaps one reason is the proliferation of what some have referred to as semi-legitimate charities. Often they use modern telemarketing methods to get people to contribute to organizations which direct some of the funds raised to legitimate needs but usually keep a higher percentage for hefty overhead expenses and even the financial gain of those who devise them.

Perhaps appeals from questionable operations have left some people feeling rather cynical toward charitable involvement. Maybe another factor has to do with where people are coming from today.

Buster Attitudes

In his excellent book *Baby Busters,* marketing research specialist George Barna profiles a typical "buster" named Alan, a twenty-three-year-old part-time student and part-time worker who used to spend quite a bit of time volunteering at the regional office of a well-known not-for-profit organization.[1] When asked why, he responded, "Good people—good cause—good work, and great pizza and parties."

When asked if he gave money to support the causes in which he believes, Alan responded defensively, pointing to his low wages, his busy schedule, his lack of trust for such nonprofit groups, and his desire to research them more carefully before becoming involved on a financial level.

As he summed up his feeling on the matter to the researcher, Alan said, "There are lots of good people and good organizations out there, but you have to be careful—there are lots of thieves too. I don't want my money sucked up by the scam artists."

Alan is part of a trend Barna and other researchers have noted that leads away from financial participation in meeting the needs of others. Only 26 percent of those who fit into the baby buster category, those born between 1965 and 1983, donate money to nonprofit organizations other than churches. Although this statistic doesn't reflect what busters may be doing in terms of contributing to their local churches or giving individually to help someone else, it does seem to indicate a growing trend away from giving to meet the needs of others.

Such a trend was definitely not present among the believers in the early church. On the contrary, even Christians in deep poverty gave freely and generously to meet the needs of others (2 Corinthians 8:2).

Nor did they allow their ability to give to provide the ultimate measure. As Paul explained, "According to their ability, yes, and beyond their ability, they were freely willing" to give (v. 3). Their heart to give was not limited by the kinds of things that typically hinder people from giving today.

So it was with the Good Samaritan. He had already disrupted his schedule to provide for the victim's immediate care. Now, faced with meeting the added needs of a helpless, destitute individual from another race and a different religion, from a people that looked down on him and his kind, he still cared enough to reach into his own pocket and come up with the necessary funds.

Warren Wiersbe observes:

> Love is costly. It was costly for Christ and it will be costly for us. The Samaritan did not set up a committee and hire somebody else to minister to the Jericho road victims. He did the work himself and paid the price from his own resources.[2]

Spiritual Bankruptcy

In another of those confrontations that so often marked the ministry of the Master, we find Jesus using money to demonstrate spiritual bankruptcy.

The occasion, the tenth chapter of Mark, involved a man who, like the Good Samaritan, has become so well-known to students of the New Testament that he has been given a title of his own, "the rich young ruler." The man in this story rushed up to Jesus, fell on his knees before Him, and asked, "What must I do to inherit eternal life?"

His question clearly parallels the one raised by the religious leader in the Good Samaritan narrative, and it is important to remember that the prevailing view in first-century Judaism was that salvation was earned by a merit system they had devised, based loosely on the Old Testament law. According to the accepted explanation, the Israelite who wished to inherit eternal life had to keep the more than six hundred commandments of Moses.

Jesus did not even choose to address the man's question right away. He first confronted him in surprising fashion regarding his assumption about Jesus. "Why do you call me good?" he asked. "No one is good but God alone."

Even though Jesus clearly knew His own goodness, He was addressing the man's failure to understand that there really was no difference between so-called "good" Jews, who were considered to have a pretty good shot at eternal life, and Samaritans or Gentiles, who were given virtually no chance of earning salvation. So Jesus laid the foundation for His case; no one, no human being, could possibly approach the goodness of a perfect God. Unless the man understood Him to be God, he could not consider Him good.

To establish His premise, Jesus next directed the man's attention to those familiar Old Testament commandments, specifically the ones regulating his relationship with his fellow man: prohibiting murder, adultery, theft, deceit, fraud, or dishonor of parents.

With the naïveté of a college sophomore who thinks he knows more than his professor, the young man smiled smugly and replied, "No problem. I've kept them all, ever since I was a kid."

Recognizing the massive denial in this young man, the Savior mercifully put His finger on the one area that could immediately demonstrate his callous disregard for both wholeheartedly loving God and unconditionally loving people.

"One thing you lack," the Master countered. "Go, sell everything you have. Give it to the poor and you will have treasure in heaven. Then come follow Me."

> IT ISN'T WHAT YOU HAVE THAT MATTERS.
> . . . RATHER, WHAT COUNTS IS THE HEART
> THAT GENEROUSLY GIVES WITHOUT
> REGARD TO ABILITY AND WITH EVERY
> REGARD FOR NEED.

The Lord had seen right through the man's professed devotion to God. The man had actually broken the first commandment! Money and the material things it could buy, rather than God, mattered most to him. He must turn from that for which he cared most to the Savior, who could meet his deepest needs. The Lord wasn't telling him that selling his assets and giving to the poor would earn him eternal life. Rather, He was simply focusing on the major obstacle that kept the man from a right relationship with God.

The young man must have been shocked at Jesus' words. After all, the Jewish rabbis taught that, while fasting, prayer, and charitable gifts were the best ways to earn favor with God, one was never to give away all his wealth at one time. In fact, those who were rich—this man was exceedingly well-off according to Mark's record—were in good shape to earn their way to heaven by giving periodically—and impressively—while the gifts they doled out had little impact on their personal "bottom line."

Peter, Mark's human source of information about the life of Christ, might have remembered this man during a later incident which occurred shortly after the Lord reminded the scribe of the demand to love God wholeheartedly and love people unconditionally (Mark 12:28–32).

Following an extended confrontation with Pharisees, Sadducees, and assorted other religious leaders, Jesus seated Himself across from the temple treasury to watch how the people cast their money into it (v. 41). After many who were rich had tossed in significant gifts of various kinds, a certain widow contributed the minimum allowed, two lepta, or one-fourth of a Roman denarius, the day's wage (v. 42). Pointing out the widow to His disciples, the Lord asserted, "This poor widow has put in more than all those who have given to the treasury; for they all put in out of their abundance, but she out of her poverty put in all that she had, her whole livelihood" (vv. 43–44).

What a remarkable example—a shocking contrast for Peter and the other disciples. It isn't what you have that matters. Nor is it being able to follow the Jewish recommendation and give large gifts that really don't affect an even larger personal portfolio. Rather, what counts is the heart that generously gives without regard to ability and with every regard for need.

NEW TESTAMENT-STYLE GIVING

A great deal has been written and said on the subject of giving, not all of it consistent with Scripture. The Old Testament established a foundation of the tithe, which actually included what we today would consider to be both support for worship, which we give to the local church, and certain taxes which support the government. The total tithe exceeded the commonly-assumed 10 percent and could actually add up to as much as 30 percent. The prophet Malachi and others in the Old Testament made it clear that refusing to give what was rightfully God's could result in His with-holding blessing and was tantamount to robbing God (Malachi 3:8–12). Refusing to support God's work could lead to personal financial difficulty (Haggai 1:6).

In the New Testament, giving to meet the needs of others provided a proof of one's love for God (1 John 3:17). Love was to be the motivation for giving, and failure to give likely indicated a lack of love.

However, this love motivation did not mean giving was only to be done spontaneously or spasmodically. Paul called on the Corinthians to give regularly, just as they were to meet together every Lord's Day (1 Corinthians 16:2). Careful planning and even budgeting for giving, including provision for the poor, was in order (2 Corinthians 8:12).

For the New Testament Christian, the primary use of money was not to build facilities, though this was not forbidden, but to support those who taught God's Word and to care for the needs of those less fortunate within the family of God (Galatians 6:10; Acts 4:34–35).

Throughout the history of the early church, Luke noted a commitment to meet the needs of the poor within the family of God. This was especially important in the early days of the church, since many who initially came to faith had made the pilgrimage to Jerusalem for Pentecost and needed to be cared for. As the work of God became established and persecution set in, it became even more critical to meet the needs of these individuals (Acts 4:34–35).

Before long, a particular group of needy individuals, widows, required special support (Acts 6:1–2). Then as time went by, the financial needs of Christians in Judea necessitated help from the newly-planted church in Antioch (Acts 11:27–30) as well as Macedonia and Achaia (Romans 15:25–27; 2 Corinthians 8:18–22).

The pattern for support of those in the Lord's work can be seen in the ministry of giving by the Philippian church to meet the needs of the apostle Paul (Philippians 4:16). Paul had called for the support of those who provide spiritual teaching (Galatians 6:6), as well as those with personal needs, both within the body and outside the Christian community (Galatians 6:10; 1 Corinthians 9:4–14). The apostle presented a strong case for the right of those involved in vocational ministry to be supported by others, as he explained why he had chosen to work to support himself in order to avoid being a burden to the Corinthians.

Priority and Opportunity

As we examine all the needs around us and wonder how we can possibly meet the needs of others, two words come to mind that can help us determine what to do with the resources God has given us. The first is priority; the second, opportunity. As Charles Ryrie notes in *What You Should Know About Social Responsibility,* "It seems that we can glean some priorities as to those who should receive financial help. First, the Lord's servants, then the Lord's people who are in need, and then others."[3]

Such prioritizing has its biblical roots in the passage on sowing and reaping in Galatians 6:6–10. While many Christians pay close attention to verses 7 and 8, as it applies to behavior, the clear context, as established by verses 6 and 10, is giving.

Verse 10 also establishes the second of our words: opportunity. It is the word Paul used in Galatians 6:10 which, in the language he used, referred to quality of time, and was often employed to refer to a certain season. Its only other use in the New Testament illustrates this meaning. In Hebrews 11, the author was discussing the citizens of heaven, who demonstrated their citizenship through faith. He noted that, had they paid attention to where they came from, they might have had the opportunity to be bent back or to return (Hebrews 11:15). But, instead of finding themselves in the season of turning back, as some of the readers of Hebrews had, these heroes of faith were identified as having stretched out toward that which is better, their heavenly citizenship (v. 16).

The point of looking at this use of the word *season* is to show that there are certain times, as the author of Ecclesiastes pointed out, when circumstances change (Ecclesiastes 3:1–8). When the season is right, God will have provided us with both the means or wherewithal to give and exposed us to the need to give. Giving is not something we are to grow weary over, wondering if we will ever receive any benefit in return. Ultimately, as Paul pointed out in the sowing and reaping passage, God will see to it that we reap in due season (Galatians 6:9; compare Philippians 4:17, 19).

Giving and Receiving

Years ago, I was pastoring a small church, struggling my way through seminary and working at a number of jobs, trying to support my wife and twin daughters and my educational career. One April I calculated my income taxes and discovered that I owed $250, which at that time seemed an insurmountable sum. Financially I felt like the victim in the story of the Good Samaritan—like a person lying by the side of the road, without prospect of help. Visions of being carted off to federal prison for nonpayment of taxes while my wife and daughters stood weeping at the door of our home flashed through my mind. In retrospect, my fears were unrealistic, but at the time, I was young and naive.

That year, April fifteenth fell on a Wednesday. With a heavy heart I prepared my midweek message and delivered it to the small group who attended. I had considered all sorts of possibilities. I thought about borrowing the money—but what banker in his or her right mind would loan that kind of money to someone of my financial status? I even considered writing a hot check, but quickly dismissed that—after all, I could then wind up with two jail sentences, for nonpayment of taxes and bank fraud.

So I did the only thing I knew to do. Without going into any detail, because I knew the people I pastored were about at the same economic level, I told the men when we broke up into groups for prayer that I had an unspoken request, for which I needed an answer by midnight that night. I would appreciate their prayers. No one said anything, and a couple of the men, as they prayed, mentioned my request along with the others.

Following the prayer time, one of the men, Elton, asked to speak with me in private. Even though they were a number of years older than we were, Kathy and I had come to appreciate Elton and his wife. We felt a kinship with them. A mechanic who owned a two-stall garage located in an unassuming tin building next to the railroad tracks in our town, he and his wife drove a ten-year-old car, lived in a small white-frame house on a quiet street just north of downtown, and generally lived a very unostentatious lifestyle.

Elton quickly came to the point. "Tell me about this unspoken request. I don't mean to pry, but do you need money to pay your income taxes?"

I had sort of assumed that no one would connect my request with April fifteenth. Not wishing to embarrass him by telling the amount of my need, I replied, as I saw him about to reach for his billfold, "That's the general area, but just pray about it, Elton."

Shaking his head in refusal, he continued to pull out his billfold. I thought to myself, "He's probably going to hand me a twenty." I couldn't imagine anything else happening—and I would still feel embarrassed, because that would leave me $230 short of what I needed to pay my taxes.

"Tell me exactly how much you need," he persisted as he opened the billfold. Feeling convicted, I finally decided to come clean.

"OK, if you insist on knowing, I need $250 to pay my taxes. But I'm not expecting you or anybody else to give."

"But what if I wanted to?" he replied. I couldn't help noticing what looked like a ten, and possibly one or two ones in his billfold. Then he unfolded what appeared to be a secret flap, exposing a much thicker collection of bills. Peeling two off one side and one from the other, he handed them to me with the exhortation, "Don't ever be ashamed to let God's people have the opportunity to help you when you're in need."

Dumbfounded, I stared for a moment at the two one-hundred-dollar bills and the fifty—I only had a vague realization that such bills even existed.

What a profound spiritual lesson. Here was a man who wasn't rich or ostentatious by human standards, but who had been blessed of God and who was sensitive, aware, and ready to spontaneously reach out and meet someone else's needs.

There have been other occasions when I have had the opportunity to play the role of giver, and what a delight it has been to be a part of the process through which God reaches out to those in need by touching others who have been blessed.

Doing Good, Meeting Needs

It's the very process Paul described with the word "equality": "that now at this time your abundance may supply their lack, that their abundance also may supply your lack—that there may be equality" (2 Corinthians 8:14). Quoting Moses from Exodus 16:18, Paul established a premise that the one who had abundance was not to have leftover waste, and the one who had gathered little was not to lack (2 Corinthians 8:15).

Let us do good—that's the way Paul put it in Galatians 6:9. The apostle urged the Corinthians to "abound in this grace" (2 Corinthians 8:7), and he pointed out his own willingness to "spend and be spent" on their behalf (2 Corinthians 12:15). It's what the Good Samaritan modeled in the Lord's parable, and what Barnabas, that world-class encourager of the early church, demonstrated during a time of great need among the persecuted Christians in Jerusalem.

First, we observe that Barnabas's giving was opportune. It was timely, in season. There was an incredible need among the body, and something needed to be done to provide for the basic needs of many Christians who had nothing. And God had provided Barnabas with the financial resources to act on the need.

Second, the need or opportunity became mixed with a willingness on the part of Barnabas. He not only had the means and the opportunity, but he also had the willingness. No one had to tell him to do this. There were no strong-armed appeals. Just like the Good Samaritan, he saw the need and cared enough to take action.

It's interesting to note that in these cases, the Good Samaritan and Barnabas, in one instance the need was met directly; in the other, the giver went through organized channels to meet the need. It has been my experience that there are appropriate times for both. Neither is always right, nor always wrong. The main thing is that we be sensitive when the Spirit of God allows us to be exposed to the needs of others and willing to use our resources.

A third observation about Barnabas's giving: Not only was his action opportune and voluntary, it was exemplary. There must be a reason the Holy Spirit had Luke single out Barnabas from all those who were engaged in giving. I'm inclined to believe that the reason is that Barnabas must have been one of the earliest, one who took the initiative, setting an example for others who had possessions and who could sell them and give. What a stark contrast he provides to the self-serving actions of Ananias and his wife! By taking action with his funds to meet needs, Barnabas must have greatly encouraged those who needed help.

Certainly Elton, with his income tax day generosity, provided me with a significant level of encouragement. So did the individuals in another church I pastored, at a time when our family faced incredible financial pressure.

Our daughter Karen had spent a lengthy time in the hospital due to a serious illness. Our insurance coverage was just about "maxed out," and she had been home for a time when she suffered a setback and needed to be hospitalized again. When we checked with the admissions office of the hospital, we discovered they would require us to make a $3,000 payment before she could be readmitted. Since we had totally exhausted what little financial resources we had, we didn't know what to do.

So we cried out to the Lord in prayer, and we asked some friends to pray that God would provide for the need.

A Tale of Two Checks

We were to take Karen to the hospital on Sunday afternoon, following the morning services at our church. I had arranged for another member of my staff to speak for the evening service so I could remain at the hospital with Karen.

That Sunday morning just before service time, one of the men in the church stopped me in the hallway. Since I was in a hurry to get to the service, I almost told him I didn't have time to speak with him.

I'm glad now that I didn't. Asking me briefly about Karen and her needs, he told me, "My wife and I have been thinking about this all weekend. We knew you had some needs. We didn't know what they were." They had not been among the small group of individuals with whom we had had the opportunity to share the specifics of our situation.

He handed me a check, which I slipped in my pocket without looking at it, thinking it was probably twenty-five, fifty, or a hundred dollars, feeling grateful for it, thanking the Lord, then putting it out of mind until after the service. Imagine my surprise when I returned home and looked at the check. It was made out for fifteen-hundred dollars! We were halfway to what we needed.

THE IMPORTANT ISSUE IS NOT THE AMOUNT IN OUR POCKETBOOKS OR BANK ACCOUNTS. IT'S THE ATTITUDE OF OUR HEARTS.

We sat down to lunch, giving thanks to the Lord for what He had provided, then we began packing Karen's things for her return to the hospital. We were just walking out the door to the car when someone pulled into the circular drive in front of our house. I whispered to Kathy, "Let's make this as quick as we can. We need to get Karen to the hospital."

I still hadn't learned!

The couple who had come to see us, one of my elders and his wife, let us know quickly that they didn't intend to delay us. "We know you're in a hurry. We just have a card for you. We won't stay. You can open it on the way to the hospital if you like."

Thanking them, we got into the car and began our journey to the hospital. As we pulled out of the driveway, I made one of those observations that range somewhere between the profound and the ludicrous.

"I guess someone will have to chase us down on the way to the hospital if God's going to provide the rest of what we need. Maybe I'll tell the hospital we have fifteen-hundred dollars and try to convince them to let us in anyway."

As usual, the Lord was a step ahead of me. About that time, Karen opened the card and let out a shriek that almost caused me to run off the road.

Folded inside the card was another check—also for fifteen-hundred dollars!

God had led two twentieth-century Good Samaritans to combine resources to meet what seemed like an incredibly impossible need.

Today, as I think of Karen and her husband and their two daughters, and the ministry God has given them to hurting people, I can't help but think of how God met a need to enable her to receive much-needed medical care at a time when we didn't have the resources. And He did it through modern-day Good Samaritans who cared enough to get involved with their money as well as their time.

PRACTICAL SAMARITANISM

So how can we, on a practical level, implement the principle we've been discussing? First, we can realize that the important issue is not the amount in our pocketbooks or bank accounts. It's the attitude of our hearts. Again I'm reminded of how Jesus said the Good Samaritan became involved and gave financially because he was moved with compassion. He was genuinely touched with God's kind of care for others.

Second, a heart of compassion will always manifest itself in action. I cannot claim to care and then turn away from the needs of others when I am capable of meeting them:

> But as for the well-to-do man who sees his brother in want but shuts his eyes—and his heart—how could anyone believe that the love of God lives in him? My little children, let us love not merely in theory or in words—let us love in sincerity and in practice! (1 John 3:17–18 PHILLIPS)

So we need to sharpen our awareness to the needs and desperate circumstances of those around us. Perhaps the best place to begin is with those with whom you assemble on a regular basis, the people at your church. There may be a benevolence fund to which you can contribute. Or you may become aware personally of specific needs, perhaps of missionaries, seminary students, others preparing for ministry, or those who preach and teach God's Word, including your pastor and other vocational staff members. Or there may be some in the church family who have lost their jobs or taken a hefty cut in pay. Special sensitivity around times such as Christmas or Thanksgiving, and at times when people have encountered disasters such as a traffic mishap or a serious disease, are also occasions when Good Samaritanism may be called for.

Another possibility is to consider giving your life in service to others. Mother Teresa of Calcutta is probably the best-known contemporary role model of someone whose life has been committed to caring for those in desperate need. You may not agree with all her theology, but you can't argue with her world-class compassion and concern for those in need.

It was Mother Teresa who delivered a stunning indictment to an audience of three thousand influential leaders in the United States, including President Clinton and his wife, Hillary, in Washington, D.C. The physically frail, eighty-three-year-old nun, speaking at a National Prayer Breakfast, gave an address that, according to syndicated columnist Cal Thomas, "cut to the heart of the social ills afflicting America. She said that America, once known for generosity to the world, has become selfish."[4]

According to Mother Teresa, abortion, the willingness of a mother to kill even her own child, provides the greatest proof of that selfishness. Speaking without raised voice, dramatic gesture, or rhetorical flourish, she pointed out that "many people are very, very concerned with people in India, with children in Africa where quite a few die of hunger, and so on. Many people are also concerned about all the violence in this United States. These concerns are very good. But often these same people are not concerned with the millions who are being killed by the deliberate decision of their own mothers."

Although he and his wife remained conspicuously seated when Mother Teresa's remarks prompted a standing ovation from most of those present, President Clinton, in his remarks that followed her address, acknowledged that Mother Teresa was beyond criticism because of the life she had lived in service to others.

Two things flow from this observation. First, it may be that some of us can follow the example of Mother Teresa, giving our lives to meet the needs of the hungry, the homeless, or the destitute. After all, she didn't enter the career which has won her so much recognition by calling a press conference. She simply began working quietly behind the scenes to meet the needs of many in Calcutta. She followed the pattern called for by the Lord Jesus, as reflected in a poem she often quotes.

> When I was homeless, you opened your door;
> When I was naked, you gave me your coat.
> When I was weary, you helped me find rest;
> When I was anxious, you calmed all my fears.
> When I was little, you taught me to read;
> When I was lonely, you gave me your love.
> When in a prison, you came to my cell;
> When on a sickbed, you cared for my needs.
> In a strange country, you made me at home;
> Seeking employment, you found me a job.
> Hurt in a battle, you bound up my wounds;
> Searching for kindness, you held out your hand.
> When I was Negro or Chinese or White,
> Mocked and insulted, you carried my cross.
> When I was aged, you bothered to smile;
> When I was restless, you listened and cared.
> You saw me covered with spittle and blood;
> You knew my features, though grimy with sweat.
> When I was laughed at, you stood by my side;
> When I was happy, you shared my joy.[5]

If God hasn't led you to give your life to the kind of vocational service Mother Teresa does, you can still follow the example of looking for the kinds of opportunities of which she spoke in the poem sung by her and her colleagues. One of those is certainly becoming involved in taking a stand against abortion, reaching out on behalf of those unborn babies who cannot protect themselves, and thereby working to counter the inherent selfishness of a society that says we should be able to kill our unborn on demand.

Finally, let's be willing to use our money, our time, and our energy to reach out to those we know who are hurting, wherever the need arises.

Some time ago, author and seminary professor Lewis Smedes learned that a friend of many years who lived in faraway Michigan had been diagnosed with cancer. The case was said to be terminal, and Smedes immediately interrupted his schedule, purchased an airplane ticket, flew from California to Michigan, and spent several days visiting his friend.[6] The airplane ticket, the meals, and the cost of lodging must have been expensive, the time from his schedule disruptive. But Lewis Smedes cared enough about his friend Cal to spend the necessary time and money.

On the last day of his visit, as he left his friend's room, Cal said, "Lew, it's all right."

Even though the friend died a few days later, profound ministry had taken place. Perhaps some of the most important ministry ever done by this seminarian. Not Bible-teaching ministry. Not theological insights. Not writing. But the ministry of a Good Samaritan who was willing to spend and be spent for a friend in need.

NOTES

1. George Barna, *Baby Busters: The Disillusioned Generation* (Chicago: Moody, 1994), 92–93.
2. Warren Wiersbe, *Meet Yourself in the Parables* (Grand Rapids: Baker, 1980), 64.
3. Charles C. Ryrie, *What You Should Know About Social Responsibility* (Chicago, Moody, 1982), 92.
4. Cal Thomas, "Startling Proclamation of Truth to Power," *Los Angeles Times Syndicate* (3 February 1994).
5. From the unpublished collected Missionaries of Charity hymns.
6. Guy Greenfield, *We Need Each Other* (Grand Rapids: Baker, 1984), 125.

CHAPTER ELEVEN

THE DANGER: WHAT THE GOOD SAMARITAN DIDN'T DO

Bear one another's burdens, and so fulfill the law of Christ.
(Galatians 6:2)

For each one shall bear his own load.
(Galatians 6:5)

Read between the lines."

Have you ever been given that suggestion by someone and felt a measure of frustration? After all, reading between the lines isn't easy, even though some people may think it is.

Some time ago when I was studying the passage on the Good Samaritan, long before I ever considered writing a book on the subject, I was struck by two observations. First, it's obvious that there's a great deal we can learn from what the Good Samaritan did.

But there is also much to be learned from what the Good Samaritan didn't do.

In a day when terms like codependency, dysfunctional families, and enabling have become buzzwords, often used but less frequently understood, perhaps it would be good for us to look at what Luke didn't record Jesus as saying about the Good Samaritan. For in seeing what this man didn't do, we might discover some important insights into the way healthy giving and relationships ought to function.

Let me list several things the Good Samaritan didn't do, then we can look at these and how they relate to our lives today in more detail.

While the Good Samaritan became involved financially in the life of this victim, he didn't pay or agree to stand good for all this man's expenses for the rest of his life.

Second, he did not adopt him as a major long-term personal project. In fact, his involvement seemed to extend only to the needs left by his present situation.

Third, he did not allow his relationship with this man to develop beyond an appropriate level of involvement.

Fourth, he did not allow the situation to hinder his own life purposes.

Finally, he didn't take control of the other man's life or allow the other man to take control of his.

COMPASSIONATE ACTIONS, HEALTHY BOUNDARIES

In other words, the relationship Jesus described between the Good Samaritan and the Jewish victim was characterized by both compassionate action to meet needs and healthy boundaries to establish appropriate limits.

I believe a biblical principle validates this kind of approach in relationships. It's a principle that, when understood, can free us from a lot of false guilt over what we cannot do and a large measure of entangling bondage we shouldn't be experiencing.

The principle is found in Paul's letter to the Galatians, the sixth chapter. It provides God's perspective on a problem that, while ignored for much of human history, has recently been given a great deal of attention—particularly since the 1970s when the term codependency was originally coined to describe behavioral patterns associated with family members of those who were addicted to alcohol or drugs. I think it's important not to fall into the trap of blaming everything on a term that has become a buzzword for pop psychology. Nor should we neglect the legitimate problem at the heart of the issue, which can and should be addressed biblically.

The term codependency came into popular use by secular therapists Sharon Wegschieder-Cruz, John and Linda Friel, and Dr. Timmen Cermack in the mid-1980s. One of the individuals generally recognized with originating the term, Melody Beattie, defines a codependent person as "one who has let another person's behavior affect him or her, and who is obsessed with controlling that person's behavior."[1]

Now controlling another person's behavior doesn't sound good, but when a person is addicted to a substance and his behavior is destructive to himself and others, controlling that person's behavior in order to change him for the better may seem like a worthwhile and positive goal.

Although it may appear that way on the surface, the reality is that any controlling or manipulative action, may, instead of providing help for the addicted person, actually add to the destructive effect of the addiction on both the addict and those around him.

Healthy or Manipulative?

One of the most difficult things for us to recognize is the difference between healthy, loving help for others and a codependent kind of controlling entanglement in the life of someone else. Gayle Irwin helps explain the distinction between service and manipulation by observing:

> A servant's job is to do all he can to make life better for others, to free them to be everything they can be. A servant's first interest is not himself but others, yet enslavement is not what I am talking about. Servanthood is a loving choice we make to minister to others. It is not the result of coercion or coercion's more subtle form, manipulation.[2]

Before we consider our subject, let's go back to Paul's letter to the Galatians to see the contrast reflected in two statements that seem like a paradox: the exhortation to bear each other's burdens in Galatians 6:2, and the statement shortly following: "Each one shall bear his own load" (Galatians 6:5).

In this seeming contrast of biblical statements, we find the essential balance that helps us practice Good Samaritanism without going beyond what is healthy and appropriate into the realm of what may be manipulative, codependent, or unhealthy.

In his landmark epistle to the Galatians, Paul wrote to correct what he saw as a move back from the grace of God into legalistic bondage on the part of those to whom he has written. He first established that the Christian faith is not a set of rules, but a relationship with Christ (3:27–28) which is to be lived in the experience of freedom (5:1). This is made possible by the power of the indwelling Spirit (5:16, 22–23), and walking in the Spirit touches every area of life, including the way we relate to those who have failed.

The immediate subject Paul addressed suggests the kind of thing that happens in the life of an individual who is addicted to drugs or alcohol. Paul wrote to the believers regarding a man who has been overtaken in a fault. The word suggests a modern-day picture of one who has slipped out of bounds while attempting to advance a football or a basketball; it's the idea of a "slip" or a "lapse."[3]

Personal involvement in the life of such an individual is expected, just as the Good Samaritan became involved in the life of the man fallen beside the road. "Restore him," Paul instructed. The term he employed was used of mending the holes or tears in fishing nets (Matthew 4:21), of outfitting a ship with supplies for sailing, of educating a disciple so he will become like his mentor (Luke 6:40), even of setting a broken bone. The idea I see in this rich New Testament term, which had such a variety of uses in first-century life, is that of supplying whatever is needed to put things in proper order. It was even used mathematically by Pythagoreans, the followers of Pythagoras, who invented one of the basic theorems of mathematics, which had to do with the order and symmetry of numbers.[4]

The practical implications of Paul's instruction for these believers is obvious. Qualified individuals are called for—those who are spiritual, rightly related to the Spirit of God. And not just a single individual, but a plurality of them were to become involved in following a specific procedure that led to restoration. Such effort was to be carried out in meekness or humility, rather than proudly or angrily confronting the fallen individual. Furthermore, those who attempted such rescues were to consider the danger of themselves falling into the snare of temptation (Galatians 6:1).

While studying this passage in the aftermath of a Midwest snowstorm, I reflected back to a time some years ago when a friend had become stuck in a snowbank. Convinced that I could rescue him because I had studded tires on the back of my old Plymouth station wagon and some experience driving on snow and ice, I attached a chain to his front bumper, began to pull, and promptly became stuck myself. Such danger to those who would rescue is evident in the spiritual realm and must be taken into consideration.

However, just as in the case of the Good Samaritan, the risk is not so great as to keep us from bearing each other's burdens. Burden-bearing fulfills Christ's law, according to Paul. The apostle must have had in mind the "new commandment" Jesus gave His disciples in the upper room, to love each other as He had loved them—a mandate we have cited often, and which has great significance to us today. It is the royal law of liberty, spoken of by the apostle James, and it is fulfilled as we bear each other's burdens.

Overloads and Backpacks

Paul's terminology parallels the language John used of Jesus bearing His cross out of the city of Jerusalem toward Golgotha (John 19:17). The word for burden comes from the same word, to bear. The word originates from a simple Greek term which means weight.[5]

The term burden was often used of the cares and pressures of life (Luke 21:34), of afflictions experienced in serving God (2 Corinthians 1:8–9), and of the general burdens we carry through this life (2 Corinthians 5:4).

If you've lived in the South for most of your life as I have, you can appreciate the absence of the consistent burden of regular snowstorms. The winter of 1993 to 1994 was particularly cruel to those who live on the east coast. One network weather guru reported that the major metropolitan areas of the East had anywhere from twelve to fifteen "plowable snows." I don't know about "plowable," but "shovelable" can mean overload or burden. It's the picture Paul gives us in Galatians 6:2.

It's a picture that occurs in the lives of individuals as well. Just within the last twenty-four hours I talked with a woman in her seventies, a godly woman, who had become plagued by intrusive and obsessive thoughts, a reflection of the terrible abuse she suffered in childhood—thoughts that intrude so strongly into her consciousness that she fears they will surface verbally while she teaches children in Sunday school. A successful Christian businessman told me of financial pressures with which he is struggling, pressures that at times bring him to the point where he feels like giving up on both his personal business and his ministry for Christ. A woman in her forties who has successfully raised her family and is now actively involved in a Christian ministry feels the intense burden of having her husband abandon her and file for divorce, seemingly for no reason. And another woman, who lost her husband to a heart attack just a year ago, has received the disturbing news that the lump she has just discovered on her breast is in fact malignant, and she must now have surgery, followed by chemotherapy and radiation treatments. A man involved in an administrative capacity in a Christian ministry has been unable to carry out the many tasks he needs to fulfill because of a persistent illness that has left him only the option of heading for home to spend time in a sickbed. One of his colleagues has been in the hospital recuperating from a surgical procedure made necessary by gallstones, feeling frustration over his own work that has either gone undone or had to be shifted to other, overworked colleagues.

No doubt about it. Life is tough. The overload is present in the lives of many. The burdens are great to bear. In fact those I just mentioned only covered one twenty-four hour period.

IT IS ESSENTIAL THAT WE HELP ONE ANOTHER WITH OVERLOADS. IT IS ALSO CRUCIAL THAT EVERY INDIVIDUAL TAKE CARE OF HIS OR HER OWN PERSONAL RESPONSIBILITY.

Bear one another's burdens. It's what Christian love is all about. So why then does Paul add just a few words later, "For each one shall bear his own load"?

Ironically, the word Paul uses in verse 5, which is also translated burden, is a different term than the "overload" of verse 2. It's the word Luke used to describe the cargo a ship was designed to carry (Acts 27:10), and that Christ used to describe His own responsibility in life (Matthew 11:29), even though He later noted that the Pharisees had a tendency to make the burdens of others heavier than they should be (Matthew 23:4).

I think the best way to understand the distinction between these two terms is to translate the first word as overload and the second as responsibility.

What Paul is telling us here is understandable and makes good sense. It is essential that we help one another with overloads. It is also crucial that every individual take care of his or her own personal responsibility—or as a friend of mine likes to put it, "carry his own backpack."

Some years ago, our family went on a camping trip into the mountains of New Mexico. Leaving our car in a parking area, we hiked up to the shore of a small yet beautiful lake near Cloudcroft. We spent the night in a tent.

On our hike up to the campsite and the trek back down the following day, all of us had things to carry. Being the father and, at that time, the only male in the family, I carried the largest load. I think it would be somewhat accurate to call it an overload.

On the other hand, everyone else had something to carry as well. During at least one point during the trip, both of our young daughters appealed, "Daddy, won't you carry my pack?"

Being a loving father, I considered their pleas. Being overloaded myself and recognizing the benefits each would gain by fulfilling her responsibilities, I chose to refuse their requests.

An Interdependent Balance

In that balance of dependence and independence comes an interdependence which is the characteristic of healthy relationships. Refusing to help someone with an overload isn't Christ-like. Taking someone else's responsibility on ourselves isn't what Christ called us to do either. Nor is it what the Good Samaritan did.

The other evening I watched the conclusion of the 1994 Winter Olympics. Jayne Torvill and Christopher Dean were reprising their gold-medal-winning ice dancing routine from the Winter Olympics of a decade earlier, to the tune of Ravel's *Boléro*. The television analysts, as might be expected, were speculating over why Torvill and Dean hadn't won the gold medal this year, even though almost everyone except the judges seemed to agree that their competition routines were superior to the other pairs.

I was reminded of how my friend and colleague Robert Hemfeldt had used Torvill and Dean to illustrate the difference between healthy interdependence and codependency.[6]

Robert suggested watching these two skaters carry out their routine, skating apart and coming back together, then attaching the skaters by a rubber band at the waist and watching to see if they could continue skating at their previous level. The answer is obvious: Despite their incredible skills, Torvill and Dean would be unable to carry out their routine if attached together in that manner. That, as Hemfeldt explained, is what happens in codependency.

Another friend and colleague, Pat Springle, has written on the subject out of both study and personal experience. He describes the problem this way:

Codependency, which occurs as a result of involvement in a dysfunctional relationship, produces a host of painful effects that come in many combinations and take a variety of forms. Many codependents can accurately analyze everyone else's problems, but they can't see their own. Many feel that they are responsible for making other people both happy and successful. They can't say no to any need, or they feel very guilty if they do. They are extremists. Everything is either wonderful or awful. Some need to be in complete control of their lives, homes, and families at all times. Others have given up on life and are irresponsible and out of control. All codependents, when they are honest with themselves, feel that they are unworthy of love and acceptance.[7]

Springle identifies three primary characteristics of codependency: a lack of objectivity, a warped sense of responsibility, and being easily controlled and controlling others. In other words, either refusing to bear my own burden, or trying to bear everybody else's responsibility.

Perhaps you are at the point of protest. "Wait, Don, we don't find these words in Scripture. Codependency, dysfunctional families—those aren't biblical terms."

But consider that whatever label we paste on them, they are certainly concepts found and addressed in Scripture. Think of Abraham's family and the incredible dysfunction that spanned several generations: the conflict between Jacob and his brother Esau, the manipulations of Jacob and his mother, Rebekah, over the birthright and the blessing. Think of Jacob's need for his father Isaac's love and respect, and of the manipulative way he sought to gain it. Consider Ahab and Jezebel—his passivity, her attempts to control him and to manipulate circumstances so he could have what he wanted. Think of David and Joab, in an unhealthy relationship in which the king's military leader said, on more than one occasion, "I'm your friend, right or wrong. You want Uriah to die on the battlefield, I can arrange it—no questions asked."

"But those are in the Old Testament!" you protest.

Consider then Martha, sister of Mary and Lazarus, friend of the Lord Jesus. It is not surprising that some of the evidence for her strong drive to control others, characteristics we might label today as codependent, appeared in the paragraph immediately following the account of the Good Samaritan. When Jesus continued His journey (Luke 10:38), entering the village of Bethany, it was Martha who greeted Him, a welcoming party of one. And Luke specifically recorded it was her house, even though Mary and Lazarus lived there as well. Everything was always identified in terms of Martha. Mary was *her* sister, and Lazarus was *her* brother. While we aren't given the information in the text, I rather suspect that Martha was the one who had the last word on many of the major decisions reached in that household.

The Martha Complex

My wife, Kathy, who has studied Martha's life extensively, has identified a number of traits that show the unhealthy nature of Martha's existence. She refers to these as "The Martha Complex."

While Mary chose to sit at Jesus' feet and listen to His words, Martha had to be doing something. She was "tied up in knots" over the much serving she felt she had to do (Luke 10:40). She also exhibited significant anger and hurt, emotions identified by Springle as among the corollary characteristics or side effects of codependency.[8]

Martha's anxiety level was extremely high. She was agitated or stirred up over many things (v. 42)—in other words, she was capable of a crisis at any time. Her life was extremely performance-based. She obviously felt if she wasn't serving, she wasn't anything.

But the most interesting trait in Martha's life is the drive she exhibited to give everybody advice, even the Lord. First she accused Him of an uncaring attitude about her responsibilities and demanded that He instruct her sister to leave her seat at Jesus' feet and come help her (Luke 10:40). Then, after her brother's death, when Jesus arrived on the scene, she accused Him of being late and suggested that if He had just been there on time, He could have kept her brother from dying (John 11:21). Finally, as Jesus stood before Lazarus's grave and ordered those nearby to "take away the stone," Martha rebuked Him, reminding the Lord that "by this time there is a stench, for he has been dead four days" (v. 39).

Here is a dear woman, gravely concerned that someone will be offended by an odor, seemingly unaware that she is rebuking the Creator of the universe. I chuckle until I think about the number of times I've tried to give the Lord advice or instructions or to suggest that He work things out a certain way. Sometimes our controlling, "codependent" traits extend beyond human relationships to the point where we treat the Lord of Glory like some kind of genie out of Aladdin's lamp, whose sole purpose is to come forth to do our bidding whenever we desire.

Needless to say, that's not the way He intends our relationship to be. The God who delights in meeting all our needs also demands the submission of our lives and wills to Him.

There's another interesting trait worth noting about Martha. Even though she was upset that Mary had refused to help her, she apparently had conveyed to those around her that she didn't need the support of other people. Some time ago Kathy asked me why I thought none of the Jews who had come to mourn the death of Lazarus went with Martha when she went out to meet Jesus, but as soon as Mary got up to leave, the Jews who were with her noticed Mary leaving and went with her saying, "She is going to the tomb to weep there" (v. 31). They then followed along, weeping with her as she met with Jesus (v. 33). When I responded that I really hadn't thought much about it, Kathy suggested to me that perhaps the reason was that Martha had conveyed a sort of "lone ranger" mentality to their friends from Bethany. So they may have figured she didn't need anybody to weep with her. On the other hand, Mary had responded like a normal person, rather than "superwoman." She therefore became the object of grieving support from the neighbors at her time of loss.

THE ROOTS OF TODAY'S PROBLEM

So where does this modern problem originate? What causes codependency? It's certainly not borne by a virus, nor is it contagious in the medical sense.

However, there is a sense in which codependency is contagious because of its origin, in homes where there is an addiction or some other form of dysfunction. Because of the effect of sin and the Fall, every home is dysfunctional to a certain extent, but in some families, there is a great deal of healthy love expressed between husband and wife and extended to each of the children. So everyone feels accepted, loved, and approved. However, in other homes, often because one or both parents didn't receive love in their family of origin, or due to a divorce or separation or some form of abuse, love needs have gone unmet. Or perhaps a workaholic dad or mom or both left the children with an intense fear of abandonment, or physical, emotional, verbal, or sexual abuse left the child fearing still more abuse.

As a result, the individual winds up having low self-esteem and feeling a great deal of false guilt and responsibility over the pain and chaos within the family. Many times he or she will assume the role of family hero, feeling responsibility for everyone else—or even coming to the conclusion that "my family system is terrible, so I must be a terrible person" or "life is out of control, so I must somehow get things under control." Such individuals often appear strong on the outside, encouraging others to turn to them with any needs. However, on the inside they are as confused, anxious, and perplexed as the Lord saw Martha to be.

So what happens to these individuals who have grown up in chaotic families? Typically, their primary goal has become survival. Seldom are they able to experience much in the way of personal development. Their self-worth is limited; their "love tanks" are running on empty.[9] So to cope with the pressures of life, they typically adopt one or more of the following roles, developing them during their growing-up years and continuing to play the roles throughout life.

The *enabler,* often the spouse of an addict, tries to make everything OK, to help the pain go away. The *hero* thinks that by being perfect he or she can somehow remove the addiction or the pain. The *scapegoat,* believing he or she is the problem, rebels against the family and against standards and authority. The *lost child* pulls into a shell, withdraws, and isolates from meaningful relationships. The *mascot* tries desperately to make everyone laugh in the midst of the family tragedy.[10]

Rescue Compulsion

So the essential components of codependency involve three factors. The first is a compulsion or drive to care or rescue or get close, based on the myth that closer is better, more is better, and a controlling form of caring is essential. The second component is caring that has gone out of control, a *Rescue 911* focus to life, or, on the other hand, adopting a mentality that "my husband must make every decision in my life; after all, he is the head, and if I care for him, I'll always let him decide." A third component is a control focus where healthy boundaries are distorted, people become enmeshed, and self-esteem is invested in the ability to control and influence the feelings and behavior of others.

When I was growing up in Alabama, several different kinds of vines appeared on the red clay hills of the area where I lived. Some were harmless. Others, like poison oak and poison ivy, could create devastating problems. It was important to be able to tell the difference.

Telling the Difference

So how can we tell the difference between healthy Good Samaritan behavior and codependency? Here's a list of five characteristics that, when present, indicate a fairly high degree of "codependency factor."

> # *A CONTROL FOCUS . . . IS THE REAL UNDERLYING ISSUE IN CODEPENDENCY BECAUSE, FOR THE CODEPENDENT, SO MUCH OF LIFE HAS BEEN OUT OF CONTROL.*

The first is a lack of objectivity, something that has been described as the "stock market syndrome." It's the sort of thing that happens when one individual bases his or her happiness or worth on how someone else feels about him. "I just don't understand it," Suzy said. "My life is miserable. It's ruined. I'll never count for anything as a wife or mother." It turned out her husband had become disenchanted with the marriage relationship and was going through a sort of a mid-life crisis. His own inappropriate response to the marriage relationship and to his wife had been triggered by unresolved pain from his own life and from unmet emotional needs in his childhood. Suzy, however, had surrendered her objectivity and her happiness, making her husband's response to her the benchmark for how things were in her own life.

A second characteristic is a distorted sense of responsibility. "There's no way I can take a weekend away with my husband," Lana insisted, her voice almost reflecting anger that her dedication to her little ones would be questioned. "When God gives you children, He intends that you take responsibility for them. There are abusive people out there in the world! I don't intend to let my children out of my sight until they are grown. That's why I'm already preparing to home-school them. And if my husband thinks I'm going to take a weekend away with him and ignore my responsibility at home, he's got another thought coming!" How I wished for the ability to hold up an objectivity mirror in front of Lana to let her see just how out of balance her sense of responsibility toward her children had become.

A third mark of unhealthiness in relationships is a control focus. This is the real underlying issue in codependency because, for the codependent, so much of life has been out of control. Jude was insistent. "All my children will attend Christian college, and every one of them will enter some kind of vocational ministry. The time is too short, the world too evil for them to waste their time in some secular pursuit. Let somebody else support the missionaries. I want my kids on the front lines, serving the Lord. That's the only way I'll be happy." Again, I wished for a mirror to be able to hold up before Jude to show him the incredibly inordinate amount of control he was expressing toward his children. I remembered hearing him tell how chaotic his own early years had been: the addiction of his father to alcohol and rage, the emotional breakdown experienced by his mother, the role he had adopted as a substitute parent for the three younger children in his family. Control had been absent in his childhood, so control had become the focus of his adulthood.

Intense emotion is a fourth characteristic that indicates unhealthiness in relationships. It's been described as like "living in a volcano" or, as my friend Dr. Chris Thurman put it, "fifty cents' worth of emotional reaction for a nickel's worth of cause." Ironically, for the codependent individual, there can be an almost numbness or under-reaction to serious problems like abuse, yet an intense overreaction to the least little disruption of life, such as lost car keys, a check returned for insufficient funds, or even a broken fingernail.

The fifth and final characteristic involves a compulsion to fix the past or to repeat it, which often leads to a sort of "stuckness" in life. Marvin and Lisa both experienced this in different ways. Marvin had watched the chaos and confusion in his own home because of his mother's alcoholism that led to a broken home and to a great deal of misery. "I'll never be an alcoholic like her," he vowed. But when he grew up, Marvin found himself addicted to work. As a workaholic neglecting his family, he saw his own marriage dissolve, just like that of his parents.

Lisa had never been able to win the approval of her father. Even though as the older sister, she had been accepted by her mother, her dad always seemed to like her younger sister, Martie, better. Lisa didn't realize just how strongly her compulsion to have a healthy relationship and fix the past had led to a repetition compulsion until she found herself caught in an unhealthy relationship with a man at her office, a relationship which affected both her social life and her self-esteem. For both Lisa and Marvin, the compulsion to fix the past had led to, if not an identical repeat of the pattern, at least some form of repetition.

STEPS TO RESOLUTION

So how do we release unhealthy relationships, codependency, and the tendency to carry someone else's "backpack"? While volumes have been written on the subject, let me suggest seven biblically-based steps, based on the experience and research of many who have studied both the Scriptures and human behavior.

First, break through any lingering denial with the truth. Unhealthy rescuing and codependent manipulation are commonly camouflaged with denial. The problem can never be resolved as long as denial lingers. Jesus clearly told those who would be His disciples, "You shall know the truth, and the truth shall make you free" (John 8:32). Unfortunately, the majority of those who heard His warning continued in denial, refusing to see the bondage of sin in which they were living. When we refuse to continue in denial, we are taking the biblical step of confession, of admitting what is wrong. Then we can take responsibility for whatever our part is, and assess what factors, such as Dad's sinful alcohol abuse, were not our fault.

Second, inventory the damage. When a tornado roars through a community, it sometimes causes physical injury and loss of life, and it always leaves hundreds of thousands, perhaps millions, of dollars in damage. In the days that follow, officials go through the damaged buildings, carefully surveying the destruction—the broken glass, twisted metal, shattered brick—carefully writing down their observations on legal pads, then tallying up and announcing the total amount of damage done.

When codependent traits or abusive hurts have been present in our lives, it's important that we inventory the damage we have experienced, whether from a dysfunctional family, from abuse suffered in early life, or from any other cause. The third step is identifying the extent of the problem, the pain caused by the problem, and the cost of the problem. Both Joseph and the apostle Paul identified the hurts each had suffered, the former at the hand of his brothers, the latter from a persecutor named Alexander the coppersmith. Each measured the damage while, at the same time, expressing forgiveness.

A third step involves reshaping personal boundaries or, as Pat Springle describes it, detaching. Sometimes a total break in a relationship is essential. At other times, boundaries may simply need to be redefined. Perhaps a young person will need to move farther away from his or her parents when stainless steel apron strings continue to be pulled by a controlling parent. In the case of a relationship where others have taken advantage of the caregivers, an assertive new approach may be needed.

Hannah, a shut-in member of a local church, felt like one of life's classic victims. Like many codependents, she just couldn't get enough time and attention from others. But friends became weary of hearing Hannah always talk about herself and how terrible her life had been. Pretty soon people from the church stopped visiting, so Hannah took matters into hand. Rather, she took telephone in hand and began calling others. Marge and Marie were two of the women who began receiving regular, lengthy calls from Hannah. Marge, who had been raised in a home where she and her siblings were made to feel guilty if they didn't do everything they could to help others, felt obligated to stay on the telephone for as long as Hannah wanted. One day a call lasted more than seven hours!

Marie, on the other hand, had been learning to give and receive unconditional love, and she was working through issues from her past. It didn't take her long to learn how to be lovingly assertive, to establish boundaries, and to say to Hannah, "I can talk with you ten minutes," or, "I have fifteen minutes to give you right now," and to be firm and assertive with those personal boundaries. She was sensitive to another's overload, while refusing to accept another's backpack.

[GOD'S] ACCEPTANCE OF US IS BASED ON WHAT CHRIST DID AT THE CROSS, NOT ON ANYTHING WE COULD EVER DO.

The fourth step for resolving these issues is to grieve losses and learn to resolve the attached emotions. Many books and articles have been written on the stages of grief, and it would serve no useful purpose to repeat their material here. The bottom line is, to

grieve is to decide to recognize that a loss has happened. It's important that we recognize that we must grieve the people we've lost in
our childhood and adult life, express and resolve the related emotions, and move on. Jesus set the classic example for grief. He wept
at the grave of His friend Lazarus in the presence of his sisters, Mary
and Martha. Since He did, it's certainly OK and appropriate for us to
weep and process our grief. Furthermore, as the psalmist reminded
us, when father and mother forsake us, the Lord will lift us up
(Psalm 27:10). Learning to grieve for the parent who was absent in
the past due to divorce, abuse, addiction, workaholism, or death can
help us toward a more healthy life in the present and in the future.

Bill had always felt driven to try to rescue others, to try to meet
their needs. However, he frequently caused others to resent his efforts because, at the same time he tried to help, he sought to control them. It wasn't until he learned to grieve for the workaholic
father who had abandoned him and his family for a successful career that he finally began to learn to relate to others in a more
appropriate fashion.

Fifth, we need to develop a new and healthy self-perception,
based on our being loved and accepted in Christ. It's important for
each of us to recognize that we're not garbage, that God loves us
and has forgiven us in Christ. Furthermore, we don't have to rescue
others or to perform in order to please God. His acceptance of us is
based on what Christ did at the cross, not on anything we could
ever do.

Donna had struggled for years with behaviors that skirted from
codependent to downright dangerous, primarily because of terrible abuse she had suffered as a child, which had left her with a self-
image that was crushed seemingly beyond repair. However, loving,
healthy relationships and a week spent working through issues of
personal significance with Dr. Jim Mahoney helped Donna understand that her self-worth was not based on anything in her past, nor
on any performance in her present. She learned to accept herself
for who she was in Christ. She was able to develop a healthy marriage relationship and to relate in better fashion to her children.

Sixth, it is important to develop healthy friendships and accountability. Those who have struggled with codependent relationships often draw away from accountability. Yet the author of
Hebrews makes it clear that we need to exhort each other daily so
that none of us will become hardened by the deceitfulness of sin
(Hebrews 3:13). For years Daniel had struggled with an addiction to

pornography, which was triggered in part by sexual abuse he had suffered in childhood. When he committed his life to Christ, he thought the desire to watch sexually explicit films would go away. For a while it seemed to, but then the temptations came back more overwhelmingly than ever, bringing failure, shame, and despair.

Daniel's pastor recommended an accountability relationship with a Christian brother who was older in the Lord. When Daniel established this relationship with Will, he shared his problem candidly, gave Will permission to ask him the tough questions, and promised honesty in his answers. This regular accountability in his area of weakness helped Daniel develop healthier relationships in other areas of his life and to overcome his persistent sin.

Finally, it is important that codependent individuals grow spiritually, based on a new, healthy perception of God. This can only come about as we understand who God the Father really is, based on His self-disclosure in Scripture. The Word is our ultimate source of spiritual food and growth. It alone can bring joy and new values and give us strength to reverse the tragic effects of codependency.

A Sharper Focus

The other day, after walking outdoors for some time near the office where our ministry is located, I noticed that what had previously seemed to be a bright, cheerful day looked somewhat dark and clouded. I couldn't figure out what was happening, since it appeared the sun was still out.

Then I realized that a fine layer of dust from the site of a nearby construction site had coated the lenses of my glasses. Without my realizing it, my perception of reality had become distorted. When I washed my glasses and allowed my vision to be refocused, I gained a new and more accurate perception of how things really were.

That is what God's Word does. It cleanses us and gives us a clear and more accurate perception of who God is and how things really are. This, then, gives us the opportunity to fulfill what God has called us to do in helping others in a healthy way.

An Example of Balance

That balance in relationships came home clearly to me in a couple of events from the life of Gill, a friend of mine. He was the foreman on a construction site. One day he met a man we'll call Bob, who was homeless and said he desperately needed a job. Gill gave Bob a job, helped him find lodging, and promised added help for Bob and his family. Gill and his wife provided food for the family, delivering it to the small home where Bob and his wife and children lived. At Christmas time they shopped for the children, securing the sizes of their clothing, and purchasing a wide range of things to help the family.

However, Gill found it necessary to show love in a different way when, shortly after Christmas, Bob began showing up late at work and failing to fulfill his responsibilities. On the day Gill finally confronted him, it was evident that Bob was suffering the effects of a prolonged drunk.

With tears in his eyes, Gill fired Bob, telling him that he could not allow him to continue to abuse the work situation and create problems for everyone else there. Later Gill and Bob's wife, Tonya, along with their pastor, participated in an intervention, during which they insisted that Bob seek help in a Christian treatment program to deal with his chronic addiction to alcohol.

As Gill explained later, "It was really tough for me to confront Bob—even worse to fire him, knowing his kids needed their father to work and provide for them. There had been a time when I would have refused to do so. After all, I used to be one of those people who felt like it was my duty to rescue the entire world. But as I came to understand what God's Word teaches about bearing the burdens of others and the responsibility each of us has to bear his own burden, I realized I really didn't have a choice."

What a great example for us in avoiding one of the primary dangers to becoming authentic Good Samaritans.

NOTES

1. Melody Beattie, *Codependent No More* (New York: Hazelden, 1987), 31.

2. Gayle Irwin, *The Jesus Style* (Dallas: Word, 1983), 48.

3. A. T. Robertson, *Word Pictures in the New Testament* (Nashville: Broadman, 1931), 4:315.

4. Gerhard Kittel, *Theological Dictionary of the New Testament* (Grand Rapids: Eerdmans, 1971), 1:476.

5. Ibid., 1:553.

6. Robert Hemfeldt, Frank Minirth, and Paul Meier, *Love Is a Choice* (Nashville: Nelson, 1989), 126.

7. Pat Springle, *Codependency* (Houston: Rapha, 1989), 11.

8. Ibid., 12.

9. Hemfeldt, 34–35.

10. Adapted from "The Family Trap" by Sharon Wegschieder-Cruz.

CHAPTER TWELVE

THE COMMITMENT: HE WHO SHOWED MERCY

"'So which of these three do you think was neighbor to him who fell among the thieves?' And he said, 'He who showed mercy on him.' Then Jesus said to him, 'Go and do likewise.'"
(Luke 10:36–37)

You could almost hear his teeth gritting, his jaw grinding, as he found himself put on the spot.

He hadn't intended for things to turn out this way. After all, as a lawyer thoroughly versed in Old Testament Mosaic precepts, he felt he was well-equipped to test this rabbi from Nazareth. Sure, others had challenged Him, and they had found themselves put in their place. But he thought he was on pretty safe ground when he raised the question, "What shall I do to inherit eternal life?"

Not only that, he felt he had handled himself well when the Master threw that question back at him about what the law said. After all, it was no little thing to have this Jesus admit that you were right. He had felt pretty good about himself when the rabbi replied, "You have answered rightly; do this and you will live."

If he had just kept his mouth shut at that point. But no, he always seemed to have this drive to press for a clear-cut victory. The lawyer in him just had to raise one more question, make one more point.

Besides, wasn't the question he raised a valid one? After all, there had been a great deal of debate in Israel on the subject of who one's neighbor was. Certainly any other Jew fit that category—especially one who was a Pharisee, or a member of the Sanhedrin.

But not Gentiles. No way. The Old Testament prophets may have talked about Gentiles coming to the light, but it seemed to him that was more for another day, not those filthy Romans and people from other nationalities.

And the Samaritans! Of all people! Acting like they were Jews, showing incredible disrespect to the Israelites.

Why, a self-respecting Jew wouldn't even go through Samaritan territory. And it didn't matter how hot you were or how thirsty, you wouldn't drink from the same cup or bucket drawn from a well as a Samaritan. No, good Jews just didn't do things like that.

But here was Jesus, telling this story that had obviously captivated the surrounding crowd, about a man traveling from Jerusalem to Jericho. He had been victimized by a band of robbers and left half-dead—there was nothing new about that. It happened all the time.

And a priest and Levite, passing by on the other side? Why, that was pretty common too. After all, priests and Levites had important work to do in the service of God. They didn't need to waste their time by becoming ceremonially unclean.

He had spotted the trap when Jesus said the word Samaritan. The rabbi's story wasn't all that credible anyway. He certainly didn't know of any Samaritans who would do a thing like that. And to think of a Samaritan taking the time, not to mention the money, to risk his own life—and risking what a group of self-respecting Jews would have done to him if they had found him carrying a half-dead Jew on the back of his donkey.

He had just been thinking, "I wish this rabbi would hurry up with this story," especially since his own feelings had shifted from confident to uncomfortable.

WHO WAS NEIGHBOR?

Now, suddenly, the story was over, and Jesus had turned back to him personally, raising the question he dreaded most of all.

"Which now of these three do you think was neighbor to him who fell among the thieves?"

Did you feel just a little bit of the emotion the religious leader felt when Jesus put him on the spot with His probing question? Did you sense the drop in his comfort level? Could you identify with his wish to be somewhere, anywhere but where he was, facing the question he was hearing? After all, he might even have to use the "S" word, refer to this Samaritan by his ethnic group. No, he didn't intend to do that, even if he answered Jesus' question.

Perhaps he paused for a moment. Luke didn't tell us for certain. But his answer certainly indicates how uncomfortable he was with Jesus' question. He didn't even refer to the man as a Samaritan like Jesus did. He said, "He who showed mercy on him."

It is my suspicion that Luke intentionally wanted us to feel the discomfort, the agitation, even the irritation this religious leader felt when Jesus put him on the spot.

At this point the Lord completed His story, then drove home His point, first with a probing question, followed by an authoritative word of instruction. The mandate was as specific as the Greek language can be. The second person singular "you" precedes the action verb and is stated for added emphasis.

Jesus' point is clear. He didn't tell this story just to engage in a debate or to entertain His hearers. Nor was He simply seeking to teach some abstract truth.

WHERE ARE THOSE WHO WILL OBSERVE THE NEEDS OF OTHERS, BE MOVED WITH COMPASSION WHEN THEY SEE THOSE WHO HURT, THEN ACT ON THAT EMOTION WITHOUT THOUGHT OF A RETURN?

No, the Lord wanted action. "Go and do likewise." In fact, it seems clear as I read this text and try to put myself back into the first-century narrative that the Lord was asking all those who could hear His voice, "Where are the Good Samaritans?"

We know where the priests are and the Levites, the teachers of the law. We know where the common people are. But where are the Good Samaritans? Where are the individuals of whatever race who are moved with compassion when they see another human being overwhelmed by the circumstances of life? Where are the people who care enough to make contact, who will risk their reputation, their possessions, even their own personal safety? Where are the people who will get involved, even in the unpleasant business of cleaning up the devastation caused by others? Where are those who will wade into someone else's pain and help relieve that pain? Where are the individuals who will care enough to expend their energy, use their resources—in fact, do everything they possibly can to help another human being, even someone who is different? Where are those who will observe the needs of others, be moved with compassion when they see those who hurt, then act on that emotion without thought of a return?

Where are the Good Samaritans?

A Question for the Nineties

Jesus' question echoed over the dusty Judean landscape, leaving the religious leader and others gathered around silent, and the individuals who were a part of the tableau that day left the scene. It seems the question still echoes today. In fact, the words of Jesus, "you do likewise," reverberate down the years, providing us with a mandate for action in the 1990s as well. Christ's mandate repeats the question for our day. Where are our Good Samaritans? Where are those who will observe the needs of people around them? Where are those who will care? Where are those who will act, who will follow through on their action, putting themselves at risk and their financial resources on the line?

The Ultimate Good Samaritan

In short, where are those who will be Christ-like? That this pointed parable pictures the ultimate Good Samaritan, the Lord Jesus Christ, goes without saying. It's not the main point Jesus has in mind, but we can certainly draw the application, as the Lord will later, to the "Son of Man [who] has come to seek and to save that which was lost" (Luke 19:10).

Without question, every single member of the human race can identify with the half-dead victim, helplessly lying beside the road, unable to save himself. Every one of us needs a Good Samaritan. We don't need someone to give us directions to the nearest hospital or to hand us a first-aid kit, a bottle of aspirin, or any of the other painkillers available.

No, what we need is someone to save us. The prophet Isaiah said centuries before, "All we like sheep have gone astray; we have turned, every one, to his own way; and the Lord has laid on Him the iniquity of us all" (Isaiah 53:6).

In fact, the Lord went even further than the Good Samaritan. Rejected by His own people (John 1:11), He paid the ultimate price, dying in our place to secure the salvation we could never gain for ourselves, and making it possible for God to extend to us the gift of eternal life (John 1:12).

If you have read this far in *Friends in Deed* and have yet to receive that gift, there is no better time than today. Just as the victim lying beside the Jericho Road freely received what the Good Samaritan offered, trusting him to meet his need, so you and I must receive as a gift the life offered by Jesus. We trust Him as Savior, just as we would trust a surgeon to operate on our bodies, an attorney to defend us before the bar of justice, or a mechanic to repair our automobile.

And for those who have trusted Him, the lesson is clear. We who have received so much by trusting the Lord Jesus are now in a position to reach out and extend a hand of love and compassion to those around us who are in need.

So what will we do about it?

A Self-Centered Society

In recent years, a great deal of attention has been paid to two significant segments of society: baby boomers, those born between 1946 and 1964; and baby busters, those born between 1965 and 1983. The 79 million boomers constitute almost 32 percent of the population in the United States, while the nearly 68 million busters constitute just over 27 percent.[1]

It is against the backdrop of the values of boomers and busters that we have looked at Jesus' account of this Good Samaritan and heard His call for Good Samaritans in His day and ours.

So far the response from our day may be less than overwhelming.

In fact, researcher George Barna recently wrote, "The drive that baby boomers initiated back in the late sixties to discover the ultimate purpose of life and to restructure the universe around their discoveries remains active today."[2]

Quoting a member of the busters as viewing boomers as "selfish-to-the-bone,"[3] Barna points out that boomers do have an unspoken perception of other people as a means to an end. He sums up the contrast between boomers and busters this way: "Boomers live to work, while busters work to live."[4]

From Barna's research we might conclude that neither of these groups has a strong inclination to become involved in Good Samaritan kinds of activities. He notes the determination of busters "to engage only in those efforts which hold high promise of resulting in sufficient personal benefit to justify the effort."[5]

In other words, the inherent selfishness we all must face when we look in the mirror is still a part of the human race, even in the idealistic younger members of society. Sure, some individuals are willing to get involved in Good Samaritanism. There have even been efforts to make it our nation's official policy. When George Bush became the forty-first president of the United States in 1989, he affirmed in his inaugural address that the Bush years would be "the age of the offered hand."[6]

"Are we enthralled with material things, less appreciative of the nobility of work and sacrifice?" he asked, with assurance that the question was rhetorical. "We cannot hope only to leave our children a bigger car, a bigger bank account, we must hope to give them a sense of what it means to be a loyal friend, a loving parent, a citizen who leaves his home, his neighborhood and town better than he found it."[7]

During his presidency, Mr. Bush initiated a program called "a thousand points of light" in an effort to motivate more personal compassion to make a difference in society.

However, as President Bush would undoubtedly recognize, no presidential mandate can force compassionate involvement in the lives of others. Ultimately, it must come from the motivation of the heart. Good Samaritanism is, if nothing else, intensely personal.

That's why I'm convinced that the mandate to "go and do likewise" will only be fulfilled as we personally come to grips with what it meant for this Samaritan man to show mercy, then commit ourselves to making this concept a part of our attitude and lifestyle.

REQUIREMENTS FOR GOOD SAMARITANS

First it might be helpful to note what the requirements for being a Good Samaritan are and, conversely, what they are not. The story Jesus told seems to make it quite clear that being a Good Samaritan does not require having attained a certain level of spiritual maturity or degree of theological insight. Jesus makes no issue of the level or existence of his faith, knowledge, worship habits, or even his personal lifestyle.

What we are told is that, ultimately, he cared. Seeing the hurting man, he felt compassion, which moved him into action. That's why when Jesus directed His pointed question to the esteemed scholar of Old Testament law, who had intended to trip Christ up, the man was left with only one possible correct response.

He knew it. Jesus knew it. The crowd knew it. And we know it today.

He replied, "He who showed mercy on him."

He Who Showed Mercy

In that simple statement can be found a world of significance. The term *eleos,* according to New Testament scholar W. E. Vine, is "the outward manifestation of pity. It assumes need on the part of him who receives it and resources adequate to meet the need on the part of him who shows it."[8]

Although two other words are translated mercy in the New Testament, they look more at inner feeling. The term used here includes the inner feeling, but it focuses on that feeling as demonstrated in concrete action.

This is the word most frequently used in the Septuagint, the Old Testament translated into Greek, for the Hebrew term *hesed,* meaning lovingkindness, steadfast love, mercy, or loyalty. It is used 240 times in the Old Testament, and its meaning contains three basic components: steadfastness, love, and strength.[9] The word's primary use in the Old Testament is to describe the covenant love and mercy shown by Yahweh, the Lord, toward His people Israel. It reflects a loyal commitment, freely extended by a stronger party to one who is weaker, and "implies personal involvement and commitment in a relationship beyond the rule of law."[10]

Hesed was used of men as well as of God—one classic case in point is David's response in showing loyal love toward Mephibosheth for the sake of Mephibosheth's father, Jonathan (2 Samuel 9:7)—and is demanded rather than external religious sacrifice of those who would please God (Hosea 6:6). This principle was studiously overlooked by the religious leader Jesus confronted and the contemporaries with whom he associated. When Micah the prophet summarized the responsibility of man in relationship to God and others, he called for three specific things: Do justly, love *hesed,* and walk humbly with your God (Micah 6:8). In essence, since God abounds in *hesed* (Exodus 34:6; Psalm 103:8), the person who responds this way demonstrates God's compassionate character to others. Yet the religious leaders in the time of the gospels had totally perverted Micah's requirement. They were living unjustly, foreclosing on widows, and praying long prayers for justification. They had no interest in loyal love, as pointed out in this parable. And their lack of humility could be seen by their loud prayers on street corners and other forms of public religious show.

But before we condemn them, it is imperative that we ask ourselves, *Where do I stand in this regard?*

I'm convinced that, for me personally, it begins with having a heart for God, a true wholehearted love for Him, that chooses to make Him the focal point of my life, my affections, and my loyalty. Once it starts there, *hesed* just naturally flows into the lives of other people.

That's how it worked for Jerry, one of the most unselfish men I have ever met. I've known him over the past fifteen years, seen him give himself, his time, and his resources to others. He's come to be a true Good Samaritan.

But it wasn't always this way, as Jerry explained to me one evening. I had been commenting to Jerry on a recently observed act of unselfish "Good Samaritan" behavior on his part, a time when he sacrificed time and money to reach out to help someone when there was not a chance in the world he would ever receive anything in return.

> *THE MORE INTIMATELY I WALK IN FELLOWSHIP WITH HIM, THE MORE I UNDERSTAND HIS HEART FOR PEOPLE AND RESPOND IN WHOLEHEARTED LOVE TO HIM, THE MORE I'M PREPARED TO BE A GOOD SAMARITAN.*

"How did you develop this kind of compassion?" I asked.

At first reluctant even to respond, Jerry finally acknowledged that his sensitivity to the needs of others had grown from his heart relationship to God. A Texan who held a strategic management position in a Texas-based corporation, Jerry admitted to having been "just about as selfish as anybody" for a good portion of his life. The shift in his values toward people had begun to take place as his relationship with God became a priority.

The Source of Samaritanism

"I hadn't spent much time in the Word," he admitted, "even though I trusted Christ earlier in life. I had very little use for spiritual things, until I met a man who motivated me to get plugged into God's Word on a regular basis. The more I studied the Word and came to know the Lord better through my studies, the more I came to understand the priority of loving others.

"But even then, it wasn't an easy transition. It took the power of the Spirit of God. After all, I still have that selfish old nature—don't we all?"

As I reflected on his words, I thought about how Paul described love as the fruit of the Spirit (Galatians 5:22). That's where the ultimate motivation for Good Samaritanism comes from. Sure, we'll always have Boy Scouts helping little old ladies cross the street and lifeguards rescuing those who encounter trouble while swimming. But the ultimate kind of Good Samaritanism grows right out of a heart of love for the Lord, and such love is always a product of the Spirit's work in our lives.

So, on a practical level, the closer my relationship with the Lord becomes, the more intimately I walk in fellowship with Him, the more I understand His heart for people and respond in whole-hearted love to Him, the more I'm prepared to be a Good Samaritan—one who not only loves his neighbor unconditionally as a matter of character, but one who is ready to demonstrate that love in action when the need occurs.

That raises the second element, that of developing sensitivity toward people and their needs—an "others focus" as opposed to the more typical "self-focus."

An "Others Focus"

Dan, who was going through an intensely difficult time in his family because of a serious illness affecting his wife, demonstrated the kind of "others focus" that provides a twenty-four carat example of Good Samaritanism on the "loyalty" side of showing mercy. The director of a large ministry, Dan heard from two of his senior staff members that a young colleague he had been counting on to help carry the load for him through a difficult time had failed significantly. It would have been easy for him to agree with their assessment of the situation as hopeless and fire the young man outright. He could have nodded agreement, responding with a comment like,

"Yes, isn't it a shame to see the lack of commitment today, the failure of people like this?"

But Dan decided on a different course of action. First, he called a meeting of his management team, including the two staffers who had alerted him to the situation. He asked for input, then he told his plan of action.

The next day he called the young man into his office and confronted him over the failure. Tears were in both men's eyes as Dan gently probed the pain behind the failure, being careful to affirm the young man's person while correcting his performance.

As an outgrowth of that initial meeting, Dan made time in an already packed schedule to meet with the young man at least every other week for the next six months. Before long the failure was corrected, the young man became an asset rather than a liability, and Dan's entire team was strengthened. Dan even gained encouragement himself as he met bi-weekly with his young colleague.

Remarkably, we can demonstrate mercy and compassion no matter what our station in life. The Samaritan had been an outcast in Jewish society, rejected by those who were proud of their Abrahamic heritage. Yet those who were members of the highest element of Jewish society showed no compassion—they passed by on the other side. Like the rich man in the story Jesus would tell a short time later (Luke 16:19–31), they were not affected by the needs of those around them. In short, they were *un*moved with compassion.

The rich man of whom Jesus spoke is a classic example of one with no compassion. During his life, he never noticed Lazarus's need, pain, or hunger, though he seemed willing to allow the man to pick through the crumbs or garbage left over from his own sumptuous fare. Ironically, even after his death, his cry to Abraham for mercy involved having Lazarus meet his needs.

How sad that, like this man, we are so often blinded by self-focus to the hurts and needs of others.

The name Eric Liddell may bring different things to mind for different people. For those who viewed the critically acclaimed motion picture *Chariots of Fire,* he may be remembered as the incredible athlete who successfully ran with an unusual style, with his head thrown back. He refused because of personal conviction to race on a Sunday during the 1924 Paris Olympic games, but later he won the gold medal and established a world record in the four hundred meter run.[11]

Others, more aware of worldwide mission endeavors, may remember Liddell's twenty-year investment of his life in missionary service in China.

A World-Class Good Samaritan

But those who lived in his area of China during the late 1930s, a time when hostilities between the Japanese and Chinese were intensifying, knew Eric Liddell not as a world-class runner or even a world-class missionary, but rather as a world-class Good Samaritan. Hearing about a wounded man who was dying in an abandoned Buddhist temple nearby, Liddell's heart was touched when the local villagers, fearing reprisals from the Japanese, showed no willingness to help the man. Liddell and a single workman, who had been persuaded to accompany him with his cart, left immediately to attempt a rescue.

During his journey, Liddell encouraged himself with the words of Jesus from Luke 16:10, "He who is faithful in what is least is faithful also in much."

This act of service may have seemed like quite a comedown for the man who had run before thousands and captured the attention of the world during the Olympics in Paris and who had been commissioned for missionary ministry in a service where more than one thousand people were unable to get in. Here there were no human spectators, just an injured man lying in a deserted temple in a danger-filled war zone.

Eric Liddell and his companion placed the wounded man on the Chinese laborer's cart, then picked up yet another man who had been seriously wounded by Japanese soldiers and left for dead with a deep gash in his head. The two men pulled the cart a total of eighteen miles on foot to a mission hospital. Both of the men they rescued survived. The second, who had suffered what should have been a mortal wound, ultimately trusted Christ as his Savior.

But Eric Liddell's career as a Good Samaritan didn't begin or end with that incident. In 1943, Liddell was one of eighteen hundred individuals confined at the Weihsien prison camp, packed into a camp area measuring only 150 by 200 yards. Both David Michell, who was one of the children present at the camp with Liddell, and Sally Magnusson, who wrote Liddell's biography *The Flying Scotsman,* were impressed with the Christ-like treatment he showed to those who were confined along with him.[12]

According to Magnusson, many of the other missionaries held in the camp treated their fellow prisoners with cold indifference. Yet

Liddell spent one day each week looking after the younger children to give the teachers and parents a break from their responsibilities. He organized athletic meets without calling attention to his previous Olympic career. He spent many hours tutoring and teaching others and caring for older people, the weak and the ill. Magnusson discovered he had befriended a Russian prostitute who had been shunned by all the others, and described his persistent cheerfulness, despite horrible external conditions and the internal pain he was suffering from the brain tumor that would take his life just months before the prisoners would be liberated.

So, in several respects Eric Liddell provides a classic model for those of us who would become twentieth-century Good Samaritans.

First, his unconditional love for people and his willingness to reach out to them as a Good Samaritan flowed from a close, loving relationship he had with Christ. As Michell described it:

> He unreservedly committed his life to Jesus Christ as his Savior and Lord. That friendship meant everything to him. By the flickering light of the peanut oil lamp early each morning, he and a roommate in the men's cramped dormitory studied the Bible and talked with God for an hour every day.[13]

Second, his unconditional love for people was evident. An obvious "fruit of the Spirit" kind of love, it stood the test of pressures and time. As months stretched into years in the cramped concentration camp, it manifested itself in joy, peace, longsuffering, gentleness, goodness, faith, meekness, and self-control, even while others were engaging in backbiting, strife, selfishness, and disdain.

Third, Liddell's love demonstrated itself toward those who could not reciprocate; hours spent caring for younger children, Christlike friendship extended to a prostitute of a different nationality.

Fourth, it generated the ultimate product of unconditional love for people: encouragement. Both Magnusson and Michell used the word encouragement to describe the persistent efforts of Eric Liddell on behalf of his fellow prisoners.

Furthermore, Liddell did not allow either external circumstances or personal pain to stand in the way of his Good Samaritan behavior. When I think of the intense pain my sister, who has had two surgeries for a brain tumor, described, I became even more impressed with the testimony I had read about this man. Instead of allowing his pain to discourage or embitter him, Eric Liddell apparently either ignored it completely or used it as a means of motivation to reach out to help others who were in pain or in need.

Finally, Liddell refused to live on the laurels of his past. He was more concerned with being an authentic servant of the Lord and others in the circumstances in which he found himself than in basking in the past glory of Olympic victories or missionary heroics.

Clearly, Eric Liddell was an authentic Good Samaritan.

Good Samaritan Activities Today

So what are we to do, and how are we to do it? There's no way a book like this could list every single potential Good Samaritan activity. But from recent days and previous experiences, I've listed a wide-ranging sample of such behaviors.

- A friend helping a family of blind people steer their shopping cart and pick up their purchases at a nearby grocery store.
- A young executive shoveling snow for an older lady who lives nearby.
- Three teenagers helping a lady change a flat tire on her car.
- Several Christian friends helping a family move their furniture from a rental truck into a new home.
- Three friends helping a young single woman by hauling her heavy upright piano to a second floor apartment.
- A group of men from a local church taking time off from their jobs to help a missionary construct a home for his family.
- A Christian man driving more than two hundred miles out of his way to pick up a friend who had flown into a more distant airport in order to save several hundred dollars on a plane ticket.
- A ministry colleague taking the time to drive a friend to the garage to pick up his automobile after it had been repaired.
- Countless people opening their homes for a day or longer to provide others with hospitality.
- A housewife spending regular times with a friend who had just been diagnosed with cancer.
- A Christian organization mobilizing a wide range of resources to help the spouse of one of the organization's leaders who was dying of cancer—providing a pager and a portable phone, helping to do laundry, picking up supplies, even helping financially to relieve the load.

And this is only a small sampling of the many ways I've seen Good Samaritan works carried out.

The essence of what we are to do as Good Samaritans can be seen in what Michael Slater points out in his practical analysis of what happened when Martha's brother, Lazarus, was raised from the dead.[14] It involves our doing whatever God has empowered and entrusted us to do.

As Slater points out, we are obviously not expected to do what God alone can do. Only Jesus, among all those present at the tomb that day, could raise Lazarus from the dead. Clearly, we cannot raise the dead, forgive sins, or grant eternal life.

However, we can support what God is doing in a given situation. As Slater observed, Jesus did call on the people nearby to help Him before He raised Lazarus. All the things He asked of them were within their capability, and all needed to be done to facilitate His working the miracle that He alone could do.

First, He asked the people to show Him where the tomb was located (John 11:34). Now as the omniscient Lord, He could have made His way to that tomb without any human help. But I believe He was asking them to get involved, perhaps even forcing them to choose between involvement and non-involvement.

He also asked them to roll back the stone (John 11:39). John the evangelist points out that Martha voiced the question that may have been on the minds of many of those who heard Jesus' request. "He's dead. All this will accomplish is to raise a stink!"

Sadly, there are times when we respond to opportunities to help in that kind of negative fashion as well. But instead of listening to Martha, several individuals took Jesus' invitation seriously and rolled the stone away.

Following the miracle, Jesus asked the people to remove the grave clothes that were tightly wrapped around Lazarus in mummy-like fashion and let him go.

As Slater points out, these actions were secondary to the major focus of the text, which is on the restoration of Lazarus to life. But I agree with his conclusion that such secondary issues, the things God calls on us to do in a given situation, are important.[15]

For one thing, it is the secondary issues that frequently discourage or dishearten people. They are the things that become "the straw that breaks the camel's back."

That's why it is so important that we be available for the Lord to use. We may not have the ability to cure someone's inoperable cancer, but we can provide him or her with a cheerful word of encouragement or ongoing personal contact, by being there for him or her. We cannot reverse the grief of parents who have lost a child in an accident or restore the child to life, but we can provide food for the family, a loving presence, and a hug of compassion.

OUR BOTTOM LINE IS NOT SIMPLY TO FIGURE OUT AND CATALOG ALL THE DIFFERENT WAYS WE CAN BE GOOD SAMARITANS. IT'S TO MAKE OURSELVES AVAILABLE TO DO WHATEVER HE EMPOWERS AND LEADS US TO DO.

Also, our involvement in secondary issues often opens doors for additional ministry on the part of others. Think about the scene at the tomb, at the moment when Jesus issued the call to roll away the stone, or a moment later, when He urged them to unwrap Lazarus. *Someone* had to respond first. Then the rest had both the Lord's word and the example of someone else to follow. When we choose to get involved, even when others haven't, we may be setting the example, providing a pattern, and motivating others to help when otherwise they might not.

Our involvement in secondary issues can be a source of great personal satisfaction, even motivating us to do additional ministry. Think of how it might have felt to have actually been one of those individuals who helped roll that stone away. It might not have seemed easy or pleasant at the time, but the fact is, it's the kind of thing that probably would motivate us to jump quickly to volunteer if such a situation presented itself. It's also something we could look back on with great satisfaction. "I was there. I participated. Thank the Lord. I had the opportunity and, by His grace, I seized it."

So our bottom line is not simply to figure out and catalog all the different ways we can be Good Samaritans. It's to make ourselves available to do whatever He empowers and leads us to do. It's to develop our love for God and people to the point where we are ready to step forward whenever circumstances appear that echo the question the Lord left hanging over the Palestinian landscape that first-century day when He originally told the story.

"Where are the Good Samaritans?"

Eric Liddell answered the call when circumstances presented themselves to him. In fact, being a Good Samaritan was one of the reasons Eric Liddell finished the race of life well.

May we do likewise, by responding positively whenever we hear the call for Good Samaritans.

NOTES

1. George Barna, *Baby Busters: The Disillusioned Generation* (Chicago: Moody, 1994), 15–16.

2. George Barna, *The Barna Report* 1992–93, (Ventura, Calif.: Regal, 1992), 29.

3. Barna, *Busters,* 19.

4. Ibid., 101.

5. Ibid., 104.

6. *U.S. News & World Report* (30 January 1989), 19.

7. Ibid., 20.

8. W. E. Vine, *Expository Dictionary of New Testament Words,* 732.

9. *Nelson's Expository Dictionary of the Old Testament,* ed. Merrill F. Unger and William White, Jr., (Nashville: Nelson, 1984), 232–33.

10. Ibid.

11. David J. Michell, "The Last Triumph of Eric Liddell," *Power for Living* (12 February 1984), 2–7.

12. Cited in James Hilt, *How to Have a Better Relationship with Anybody* (Chicago: Moody, 1984), 9–10.

13. Michell, "Liddell," 7.

14. Michael Slater, *Stretcher Bearers* (Ventura, Calif.: Regal, 1985), 99–103.

15. Ibid., 103.